Praise for

MEN IN GREEN

"Marvelous . . . Put a birdie down on the card for *Men in Green*."

—Garry Smits, *The Florida Times-Union*

"Until roughly the mid-1980s, the PGA Tour really was a tour, not the geographically dispersed collection of big-money events it is today. The players and often their wives drove from event to event or hopped on chartered flights together. . . . In a new book, *Men in Green*, author Michael Bamberger re-creates that tour through a series of surprisingly candid interviews with players, caddies, wives, and others who were there. It is a world of booze-fueled friendships and feuds, of deep bonds and annoyances, of hurts that still fester and memories that still glow. Braiding it all together is the power and addiction of golf. . . . Bamberger doesn't flinch at portraying the Tour's earthier aspects. Drugs, sex, and alcohol, although not sensationalized, take their appropriate place in his narrative. But the book is overwhelmingly a love song. . . . Above all, what comes through is the sense of the Tour back then as an extended family, sometimes dysfunctional but never dull."

—John Paul Newport, *The Wall Street Journal*

"Compelling . . . This is the golf version of Roger Kahn's classic *The Boys of Summer*. . . . A fascinating portrait of a time in golf much different from the corporate version of today."

—*Chicago Tribune*

"*Men in Green* is peppered with appealing vignettes—such as Billy Harmon on what Bob Goalby said to himself standing over a four-foot putt on the last hole of the 1968 Masters—but Bamberger has a higher purpose. Identifying legends and trying to find out what makes them tick, he and Donald provide exceptional insight into some of America's greatest players over the last half century."

—*The Philadelphia Inquirer*

"Michael Bamberger is a hard-boiled reporter with a sly wit, but his bottom-line virtue is empathy. That's made him the most penetrating and insightful golf writer of our time. *Men in Green* is Bamberger at his best: revealing secrets, puncturing myths, adjudicating never-settled feuds. His new book has the suspenseful urgency of a detective novel, a cast of characters out of a Fellini movie, and the heart of a Charlie Brown Christmas special. If I could have only one golf book on a deserted island, *Men in Green* would be that book."

—John Garrity, author of *Ancestral Links*

"Poignant . . . Consistently entertaining . . . Whether it's Gay Talese profiling heavyweight boxer Floyd Patterson, John McPhee describing the artistry of basketball great Bill Bradley, or Roger Angell writing anything about baseball, the best sportswriting is about more than the sport that is its ostensible subject. That's what makes Michael Bamberger's *Men in Green*, nominally a book about what Bamberger calls eighteen 'legends of the game,' one that will appeal to more than passionate golf fans. Less concerned with birdies and bogeys than he is with exploring the stories behind the lives and careers of his subjects, Bamberger matches a keen eye for the sport that's been the subject of two of his previous books—*The Green Road Home* and *To the Linksland*—with a knack for getting his subjects to share their candid reminiscences in revealing fashion."

—Harvey Freedenberg, *Harrisburg Magazine*

"A pleasure for fans and historians of the game."

—*Kirkus Reviews*

MICHAEL BAMBERGER was born in Patchogue, New York, in 1960. After graduating from the University of Pennsylvania in 1982, he worked as a newspaper reporter, first for the (Martha's) *Vineyard Gazette*, later for the *Philadelphia Inquirer*. Since 1995 he has been a senior writer for *Sports Illustrated*. He lives in Philadelphia with his wife, Christine.

ALSO BY MICHAEL BAMBERGER

The Green Road Home

To the Linksland

Bart & Fay (a play)

Wonderland

This Golfing Life

The Man Who Heard Voices

The Swinger (with Alan Shipnuck)

MEN
IN
GREEN

MICHAEL BAMBERGER

SIMON & SCHUSTER PAPERBACKS

NEW YORK LONDON TORONTO SYDNEY NEW DELHI

Sports Illustrated
B O O K S

Simon & Schuster Paperbacks
An Imprint of Simon & Schuster, Inc.
1230 Avenue of the Americas
New York, NY 10020

First Simon & Schuster trade paperback edition April 2016

SIMON & SCHUSTER PAPERBACKS and colophon are
registered trademarks of Simon & Schuster, Inc.

Sports Illustrated is a registered trademark of Time Inc. Used by permission.

For information about special discounts for bulk purchases,
please contact Simon & Schuster Paperback Special Sales at
1-866-506-1949 or business@simonandschuster.com.

The Simon & Schuster Speakers Bureau can bring authors to your live event.
For more information or to book an event, contact the Simon & Schuster Speakers
Bureau at 1-866-248-3049 or visit our website at www.simonspeakers.com.

Interior design by Ruth Lee-Mui

Map by Elisa Pugliese

Manufactured in the United States of America

1   3   5   7   9   10   8   6   4   2

Library of Congress Cataloging-in-Publication Data
Bamberger, Michael, 1960–
Men in green / Michael Bamberger.
pages   cm
1. Golfers—Biography   2. Golf—History.   I. Title.
GV964.A1B34   2015
796.3520922—dc23
[B]   2015001158

ISBN 978-1-4767-4382-0
ISBN 978-1-4767-4383-7 (pbk)
ISBN 978-1-4767-4384-4 (ebook)

The author wishes to express his gratitude for permission to reprint lyrics
from the following songs: "We Are Family" by Bernard Edwards and Nile Rodgers,
copyright Alfred Music, used by permission; "Driving Wheel" by David Wiffen,
copyright Bytown Music, used by permission (David Wiffen); and "Willin'"
by Lowell George, copyright Naked Snake Music,
used by permission (Elizabeth George).

This guidebook is joyfully dedicated to

my Philadelphia pathfinders,

Bob Warner *and* Jeannie Hemphill.

Birthplaces of Golfing Legends

1 Arnold Palmer, b. Latrobe, Pa., 1929
2 Ken Venturi, b. San Francisco, Calif., 1931
3 Billy Harmon, b. New Rochelle, N.Y., 1950
4 Sandy Tatum, b. Los Angeles, Calif., 1920
5 Chuck Will, b. Philadelphia, Pa., 1925
6 Mickey Wright, b. San Diego, Calif., 1935
7 Fred Couples, b. Seattle, Wash., 1959
8 Dolphus Hull, b. Jackson, Miss., 1942
9 Tom Watson, b. Kansas City, Mo., 1949
10 Jaime Diaz, b. San Francisco, Calif., 1953
11 Curtis Strange, b. Norfolk, Va., 1955
12 Ben Crenshaw, b. Austin, Texas, 1952
13 Hale Irwin, b. Joplin, Mo., 1945
14 Neil Oxman, b. Philadelphia, Pa., 1952
15 Cliff Danley, b. Pittsburgh, Pa., 1948
16 Randy Erksine, b. Springfield, Ohio, 1948
17 Mike Donald, b. Grand Rapids, Mich., 1955
18 Jack Nicklaus, b. Upper Arlington, Ohio, 1940

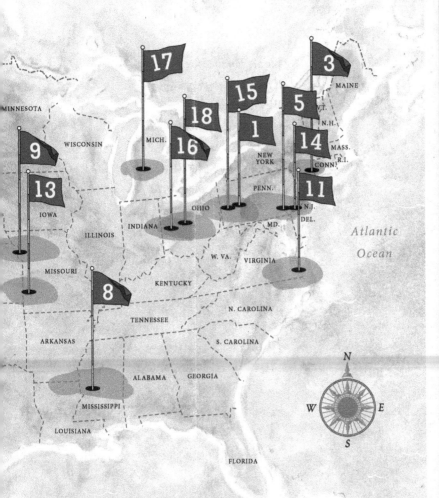

We are family.
I got all my sisters with me.
We are family.
Get up everybody and sing!

—"We Are Family" by Sister Sledge
Pittsburgh Pirates theme song, 1979

Augusta beckoned, as she does.

I was heading there by way of Charlotte, made one wrong turn, and found myself on Wilkinson Boulevard, pointing for downtown. One wrong turn and my mind went into a drift. All these old-timey motels hanging on. Which one was it?

I was remembering a day from thirty years earlier. More than thirty. It was the night of my brother's college graduation, and I was flying from Boston to Charlotte to caddie in a tournament there, a *professional* tournament, with stars in the field and a big cardboard check for the winner. Fred Graham, one of Cronkite's lieutenants on CBS News, was on my flight, sitting in first class, smoking a cigar. It was Fred Graham, for sure. He had that scar on his chin.

Scars were more common then. When I was growing up—in the village of Patchogue on the South Shore of Long Island in the sixties and seventies—there were still World War I vets on the benches by the VFW Hall with scars both visible and hidden. (We all knew the phrase *combat fatigue*.) My baseball hero, Cleon Jones, had a scar on his right cheek, the residue of a young-buck car accident that had sent him flying through a windshield. I learned about this face-changing mishap in *Cleon*, his 1970 autobiography, which I devoured when it became available at the Patchogue Library. Soon after, in that same library, I found Cleon Jones's phone number in Mobile, Alabama. What a thrill, to look at that exotic 205 area code and imagine the scene on the other end. And in that same vein, here was Fred Graham of CBS News with his positive-ID chin scar. I caught my breath. He was famous, yes, but it was more than that. He was a member of a nomadic tribe—newsmen—a group forever on the prowl, always going to some new place. It was May 1979. I was newly nineteen and looking to join the circus myself. Not Fred's. It was Golf Road that was calling.

Wilkinson Boulevard, when I stumbled on it en route to Augusta all those years later, was just another misstep in a long series of them for me, on the wrong street, likely heading the wrong direction, temperamentally incapable of using a smartphone map. No matter. Little waves of happiness were washing over me.

The accidental tourist: I know the concept well. Here I was, in the throes of middle age, and the song of the road was playing at full volume again. It plays for all of us, doesn't it? My own wanderlust is tempered by a powerful desire to get home, be home, stay home. Those urges were especially strong in the years when our kids were in the house. But they had grown into collegians. (My wife, Christine, once brought home a small sign: CHECKOUT TIME IS 18.) And even in our Swim Meet years, the pull of the road was always more than background music. In my line of work—*sportswriter*—if you're home too long, something's wrong.

I've never had a true office job, and in our married life Christine

and I have both always been coming and going. Our honeymoon was
seven months in Europe during which I worked as a caddie on Europe's professional golf tour. On long drives, Christine read aloud
Richard Halliburton's *The Royal Road to Romance*. My parents had the
massive Arthur Schlesinger biography of RFK that included a photo
of Bobby in front of the King David Hotel—Jerusalem, 1948—when
he was twenty-two with a gig as a reporter on the *Boston Post*. A snap
that inspires me to this day.

My mother and father left Nazi Germany as children with their
parents, and many years later they gave long formal interviews about
their wartime experiences. They dressed up for the occasion, which my
mother does with ease and my father less so. (His dress shoes all have
Vibram soles.) My mother spoke of family vacations in a village near a
Czechoslovakian forest in the 1930s and her fascination with the Gypsies on the edge of it, with their dark skin and light feet.

In 1959, when Khrushchev was coming to the United States, Mike
Wallace was on TV conducting a contest: What one place should U.S.
officials take the Soviet leader to show him the real America? The winner would get a car, and our family—with me on the way—needed
one. In my father's entry, he said the American hosts should have
Khrushchev throw a dart at a U.S. wall map and wherever it stuck was
where he would go, so that Nikita and his comrades back home would
understand that democracy thrives everywhere in the United States.
How did that not win?

One year my brother was given a globe with raised mountain
ranges. That was a big deal. Our father had a collection of Mobil travel
guides stacked on a basement shelf. I read them front to back. On our
family trips, David would read those accordion Hess and Esso road
maps for our father like he was reading the back of a baseball card.

David and I were devoted to the fine print of American life. We
will know forever the name Lou Niss, traveling secretary of the New

York Mets in the Cleon Jones years. He was in the team photo annually. What a job. Whatever that position actually entailed, I could not know. But he was at-large. In the agate type of the sports section in the *New York Times*, under the heading "Today's Games," whole cities were in transit: New York at St. Louis, Chicago at Philadelphia, Cincinnati at San Francisco.

All my youthful heroes were at-large: the ballplayers and the golfers, the beat writers and the war correspondents, the musicians and their silent roadies. A nod here to some hits from yesteryear: Peter, Paul and Mary singing "Five Hundred Miles," Glen Campbell singing "Wichita Lineman," David Wiffen singing "Driving Wheel." If you told me any of those songs were conceived on the side of the road, it wouldn't surprise me one bit.

Just came up on the midnight special
Honey, how about that
My car broke down in Texas
She stopped dead in her tracks.

Do you like how Wiffen's car gets the feminine pronoun treatment, as ships and principalities once did? My senior-year roommate called his boat of a station wagon Betsy. Another roommate, a physics major, wanted to be a long-distance truck driver. A high school buddy who shined shoes at the village course where I played in Bellport, one town east of Patchogue, saved his tip money for flying lessons. We were all in transit, at least in our dreams. The touring-caddie thing persisted in me for years.

Golf is a road game. Professional golf, of course, but the game as it is played on Sunday mornings, too. You start in one place, head out, have various adventures along the way, turn around, come on home. Chaucer would have had a field day with it, and Updike did. In one of the most beautiful sentences I know, from a short story for the ages, Updike describes an American banker on a Scottish links: "This was happiness, on this wasteland between the tracks and the beach, and freedom, of a wild and windy sort."

I am certain of little—I am leery of the overconfident reporter—and at nineteen I knew even less. But I knew what anybody with a TV might know: Every week a group of professional golfers assembled in some new and glamorous place and played a leisurely ball-and-stick game for money and glory. I was never going to be one of those golfers. Even with the advantage of starting young, in gym class at South Ocean Avenue Middle School, I never was much better than an 85 shooter at marshy Bellport, where I knew every hump. (In middle age, I have been besieged with the yips, a putting illness that takes away your desire to write down scores.) But I was aware that the golfers on our family TV all had caddies. That's where I saw my opening and my pathway to the circus.

In the winter of '79, in the long winter break of freshman year, I had a brief stint catching T-bars flung by dismounting night skiers at the top of the Bald Hill Ski Bowl. (Named, we always said, for its distinct lack of snow.) On a Saturday afternoon in late January I was watching the Andy Williams San Diego Open in my parents' living room. If golf was on TV, I watched. (My parents and brother had no interest. I had golf for myself.) At one point, CBS decided to show a journeyman doing nothing more than playing well: Randy Erskine, a reliable voice told us, of Battle Creek, Michigan.

I located this Randy Erskine of Battle Creek as I located Cleon Jones of Mobile. I wrote to him and asked him for a summer job as his traveling caddie. If the phrase *tour caddie* existed then, I doubt I knew it. The letter led to a phone call, which led me to a flight to Charlotte, site of the Kemper Open, on a May evening in 1979, when Fred Graham was sitting up front.

I headed out of the Charlotte airport that night and walked over to Wilkinson Boulevard and found a motel room for maybe fifteen dollars. It had to be the first night I was alone in a rented room. Early the next morning, the lady owner gave me a bowl of Raisin Bran and a tiny glass of orange juice and I was off.

The hair on Randy Erskine's arms was bleached blond by the sun and he kept his heavy watch, along with his wallet and wedding ring, in a purple velvet Crown Royal bag, which he stowed in his golf bag while he played. He had narrow hips that didn't rotate much on his backswing and a big shoulder turn. He used a Ping Pal putter, the same model used by my putting hero, Tom Watson. (Watson, so bold on the greens, made *everything*.) I had brought a tiny tool to clean the grooves on his irons, and that seemed to impress Randy. He played a practice round with a golfer named John Adams.

After one practice round, I found myself sitting in the back of a camper-van set up for the week in the parking lot of the Quail Hollow Country Club. Three touring pros—Randy, Doug Tewell, and Wayne Levi—were the real occupants of that camper-van, but nobody was chasing me away. Wayne Levi's denim golf bag was parked outside, standing up on its own. A rap session, tour-style, was under way. To this day, it all seems so unlikely. A fourth pro, a lanky man named Don Pooley, came by with his wife, and Randy said, "The Pooleys!" It was like a golf commune.

Randy Erskine's golf skill was like nothing I had ever seen, not up close. But his two-day total—150 shots, each of them accounted for on scorecards and sworn to with his signature—left him outside the cutline. His presence would not be needed for the Saturday and Sunday rounds. He made nothing that week, not on the greens and not in the way of a paycheck. Still, he stayed around to prepare for the thirty-six-hole U.S. Open qualifier that would be played on Monday.

People were talking about how the United States Golf Association had essentially forced Arnold Palmer, who hadn't met any of the automatic eligibility requirements for the '79 Open, to play in that qualifier. In other words, the USGA, in its hard-boiled wisdom, had not given a special exemption to the game's most popular and revered player, who was then chasing fifty. There were people who were offended by the way Palmer was being treated. But Palmer was registering no such complaint. He would not put himself above those who had to qualify.

Randy allowed me to use the second bed in his Holiday Inn room that weekend. (Amazing.) When we showed up early on Monday morning at the Charlotte Country Club, we found out that Randy would be playing right behind Arnold Palmer himself.

"Great," Randy said. "We gotta play in his wake all day."

I felt he was feigning frustration, and noted his use of *we*. Randy Erskine was a touring professional in the vicinity of Arnold Palmer. How could that be anything but good?

There were at least a hundred people following Palmer that day, but it was never anything like bedlam. Palmer's hair was already silver and his skin was bronzed. Palmer made it—he played his way into the U.S. Open. Randy did not. Still, he paid me one hundred dollars for the day. (Half that would have been generous.) He wasn't playing in that week's tournament in Atlanta. The week after that was the U.S. Open at Inverness in Toledo, Ohio, and he had just failed to qualify. But he would be playing the following week, in the Canadian Open. He said I could work for him in Canada.

And here I was, thirty-something years later, back in Charlotte, heading to Augusta in the name of *Sports Illustrated*. I got myself from Wilkinson Boulevard to Billy Graham Parkway to I-77 and motored my way south. I could not identify my old motel. Maybe it was gone.

I found myself thinking, for the first time in forever, about that long-ago Monday morning at the Charlotte Country Club, Arnold Palmer arriving in a shiny white Cadillac from a dealership that bore his name. He emerged from his grand chariot. Everybody inhaled. Time stopped. Arnold Palmer, in the flesh.

In October 2012 the Ryder Cup was played at Medinah, outside Chicago, and my assignment for the magazine was to help Davis Love III write a deadline first-person piece about his experience as Ryder Cup captain, a task that would be fun if the Americans won and challenging if they did not. Late at night, after the first day of the three-day competition, I was in a downtown restaurant by myself at a table with a paper tablecloth, and I found myself writing names on it. The names came to me quickly. I marked one column LIVING LEGENDS, the other SECRET LEGENDS.

LIVING LEGENDS
Arnold Palmer

Jack Nicklaus

Gary Player

Ken Venturi

Tom Watson

Curtis Strange

Fred Couples

Ben Crenshaw

Hale Irwin

SECRET LEGENDS
Sandy Tatum

Jaime Diaz

Billy Harmon

Neil Oxman

Dolphus Hull (aka Golf Ball)

Randy Erskine

Cliff Danley

Chuck Will

Mike Donald

Maybe I was subconsciously filling out lineup cards for a National League game, I don't know, but when I was done I had two columns with nine names each for a total of eighteen—golf's holy number.

During dessert, I decided to add Mickey Wright to the Living Legends list. The Big Three of the modern American golf swing are Ben Hogan, Tiger Woods, and Mickey Wright, and the list just didn't look right without her. (The first golf book I read was *Power Golf* by Ben Hogan, published originally in 1948. It was a hardcover, and I read it outside with a club in hand. Where my mother found it I have no idea.) When I added Mickey, I took off Gary Player, a nod to symmetry more than anything else. That move, unintentionally, made the list all-American. Seventeen American men and one American woman.

The Living Legends were all players. The Secret Legends list included a club pro, a teaching pro, a tour caddie. A tournament director in his sixties, a TV producer in his eighties, a former USGA president in his nineties. They had all shaped my life. They all, in different ways, had driven deep stakes into the game long before I started poking around in it in the mid-1970s. Because of that, they were all elder statesmen to me—even Fred Couples, less than six months older than I.

Later, I got out a map and put a little check mark by each legend's hometown. Before long, I had red marks in Pennsylvania, Michigan, California, Texas, Virginia, Ohio, and some other states. I concocted a vague plan to try to see each of them, notebook in hand, wherever I might find them. I got a little shiver. Does anything give a man more of a sense of purpose than a list?

My combined list had built-in problems. I didn't know if Golf Ball was alive or dead. Fred was impossible. (Likable but impossible.)

Palmer could be a challenge to interview. Mickey Wright didn't even come to the USGA museum for the dedication of its Mickey Wright Room. Nicklaus was far more interested in his work as a golf-course architect than in revisiting his old playing days.

Still, it was a good list. In that great episodic TV show of my youth—American Golf in the '70s!—all eighteen had a role. Bit or starring or in between, they were all there.

My plan, to the extent that I had one, was to pack these questions in my Target knapsack, along with my Lipitor and my hearing-aid batteries and my notebooks. "What was it like? Who did you hang with? How does then look to you now?" Or ditch all that and steal a question from the Proust Questionnaire in *Vanity Fair*: "When and where were you happiest?" A difficult question to answer, at least honestly. I wondered if I could answer it myself.

I have heard Palmer, Nicklaus, and Watson all say the same thing, each in his own way: *I wouldn't trade places with Tiger Woods for all the money in the world*. Gary Player, too. "Do I wish I had Tiger's access to private jets?" Player once said to me. "Yes. Do I wish I could have played with his equipment? Yes. But would I trade any aspect of my career and life for his? No."

I don't believe that things were better, to use a phrase Woods started using when he was about twenty-six, *back in the day*. I don't think that for a minute. I like flying in smoke-free planes and playing at clubs that would not have had me back in the day. But you are not going to convince me that Dustin Johnson is a more interesting person than Lee Trevino. You're not going to convince me that *The Big Break VI: Trump National* on Golf Channel will have anything like the staying power of Gene Littler versus Byron Nelson at Pine Valley on *Shell's Wonderful World of Golf*. You're not going to convince me that any sport-centric website is going to cover the game with the depth that the *New Yorker* did when Herbert Warren Wind was writing just a few golf pieces a year for the shiny weekly.

Dip into various golf events from Herb's era—Roberto De Vicenzo of Argentina losing the Masters in '68, for example—and you'll find that Herb covered it at length, in depth, and with humanity. Yes, you had to wait a few weeks, or longer, to get his story, but it was worth the wait. His work has held up. I read Herb's story about Di Vicenzo signing an incorrect card twenty years after the fact. It's some piece. As for the editors who signed off on its title, they knew what they were doing: "Rule 38, Paragraph 3."

Or, if you like, 38:3. Golf's rules come up in the game's various write-ups, with citations that look like chapter-and-verse biblical references. Maybe your eyes are rolling. The fact is, the rules are the spine of the game, at least when it is played seriously. I am nothing like an expert, but I do have an abiding interest in how the rules govern play. Maybe this interest in laws and their application is in my DNA. My grandfather's main hobbies were collecting stamps and studying Jewish law, and his brief, one-column obit in the *New York Times* ran with this headline:

DR. S. B. BAMBERGER,
CHEMIST, TALMUDIST

When I read *The Great Gatsby* for the first time, I noted with interest that Fitzgerald made Daisy's friend Jordan Baker an elite golfer who once was accused of cheating: "At her first big golf tournament there was a row that nearly reached the newspapers—a suggestion that she had moved her ball from a bad lie in the semi-final round. The thing approached the proportions of a scandal—then died away. A caddy retracted his statement, and the only other witness admitted that he might have been mistaken."

Whenever a rules dispute comes up, you might ask yourself: How would Roberto have handled it? De Vicenzo blamed nobody but himself at that '68 Masters. He said, "What a stupid I am." In word and deed, he was saying that a golfer is responsible for his scorecard. Any society with an underlying respect for rules is off to a running start, provided the rules make sense. It helps keep things civil.

Along those same lines, golf has a weird ability to foster camaraderie. Most of my enduring friendships have come through golf. The modern golf tour, if you can even use the word *tour* anymore, strikes me as lonely. (Must be all that money.) But I don't think it was for Arnold and Gary and Jack. Gary Nicklaus, Jack and Barbara's third son, is named for Gary Player, because the older Nicklaus boys had so much affection for "Uncle Gary." I will never let go of that moment in May '79 when Randy Erskine and his buddies were sitting in the back of that camper-van, fixing their backswings and plotting their futures.

It was no great shakes, 1979. A swamp rabbit attacked Jimmy Carter during a presidential fishing trip in Plains, Georgia. But it was a good year for golf. In that same state, in the same month, Fuzzy Zoeller won the Masters in a playoff over Ed Sneed and Watson, Nicklaus missing out by a shot. (Herb Wind's account reads like a thriller.) Big Jack was at his peak, and Arnold was still at it. Trevino won the Canadian Open in '79. Younger players—Tom Watson, Seve Ballesteros, Ben Crenshaw—were taking over center stage. Watson was a latter-day Huck Finn with a Stanford degree. Seve was a Spanish artiste. Crenshaw was a matinee idol. The low amateur at the '79 U.S. Open at Inverness was Fred Couples, in his first U.S. Open. Curtis Strange, already famous for his collegiate play, won his first tour event in '79.

I would like to point out that my legends have nothing to do with the modern penchant for celebrity worship. You can become a celebrity overnight. My legends have a serious body of work behind them. John Updike, referring to Ted Williams, famously wrote, "Gods don't answer letters." No, they don't.

The Ted Williams reference (you may know) relates to his refusal to take a curtain call after the final at-bat of his career, a home run into the Red Sox bullpen at Fenway. Williams courted nobody. Why would he need the Boston baseball writers when he *owned* the box scores? Maybe a piece of his humanity got robbed along the way, going through life the way he did. If you read the books about him, it sounds that way. Regardless, his lifetime batting average was .344. You can't have everything.

Tiger Woods has some Williams in him. He'll look right through you. I started covering Tiger when he was an amateur, and it's been an honor, writing up his golfing exploits. I am well north of a quarter-million words on Woods and counting. What luck: I was able to write about one of the most dominating athletic careers ever as it unfolded. Still, I would have enjoyed it much more had there been expressions of warmth from the man, hints of humility. I wish he would acknowledge that the game has given him far more than he could ever give it. Maybe he doesn't think that—I wouldn't know. One of my goals here is to see for myself whether Arnold and Jack and the rest really put the game ahead of themselves, or if that was a myth handed down to me by sportswriters happy to god-up the ballplayers.

Only a fool would try to dismiss what Woods has accomplished. (The most common method is to diminish his competition.) When Woods won the 2008 U.S. Open at Torrey Pines, that was his fourteenth major, and he was only thirty-two. Who wouldn't want to write up all *that?*

But I can say without even pausing that writing about other golfing lives has been far more meaningful to me. Arnold and Nicklaus and Watson spring right to mind, though I arrived on the scene long after their Cold War heydays. Collectively, they owned about thirty years of American golf, starting in '58, three decades when Tom Carvel was the voice of summer and you could play street hockey with his rock-hard Flying Saucers.

While we're kicking this theme around, I should explain the concept of Secret Legends: your Mike Donalds, your Neil Oxmans, your Billy Harmons. We all have our own, and here are others from my catalog: Hilome Jose, a Haitian artist; the guitarist Jorma Kaukonen, whom I have heard dozens of times; Ed Landers, a Martha's Vineyard fisherman discussed with hushed awe when I lived there. All men devoted to doing a difficult thing well. Craftsmen. You surely have a list of your own.

You probably don't know the name Joe Gergen. Joe Gergen was a sportswriter and columnist on *Newsday* when I was a kid. He covered the Mets, the Jets, the Knicks, and the Rangers, and he wrote like a dream. At the 1986 U.S. Open at Shinnecock Hills, typewriters dying but not yet dead, I sat behind Gergen in the press tent. On U.S. Open Sunday he wore a colorful short-sleeve shirt patterned with flowers, and he wrote up Raymond Floyd's win with one guy on his left elbow and another on his right. Three writers on deadline, and every five minutes they tilted their heads and laughed about something. It was Father's Day. Do you think he minded working? Not one bit. His story in the next day's paper was excellent, and I wanted to be him. Joe Gergen is not likely a legend to you. Why would he be? But he is to me. I'd die without people like that in my head.

A note here about Mike Donald, the legend with whom I have the most personal history. I met Mike in 1985, when he was playing in the Honda Classic and was paired with Brad Faxon, for whom I was caddying. Over the next six months—as a fledgling caddie with a plan to write my first book—I saw Mike here and there. My boss, Bill Britton, would play in practice rounds with Mike, one of his closest friends. Or they'd hit balls and look at each other's swings. Or I'd see Mike on Friday afternoons, standing in front of that week's giant scoreboard, pointing at names, counting scores, calculating where the ax—the cut number—would fall. His nickname was Statman.

In '86, I caddied for Mike for one memorable week, at the Colonial tournament in Fort Worth. That week was a semi-disaster and included a mortifying rules question for which I was responsible. All in all, not my best week. My main purpose in Fort Worth was to promote the aforementioned book. I should have told Mike that when I sought his bag for the week. I now realize the week was doomed before I even arrived. It's embarrassing for me, looking back at it. Talk about young and dumb.

By the high standards of tour play, Mike was considered average in every category except three: chipping, putting, and intensity. In '89, after playing in more than three hundred tour events and having posted more than twenty top-ten finishes, he won the Williamsburg stop, the Anheuser-Busch Golf Classic. He was thirty-four and had his first tour win.

That win got Mike into the Masters for the first time, the following April. He shot an opening-round 64 in the '90 Masters, one shot short of tying the course record. Two months later, Mike played in the U.S. Open at Medinah. Hale Irwin shot a final-round 67 to come in at 280. About two hours later, in the final group of the day, Mike made a par on the seventy-second hole to post 280 as well. Their Sunday-night tie meant an eighteen-hole playoff the next day. After those eighteen holes they were still tied, which meant for the first time a U.S. Open would be decided by so-called sudden death. The next winner of a hole would be the champ. Mike and Hale went to the first tee for the ninety-first hole of the championship.

I can't imagine anybody (outside of Hale Irwin's immediate family) not pulling for Mike in that playoff. He was the classic underdog, and who doesn't cheer for an underdog? Hale Irwin was already in the pantheon, by way of his '74 and '79 U.S. Open wins. What Irwin was attempting to do, at age forty-five, was impressive. But it paled in comparison to Mike's quest. In the 1955 Open, Jack Fleck, a club pro from a public course in Iowa, defeated the great Hogan in a playoff. Mike was another lunch-bucket pro trying to knock off a legend in the most demanding event in golf.

I was working that Sunday, covering a Phillies matinee, and watched good chunks of the fourth round in the manager's office at Veterans Stadium. I watched the Monday final at home on a day off. What Mike did that day was raise expectations, for himself or anyone with middling skills, in any trade or craft or profession. Watching Mike made you realize that past performance really doesn't always predict future results. Mike was going toe to toe with Hale Irwin! All the while, watching the events unfold on ABC, we could not know that the best was still to come: Mike in defeat. There was a moment at the end of the playoff that screamed at me. Irwin made a twelve-foot birdie putt to win. He had his third Open. He had become the oldest player ever to win an Open. He was dancing around. And there was Mike, holding out a hand in a manner that was just so . . . *dignified*.

Our friendship began for real five years later, when I was writing a piece about him. Mike told me about accepting an offer to play in Sweden soon after that U.S. Open for a thirty-five-thousand-dollar appearance fee and all expenses paid for Mike and his parents. "To be honest, I felt like a whore," Mike told me with my notebook open. Who is that honest? After the '90 U.S. Open, he never revisited that level of play. I sat amazed, with the five-year anniversary coming up, as Mike tried to analyze what had happened to his game and to him.

Had Mike won in '90, I'm sure our friendship never would have developed as it did. You can't have a real friendship with a winner. You come into a person's life after the prize ceremony, you'll always be a Johnny-come-lately. I expressed this to Mike once, and he said, "If I had won, you wouldn't have been interested in writing about me." He's probably right. At *SI*, my assignment is often to write the loser. I like it.

Mike played the circuit hard, as hard as anybody. For years he played thirty to thirty-five events a year. He had a true grasp of the tour and how it worked, and the other players knew it. Even though he never finished higher than twenty-second on the annual money list, he was at the center of the game. Tiger Woods drops in and drops out when it suits him. Phil Mickelson, Ernie Els, Rory McIlroy, they all do that. Mike was *on tour*. He was at-large.

In various ways, we could not be more different. I am trusting and Mike is suspicious. Yet Mike tends to overshare and I underdo it. He watches everything and I read, too narrowly. He understands the stock market in ways that I do not. He is profane and I'm not, or at least not at Mike's level. I see gray in everything and Mike *tries* to see things in black or white. Mike likes the windows up and I like them down. But we have significant similarities, too. We're both good tippers. We both have good memories. We both like to try to figure things out.

When he was fifteen, Mike skipped school and caddied in the 1970 Coral Springs Open, near his home in Hollywood, in South Florida. He can tell you what Hale Irwin and Lee Trevino did that week and that Palmer stayed in a house on the course sponsored by Westinghouse known as "The House of the Future." (You could turn a light on and off in it by waving your arms.) Mike remembers Palmer wearing a baby-blue shirt with dark-brown pants and wondering whether that was a good match. He of course remembers who won: Bill Garrett. Mike was his caddie, and Garrett paid Mike a fortune.

I once asked Mike, "Did you do anything to help Garrett at all?"

"*Noooooooo*," Mike said. "Shit no. I carried the bag!"

One day I was looking at my legends list and thinking about the start of my tour. What the hell was I actually looking to do? Write something longer than six hundred words. Explore friendship. Have an adventure. Try to understand the lives and times of craftsmen I admired. Rekindle my boyhood excitement.

As a reporter I work solo. It's a rewarding and lonesome way to proceed. I'm not even sure why, but one day I found myself asking

Mike if he wanted to join me on the tour's first stop. I would have asked him if he wanted to sign up for the whole thing, but Mike, like me, avoids commitment. Plus, I couldn't know if there would be a whole thing. Anyway, we both do most everything on the fly. We've had many excellent meals, rounds of golf, and ballgames over the years with little advance planning, if any.

Mike said yes. No questions, just yes. He caught a flight to Philadelphia, and we hopped in my car and drove clear across Pennsylvania, off to see Arnold Palmer, in Latrobe. You got to start somewhere, right?

My Outback, the old gal, broke through the 184,000-mile mark on the way there. *Cele-a-brate good times, c'mon!* I warned Mike that the horn, with a mind of its own, could go off at any time, but he's been around beaters all his life. He wasn't fazed.

The trunk was a little crowded, what with the yard-sale tennis rackets and the Kadima paddles, a swimsuit, running shoes, a baseball glove, various cases from Bonnie Raitt CDs, and emergency reading material, plus a golf bag and various stray clubs. (Have at 'em, smash-and-grabbers. I warn you, though, that 6-hybrid is lousy into the wind.) Then there were Mike's clubs, concealed in a traveling coffin. Christine, underwhelmed by the car's aroma and trying to talk me into an upgrade, had told me more than once, "It's like a locker room." Actually, she could have dropped the word *like*. Mike had no problems with it. I've seen his car.

The Pennsylvania Turnpike yawned before us, the portal from the congested Eastern Seaboard, where I have spent my life, to the wide and open Midwest. Neil Oxman likes to say that Pennsylvania is Philadelphia and Pittsburgh with Alabama in between. The fact is once you're west of Harrisburg you might as well be in Ohio.

We stopped for gas at a drive-off plaza. A college volleyball team was there from one of the rural state schools, tall wispy athletes in flip-flops boarding their team bus on a warm, still evening. You could feel their giddiness across the macadam. They were on a road trip, too.

Along the way, Mike asked, "Who's signed more autographs than this guy?" *This guy* is Mike's all-purpose pronoun. Here it meant Arnold.

We mulled it over. Cal Ripken signed all night and he played in 3,001 regular-season games alone. Bill Clinton and Phil Mickelson are inveterate signers. But Palmer had been signing for a half century, one tournament after another, one testimonial dinner after another, one golf course opening after another.

"Nobody," I said. "Nobody could be close."

"Nobody!" Mike said.

Mike is not an autograph collector, but for years on behalf of a friend he had been trying to get all the living British Open winners to sign a poster of the Old Course. It had become a scavenger hunt for him. By the time of our trip to see Arnold, Mike had a vacancy for Roberto De Vicenzo, the Open winner in '67, and several others. He got Palmer one year at a senior event in Houston and Woods one year at Doral, in the players' locker room. Tiger recognized Mike, and Mike opened with the perfect question: "Tiger, do you sign posters?" Tiger was fine with it. I was nervous as Mike was telling me the story. I've seen Tiger be churlish at such requests, particularly with tournament officials. But I imagine with Mike it was different. I think Woods respects any pro who has worked hard, tried his best, and made a living at the game. That's what Woods has done.

Palmer has the knack of making autograph seekers feel good about themselves. George Clooney, I think, has the same skill. In a *New Yorker* profile, Clooney once talked about the post-autograph moment, when the recipient feels exposed and vulnerable. Clooney's goal, he said, is to show autograph seekers "a path back to their normal selves." How nice. Palmer would never analyze the transaction in such depth, but he instinctively does just what Clooney describes. As Palmer signs, he often says, "Nice to see you." His signature is heavy, inky, curvy, legible. It's a beautiful signature. It's part of his trademark.

At one point the Outback conversation morphed into: "Who's *bigger* than this guy?"

Your answer is going to depend on your age, the influence of your father-in-law, various other factors. Two of Palmer's rough contemporaries, Ronald Reagan and John Wayne, were vastly bigger figures on the American landscape, but they were dead. Joe DiMaggio, Elvis Presley, Bing Crosby, Johnny Carson, Paul Newman, the same. But among the living? As a pure American icon? Who was bigger than Palmer? Ali. Maybe Magic Johnson. Maybe Warren Buffett. There must be others. But not many.

Arnie (as my late father-in-law called him) held particular appeal for anybody who ever shopped at Sears. He looked and acted like a man who followed all the rules of middle-class life, mowing his own lawn and taking out the trash. But we knew that wasn't really the case, and that's the part we liked best. We knew that if Arnold suddenly had an urge to visit the Playboy Mansion, he likely got in his plane, flew to Chicago, had himself a big time, and made it back home in time for breakfast with Winnie and the girls. If you watched him in his prime, or if you've seen the clips, there's something almost lawless about his play. But his respect for the game, and the accuracy of his scorecard, was never questioned. Well, that last part should be amended. There was one murky episode, in many, many years of play. But other than that, we're talking about pretty much a spotless career. Arnold was a man who was respectful to his playing partners, warm to his fans, accommodating to the writers, a man who complained about nothing.

If Arnold was profound, or had unique insight into the human condition, I didn't know about it. And yet there he was, just south of John Wayne. And what did he do to get there? He won a bunch of golf tournaments with more than a soupçon of style. He mixed iced tea with lemonade. He stayed married. He attached his name to a hospital and other good causes. He made people feel good. And that evidently was enough. That was enough to allow a small-town man playing a niche sport for no money to wind up on the highest floor of the American Pantheon Building, in a paneled room with an open bar. How on earth did that happen? What was it about the man that *allowed* that to happen?

His home state rolled by, her craggy farms and sleepy rivers almost blotted out by the blue-black October night.

We arrived at the SpringHill Suites in Latrobe, at 115 Arnold Palmer Drive, late at night. Arnold was a part owner. Our rooms were $125 per night, make-your-own-waffle breakfast included.

At the front desk were free copies of a magazine called *Kingdom*. The walls were a collage of Arnold Palmer photographs. In the lobby, a group of middle-aged men, hotel guests, were carting around golf bags. I asked the man in front of me on the check-in line if they were playing in some sort of tournament. He showed no interest in conversation. "Could you believe that fucking guy?" Mike said later. "He's looking at you like, 'Who the fuck are you to talk to me?' "

Maybe you're wondering: Could Mike not squeeze one more *fuck* into those two sentences? Evidently, no. I'm not trying to shock anybody here. I am trying to capture people as they actually are. I assume that's why you're here.

When I was setting up the trip to Latrobe, I asked Donald "Doc" Giffin, Palmer's aide-de-camp since 1966, if Mike could come, too. He and Arnold knew him and were happy to have him.

"He's one of the best reporters I know," I told Doc.

He is. Mike is the best natural reporter I know. He challenges every assumption.

"I didn't know that about Mike," Doc said. Doc is a stolid man, like Arnold himself.

There were many older sportswriters who knew Arnold far better than I, but I knew him. I'd done maybe a dozen interviews with him over the span of twenty-five years. I'd been alone with him, which I note because it's uncommon. Arnold likes to have a group around him whenever possible. I've ordered Arnold Palmers at lunches with him. I once asked him what it's like when people order an Arnold Palmer in his presence. "It's a little embarrassing," he said.

The photograph of Arnold on the Arizona Arnold Palmer Half & Half cans is an interesting choice. In the shot, Arnold's hair is silver and flopped down over his browed forehead. He's in his late fifties. In other words, it's Arnold long after his athletic prime. But that was part of the marketing genius behind Arnold Palmer Enterprises. Don't sell the golfer, because his golf skill will come and go. Sell the man.

Arnold in the 1980s, when he was in his fifties, was still having a good time. Mike played with Arnold in the early 1990s at a Peter Jacobsen charity tournament in Oregon, and Arnold told Mike that his "best times" were in his fifties. But it's not like Arnold went into a cave the day he turned sixty. Far from it. Just take a look at the clips of him playing his final U.S. Open in 1994 at a sweltering Oakmont. Arnold marched up and down Oakmont's hills, sweating through a white shirt and a floppy straw hat, waving at fans like he was in a parade. Nobody cared what he was shooting. Over his ball he was still making that familiar, oomphy crazy swing. He was sixty-four and still virile.

About five years after that Open, I was in the California Pizza Kitchen on PGA Boulevard in Palm Beach Gardens, near the PGA of America headquarters. I had ordered an iced tea and lemonade mixed together. The young waitress said, "Oh, you mean an Arnold Palmer."

"Do you know who that is?" I asked.

She didn't. She just knew the name as a drink.

The check came, a computer-generated check at a national chain restaurant, and right on it were the words ARNOLD PALMER.

The next day I was with Arnold Palmer. We were in his work-room in his townhouse at Bay Hill. I told him what had happened at the California Pizza Kitchen. He got out the most slender cell phone I had ever seen, called his business manager, and relayed the story. He said, "Is there a name-rights issue here we should be looking into?"

One more thing before we go in and see the man: In 2000, as a paid spokesman for Callaway, Arnold endorsed a driver called the ERC II, a club legal for play everywhere in the world except the United States and Mexico. (The Royal and Ancient Golf Club had approved it and the USGA had not.) In an opinion piece in *SI*, my friend and fellow writer Gary Van Sickle eviscerated Arnold over his endorsement. In editing, the piece only became tougher. The headline was BENEDICT ARNOLD. The subhead was a kick in the teeth: *When Arnold Palmer said it was O.K. to cheat, his reign as the King ended.*

Word came back quickly that Arnold was really annoyed. He had won the U.S. Amateur in '54, the year *SI* began publishing, and the magazine had run a long, detailed report by Herbert Warren Wind about his win. Arnold was the magazine's Sportsman of the Year in 1960. His heyday and the magazine's were one and the same. My boss told me to call Arnold and take his temperature. Through Doc, I got Arnold on the phone with relative ease. I said, "Arnold, this is Michael Bamberger with *SI*."

"I know who you are," Palmer said. "And evidently you don't give a shit *who* you write for these days."

That's exactly what he said to me on a fall day in 2000 when I got him on the phone and he was all pissed off at my magazine. I loved it. There's too much chickenshit corporate-speak from athletes these days. It was so nice to hear something real.

Even I could not get lost, finding Arnold's offices at One Legends Lane, across the street from the entrance to the Latrobe Country Club. Yeah, sure, that address—it's a bit much, but so what? Nicklaus likes to say that you could not enjoy being whoever you are more than Arnold Palmer enjoys being Arnold Palmer. *Legends Lane.*

Arnold's offices were housed in a one-story white brick building, uncannily similar to the wings attached to the Augusta National club- house, not even a half mile from the first tee at Latrobe, where Arnold's father worked all his adult life as the greenkeeper and club pro. (As soon as he could, Arnold bought the club.) On the downhill side of Legends Lane is the house Arnold built with Winnie, his first wife, who died in 1999. That house is a modest brick rancher where Arnold and Winnie lived for forty-two years and raised their two daughters.

On the uphill side of Legends Lane is a modern wooden home, almost camouflaged by the trees that flank it. Arnold built that house with his second wife, Kit Palmer, whom he married in 2005. When they're not at Bay Hill or in the California desert that's where they live.

Mike and I arrived early, and Doc, in a sport coat and tie, ushered us into Arnold's office. Arnold was wearing a brown plaid shirt and had a green sweater draped over his shoulders.

Maybe you've had this experience, that moment of shock when you're face-to-face with a legend, even if you're semi-accustomed to seeing the person on TV. Some odd thought crosses your mind. *Man, that Doris Kearns Goodwin is . . . skinny!* I have had the moment with President Ford and President Clinton. (Golf got me to both.) I have had it with John Wooden, Henry Aaron, Caroline Kennedy. And I have it every time I see Arnold Palmer. It's hard to describe what happens, but it's kind of like his old Pennzoil ads and snapshots from his Augusta heyday and assorted other mental pictures all converge at once.

Arnold, two years younger than my father and eighteen months older than my mother, looked great, tanned and strong. He was energetic. He had recently turned eighty-three. He was sitting in a big brown leather desk chair that did not dwarf him. He stood to shake our hands.

Mike and I sat in chairs in front of Arnold's desk. Doc sat nearby with his personal Arnold Palmer record book in his lap. We went in with no agenda except to try to get Arnold to talk about something meaningful to him, to talk about a time when every day seemed exciting and fresh and new.

With gentle assistance from Doc, Mike and I opened a door for Arnold marked *1954*. And Arnold walked through it. His speech, right from the beginning, was slow and measured and precise. He began with his win at the U.S. Amateur at the Country Club of Detroit in late August 1954. He was almost twenty-five, a bachelor, an ex–Coast Guardsman, a Wake Forest dropout. He was living in Cleveland and selling paint. He came from a workingman's club nobody knew, and in the final he defeated a tall, slim member of the Long Island golf establishment. (In Herb Wind's *SI* account of the event you might detect just a hint of class warfare.) Arnold half-bellowed to his secretary and asked her to bring Mike and me copies of a slender, privately published book about the '54 Amateur called *The Turning Point*. They were pre-signed in Arnold's perfect script.

From Detroit, Arnold took us to early September '54, a few days after his win in the Amateur, when he and three buddies made the four-hundred-mile drive from Cleveland to the Shawnee Resort, on the Delaware River in eastern Pennsylvania. They went there to play in an amateur tournament over Labor Day weekend. Fred Waring was the host. He was a celebrity bandleader and the inventor of the Waring blender.

Arnold was revisiting his introduction to a nineteen-year-old

Pembroke College student named Winnie Walzer of Coopersburg, Pennsylvania, daughter of Martin Walzer, an owner of a canned-foods business, and Mary Walzer, a schoolteacher.

"I met her on Tuesday morning, she and Dixie Waring, Fred's daughter, at the hotel at Shawnee," Arnold said. "They were coming down the stairs, and I was there registering. Somebody said, 'You want to meet a couple of good-looking girls?' And I said, 'Hell yes.' I was single. And they introduced me to Dixie and Winnie. It was my shot. I could take either one. They were both available."

Some of the story was vaguely familiar to me from Arnold's autobiography, *A Golfer's Life*. But this version was unvarnished.

"So I said to Winnie, 'Why don't you come follow me?'

"She says, 'I can't follow you. We just met. I have to follow Uncle Fred.' That was the first day.

"The second day I told her again that she should follow me. So she did.

"My partner was Tommy—what was his name, guy from Detroit—Tommy Sheehan. He was a good player. And we romped the field. We won going away. And Saturday night I said to Winnie at the banquet, 'Will you marry me?'

"She said, 'Well, can I have a few days?'

"I said, 'Not really. You better decide pretty quick.'

"And she said, 'Well, give me a day or two and let me talk to my parents.'"

Let's pause for a moment to let this all sink in: He met the girl, a nineteen-year-old, on a Tuesday. He proposed four days later. He was about to turn twenty-five, and suddenly after some years of not doing very much he had an epic to-do list. Getting married was on it. He got his yes a day after he asked, but it came with an asterisk.

"She said, 'My parents don't like the idea.'

"Her dad hated my ass. He said to her, 'You're going to marry a golf pro?'"

A few days after the Fred Waring tournament, Arnold borrowed money from his Cleveland gang and bought an engagement ring. Two months later he turned pro.

There was no good reason to think that Arnold could make money at it. The previous year Lew Worsham—older brother of Arnold's Wake Forest roommate, Bud—won two events and finished first on the money list with $34,002. Arnold couldn't know how his game would stack up. The gods of the circuit, Hogan and Nelson and Snead, played a different game from Palmer. They kept the ball in front of them. They plotted. Hogan, particularly, was a thinker. He played chess on a 150-acre board.

Arnold played muscular, slashing golf that was far more suited to match play, the amateur game, than the seventy-two-hole stroke-play events the pros typically played. (*Go for broke* was not yet a phrase of golf, nor the name of one of Arnold's many books.) To make it, Arnold would have to improve, and improving in professional golf is exceedingly difficult. You have to make a series of good decisions and compensate for your bad ones. Still, the Wilson Sporting Goods Co. of Chicago was willing to put Arnold on its staff and give him Wilson Staff irons and a set of woods, a golf bag, and boxes of mushy Wilson Staff balls, and to sign him to a modest deal. Arnold drove to Miami with his father to play in his first professional tournament, the Miami Springs Open. "And at the tournament I ran into a model that I knew from Chicago," Arnold said. "And she was a good-looking broad."

The phrase *good-looking broad*, by the way, does not appear in *A Golfer's Life*.

"And I'm engaged now to Winnie. I was out with the model that evening, and I got back to the hotel where my dad was. And it was late.

"He said, 'Where in the hell have you been?'

"My father was tough. He was no patsy. And I told him I had run into this lady.

"My father says, 'Arnie, you're engaged. You make up your mind. Are you going to play the tour? Are you going to quit screwing around? Where's your fiancée?'

"I said, 'She's in Coopersburg.'

"He said, 'Well, you get your ass up there and get her and get going on what you're going to do.'

"I said, 'What do you mean?'

"He says, 'You take the car and go get Winnie and decide what you want to do.'

"So I went to Coopersburg and four days later I was married. We went to Washington, where my sister was, got a marriage license, and got married. We came here for the holidays."

Christmas in Latrobe, 1954. Their honeymoon night was spent at a motel for truckers off the Breezewood exit of the Pennsylvania Turnpike.

Get your ass up there. People my age and younger don't even know how to use the word *ass* anymore, but older people do. My father, the least vulgar of men and the most encouraging of fathers, once criticized my boyhood leaf-raking with "That's a half-assed job." Today a parent who dares to be critical is shunned during the cookie portion of parent-teacher night. The real truth is that my father wasn't being critical. He was teaching me something. Arnold's father, the same. Deacon Palmer didn't care how good-looking that Chicago model was.

I asked Arnold about earlier girlfriends, if he had ever been close to getting married before meeting Winnie.

"Well, I fucked a few," Arnold said. "But I never wanted to marry them."

Arnold was going off-script. He knew he was not portraying himself as a saint. But he was doing something better and more useful. He was telling a story that was actually believable. I think he wanted us to know the real story of when Arnie met Winnie. For our benefit, for yours, and for his own, too. You know what they say: The truth will set you free.

In his own way, Arnold expressed a deep love for his life with Winnie.

He said, "Winnie did what I wanted to do. She worked with me all the time. She didn't mind if I was practicing. And I practiced a lot. She came and watched me. And it was great."

Okay, Winnie was in a subservient role, no question about that. But in 1954 nobody was talking about feminism, at least not within the confines of the mainstream American marriage. My parents, I'm sure, had about the same setup. In 1954 *Father Knows Best* had just come on TV; Gloria Steinem, Winnie's age exactly, was an undergraduate at Smith; and Mr. and Mrs. Arnold D. Palmer were conjoined by elopement.

And it was great.

Would Winnie have said the same? We can't know. Different answers at different times, in all likelihood. As in any marriage. Right then, Arnold was remembering their early days when they shared a dream known only to them, the road in front of them was wide open, and anything seemed possible.

Christmas 1954 segued into the new year and the start of his rookie season. Arnold told us how he and Winnie started traveling the tour in a four-door Ford, lugging a trailer behind them. The first trailer, which died young, was nineteen feet long. The next model was a twenty-seven-footer, a home on wheels that toured all of California and the west, crossed the country to Florida, migrated north from there to Augusta. For nearly four months, everything Arnie and Winnie did, they did in that trailer.

"After Augusta we came home, right here to Latrobe, and pulled that trailer in my father's backyard and parked it," Arnold said. "And

Winnie looked at me and said, 'You know how much I love you. I'll do anything you want to do. But I will never go with you in a trailer again.' "

There was a beautiful portrait of Winnie on a nearby wall, her hair swooped back. She looked like a Breck Girl.

"The trailer never went again."

Arnold looked right at us. The silver hair, the massive head, the creased face. This was not cocktail chatter. It was his life.

I was struck by Arnold's coarse, plain language, by its Rat Pack cool and economy. His golf ball was "that son of a bitch." The old pro Dutch Harrison, a gambler, got Arnold into a big-bucks pro-am and wanted a "kickback." The Hall of Famer Tommy Bolt "was *so* bad." A double-date fishing trip with Bolt and his wife, Shirley, ended with the two of them "throwing knives at each other" and Arnold saying to Winnie, "Babe, we gotta split." On the road out, they saw Bolt's own son "thumbing." Regarding the successful Latrobe lumberman for whom Palmer had caddied as a kid: "I hung close." He called himself "dumber than a rock." (Fat chance.) When he made money in a Calcutta gambling game, he was "as happy as a dog going to a farting contest with six assholes." His great college friend Bud Worsham was a "bad drinker" and Arnold had to "pull him out of ditches." (Bud, along with a Wake Forest basketball player, died in a late-night car accident when Arnold was a senior.) Arnold got his "ass kicked" on the course by so-and-so. He remembered Bobby Jones once telling him, "If I ever need an eight-foot putt for my life, you're going to putt it." *For my life.* They played for high stakes.

Mike asked Arnold if there was a party in Latrobe after he won his first tour event, the 1955 Canadian Open.

"No," Arnold said. "It was quiet."

You can see clips from that win in the Arnold Palmer Room at the USGA museum in the New Jersey horse country. It also has home movies of Arnold, Arnold doing a Pennzoil ad, Arnold holing out on the eighteenth green on Sunday at Augusta in '58, when he won the first of his four titles there. You can see skinny Ken Venturi on the green with him, warmly congratulating him. The scene, in black and white, has a certain timeless grace.

Mike and I sat there listening to Arnold checking off all these old names. I knew most of them, and Mike knew every last one. Dutch Harrison, Dick Mayer, Tommy Bolt, Billy Casper. Ky Laffoon, Porky Oliver. Gene Littler. Hogan and Nelson and Snead. The Worsham brothers and Skip Alexander. (Mike played golf for his son, Buddy Alexander, at Georgia Southern.) Ed Furgol. Harvie Ward. Fred Hawkins. Al Besselink. Mike and I once spent half a day with Besselink, a tour star from the fifties with a loaf of yellow hair. Bessie was a habitué of the South Florida golf scene but also well known at the betting windows at Gulfstream and Hialeah. Mike had been quoting for years something Bessie told us that day: "Don't date no brokes."

"I'll never forget this," Arnold said. "Winnie and I are driving from Baton Rouge to Pensacola. We're watching the car in front of us. All of a sudden sparks are coming out of the back of that car. I'm watching. And I thought, *I'm seeing something that I don't understand.*

"I pulled up closer to them and there's Besselink hanging out of the back door of the car, grinding a wedge on the highway. That's what the sparks were."

You could see it like it was in a movie.

"It really happened," Arnold said.

"Al Besselink's a crazy man," Mike said.

"Oh, shit," Arnold said in casual agreement.

Arnold's wealth is vast. In 2000 he was worth over $300 million, despite earning only $4.4 million on the regular and senior tours over a fifty-year career. But Pennzoil loved him, and so did, at various times,

Hertz, Rolex, Wilson, Callaway, Ketel One, Arizona Beverage, Lamkin grips, the Bay Hill Club & Lodge, *Golf* magazine, *Golf Digest*, Random House, Cessna, United Airlines, Sears, various auto dealers in Charlotte and Orlando and Latrobe, Golf Channel, and the long list of developers who hired Arnold as a course architect.

That list barely scratches the surface. It also included Toro (lawn mowers), Robert Bruce (clothing), Paine Webber (money). Plus Palmer's forays into dry-cleaning and golf-club manufacturing and, less significantly, a product called Arnold Palmer Foot Detergent. You can still find Arnold Palmer Indoor Golf, stepbrother of Bobby Hull Hockey, at your better yard sales. In that game, the toy Arnold takes the club back shut, just as the real Arnold did. Hogan hated that move.

Mike has an abiding interest in money. He's tried, with some success, to teach me about option trading, but it was work. Arnold is more like Mike. When he talked about money—the cost of his first house, the size of his first tour check, the expense of his first engagement ring—he was always precise. Mike was hanging on every word. One of his tests for character is how people spend and save their money.

"At what point did you buy your first home?" Mike asked.

Arnold's answer took him straight to Ed Anderson, the successful Latrobe lumberman he caddied for, who gradually raised Arnold's rate from a quarter to a half-dollar to a dollar. No wonder Arnold hung close.

"I said to him, 'Mr. Anderson, I'd like to buy some land from you.' This was in '56.

"He said, 'Where's that, Arnie?'

"I said, 'Across the road from the course.'

"He said, 'You can't afford that land.'

"I said, 'Yeah, well, I'd like to try to buy it.'

"He said, 'I'll sell you enough for a house.' "

Mr. Anderson sold just under two acres to Arnold. Nearly sixty years later that land was still home to the original Arnold-and-Winnie rancher, the new home where Arnold lived with Kit, and Arnold's suite of offices at the end of Legends Lane. It was all impressively modest. It was right out of the Warren Buffett playbook.

Living within one's means happens to be a central tenet of Mike's life. You don't even want to hear him on the subject of young tour players with one or two wins who fly on private jets and live in coastal mansions with his-and-her Land Rovers on their Belgian block driveways. He knows what they don't: Someday they will stop making short putts.

Mike asked Arnold, "At what point did you feel secure, that you knew you were going to be a professional golfer for an extended period of time?"

Mike once told me that he turned pro "to avoid getting a real job." When he was starting out, he never expected he'd be able to make a living from his play.

"I never took that attitude," Arnold said. "I always remained very money-conscious." He never allowed himself to feel secure. He never allowed himself to think he was set for life.

They were comparing notes, pro to pro. The scale of achievement was different but the similarities were considerable.

Arnold talked about the old tour apprentice rules, by which a player had to wait six months before he could cash his first check. Mike knew about that system, but he was appalled all over again.

"Six months!" Mike said.

Arnold made a sad nod.

Mike then told Arnold about a prominent pro with a massive house in foreclosure, a player who'd had some excellent years and endorsement deals worth tens of millions of dollars. Arnold was all ears.

He asked, "Where is that money?"

Arnold has two grandsons. One, Sam Saunders, grew up at Bay Hill and was in his mid-twenties. Sam had a good college golf career at

Clemson and played some on the PGA Tour, often on sponsors' exemptions with Arnold's fingerprints on them. Most of Sam's professional golf has been on the Web.com tour, golf's answer to Class AAA ball. There could not have been a thousand golfers in the world who were better than Sam, but every year new ones come into the pro game and existing ones try to figure out ways to hang on. The game is actually vicious. Sam could make it on tour, but the odds are long. You have to make many smart decisions about your swing and whom to trust with it, what clubs to play, how and when to practice, whom to hire as your caddie, when to take dead aim, when to lay up. You can get all sorts of advice in golf, but when you're standing over your ball you're all alone.

Arnold's other grandson, Will Wears, was in high school. Arnold described him as the best player on his school team, breaking 80 regularly and showing interest in the game.

Arnold spent many hours with both grandsons. Will was living near Latrobe, and Arnold said he wanted golf instruction from his grandfather. Mike asked about Sam. Was he getting from Arnold the kind of golf and life lessons Arnold received from his father?

There was a longish pause before Arnold answered. It was his first cautious moment with us.

"It's a little different; I'm not his father," Arnold said.

Profound.

Before our day in Latrobe was over, Arnold turned himself into a tour guide. "Have you ever been inside the house?" he asked.

We shook our heads.

"Well, I'll show it to you."

For the first time we could see Arnold's age. With every step he took, his shoulders listed to one side and then the other.

The first stop on the house tour was in front of a gentle landscape painting given to Arnold for his thirty-seventh birthday in 1966 by its painter, Dwight Eisenhower.

It was a mountain house, really, sturdy and handsome. Mike said, "It's a house where you can tell people actually live." There was almost nothing golfy in it except the family dog, a golden retriever named Mulligan.

"Where's Mommy?" Arnold asked Mulligan.

Kit, who designed the house, came in, shook hands with us, and said to me, "Nice to meet you."

Arnold said, "You've met Michael before."

We had met, but it had been years earlier. I don't know how Arnold could have remembered. His ability to make people comfortable is astounding.

Arnold took us through the house. The tour concluded in his master bathroom. It was not ornate. No gold anything. Just a nice bathroom with a deep tub. Arnold showed it with pride. You can probably guess how it compared to the loo from his Depression-era boyhood home or even to the one in the rancher he shared with Winnie. That master bathroom was paid for, when you get right down to it, by his skill in golf. Everything in his life followed from that. You could tell Arnold knew that and never forgot it, not even for a minute.

Earlier, Arnold had taken us into his workshop, near his office. In the workshop were hundreds of golf clubs and an elaborate painting that a fan had sent, diagraming every shot Arnold hit en route to winning the 1961 British Open at Royal Birkdale.

"When I get pissed off at everybody, I come in here and work on the clubs," Arnold said. "Not as much as I used to, but I still do."

Next to the workshop was his airplane room, with models and photographs of the eleven planes he has owned. In 1976 Arnold made it into the *Guinness Book of World Records* by circumnavigating the globe in a Lear 36 in about fifty-eight hours. When he spoke of his planes he sounded like he was in his fifties again, when he was winning (on the senior tour), Peggy and Amy were out of the house, Winnie was busy with her stuff (hospital philanthropy), and Arnold could go just about anywhere he wanted, whenever he wanted. What freedom.

Arnold kept a pilot's license for fifty-five years and had given it up only recently. He told us about a "dogfight" he once had over the Atlantic with another civilian pilot, each in an F-15 borrowed from the United States Air Force. I didn't know you could borrow planes from the United States Air Force. Arnold said that was his fee for giving a clinic at the Langley Air Force Base golf course. "I threw up all over myself," Arnold said. "I'm just being honest."

Arnold's docent work concluded in the office lobby, where his presidential collection was assembled. The people at the World Golf Hall of Fame must have fantasies about it: filled scorecards, golf balls, clubs, bag tags, all connected to the many golf games and White House visits Arnold has had with many of the twentieth century's First Duffers.

Palmer hadn't met Obama and he never met Kennedy. He and JFK had a Palm Beach golf game in the works for Christmastime 1962 but it got canceled when Kennedy's back went out. Kennedy didn't forget. In the summer and early fall of '63, he had the White House photographer, Cecil Stoughton, shoot sixteen-millimeter film of his swing, with the intention that Palmer would come to the White House, review the footage, and offer the former Harvard golfer (freshman team) some tips. Then came November 22.

The film was buried in a vault at the Kennedy Library until a reporter on Cape Cod uncovered it. Many years too late to help the man, Arnold analyzed JFK's stylish, relaxed swing. In one round Kennedy is wearing pink pants and Ray-Bans and his shirttail is out. He looks like a preppy movie producer on vacation. The caddies are skinny teenagers in country-boy dungarees and white T-shirts they borrowed from James Dean. The motorized golf carts have three wheels. Jackie is in the background now and again. A few years earlier I had watched the film with Arnold. He said, "Look at Jackie—she's smoking!" Arnold's own war with cigarettes went on for years. His eye for pretty women never diminished.

Near a corner of the lobby was a golf bag stuffed with Eisenhower's clubs. A wall was dotted with presidential photos, spanning nearly a half century. One showed Arnold playing with Jerry Ford. They're cracking up about something. "He was my buddy," Arnold said. Deacon Palmer was a Roosevelt Democrat, but Arnold, like a lot of golfers, checked in early with the Grand Old Party and stayed there. There was a photo of Kissinger on a sofa with Pat Nixon and Dolores Hope. They all look sort of stuffed. The whole lobby was like a tribute to a lost world. "Jerry Ford's turning golf into a contact sport," Bob Hope used to say. Who's writing golf jokes today?

Arnold told us about a round he played recently with Bill Clinton at a course called Trump National Golf Club Hudson Valley, in New York. Mike and I played there once with Trump, who played well but didn't stop talking. I lost a dozen balls and came off the eighteenth green with a throbbing headache. I found aspirin in the locker room, where Trump's locker sits in a row with others bearing shiny nameplates for Rudy Giuliani, Joe Torre, and Lou Rinaldi, a scratch player and Trump's pavement guy. Trump made Clinton an honorary member of the club.

"Clinton can play a little bit," Palmer said. "But he hits this one shot that goes way right. A wild shot. He looks at me with this shit-eating grin and says, 'I promise you: You'll never see me go that far right again.'"

Not even a mile from Arnold's office is a giant warehouse that Arnold calls the barn. (Simplicity is one of Arnold's chief gifts.) Arnold's brother, Jerry, thirteen years younger and the former superintendent of the Latrobe course, gave Mike and me a tour. Evidently, Arnold's mother couldn't throw out anything, and Arnold was the same way. There were scores of bag tags, thousands of clubs, hundreds of books, boxes and boxes of photos, canister after canister of network film from various tournaments, the antique tractor from a famous Pennzoil ad, dozens of artworks sent to him by fans, and more leather golf shoes than you'd want to count.

"This can't be every pair of golf shoes he's ever had, can it?" I asked.

"I'm not sure," Jerry said.

"It probably is!" Mike said.

Mike loved Palmer. Being in that barn was like touring the Louvre for Mike. Jerry thought Mike was the first tour player to see it.

"You figure three, four pair a year, for fifty years, this could be *all* of them," Mike said. He picked up a shoe. "You know what I like? You feel how heavy this shoe is? It just seems like everything they made then had more quality."

"The amazing thing," Jerry said, "is that we could bring Arnold in here and he could tell you what shoes he wore at what tournament."

"Unbelievable," Mike said, responding not really to Jerry but to his awe at the whole scene. He picked up an old iron and said, "Look at these irons. Would you look at them?"

The irons were old Wilson Staffs, the forebears of the club Mike used when he nearly won the U.S. Open. I looked at them. They looked tiny, obsolete—beautiful.

The warehouse tour was the final thing we did before leaving Latrobe, but for this report I have saved lunch for last. We ate in the Latrobe Country Club grillroom. Arnold introduced Mike to the clubhouse manager as "the guy Hale Irwin beat in the U.S. Open. They had a playoff."

Arnold is an expert on the subject of losing U.S. Open playoffs. He had been defeated by Nicklaus at Oakmont near Pittsburgh in the '62 playoff, by Julius Boros at the Country Club in Brookline in '63, and by Billy Casper at Olympic in San Francisco in '66. In Arnold's day, the Masters was charming and clubby and genteel, and Arnold won it four times. In more recent years, it has become the prized jewel of golf events. It gives its winners something money cannot buy: the ultimate golf time-share, complete with a parking space near the clubhouse and a green sport coat to wear inside it. But for Arnold, for Mike, for any American touring pro who grew up in a less cushy time, the national open will always be more important. They belonged to a country-first generation and they welcomed the tournament's extreme challenge. It's a modest link between Mike and Arnold that they both know what it's like to lose a U.S. Open in a playoff. But it's significant.

We sat at a round table, Arnold, Kit, Doc, Mike, me, and Pete Luster, Arnold's pilot. I ordered an Arnold Palmer. I've seen Arnold have a martini at lunch, or a beer or a glass or two of wine, but on this day he ordered a Coke Zero. Mike was paying attention. He was going to order whatever Arnold ordered.

We talked about the Congressional Gold Medal that Arnold had just received and made a list of the five other athletes who had received it. Jesse Owens, Joe Louis, Jackie Robinson, and Byron Nelson came readily. The fifth name was elusive for a minute until Doc remembered it: Roberto Clemente, the Hall of Fame outfielder for the Pittsburgh Pirates, who died while doing relief work for earthquake victims.

We talked about the results of the World Golf Hall of Fame voting and whether Fred Couples deserved his spot. Arnold said he had voted for him. That led me to ask Arnold how he would compare Tiger and Fred, just for pure golf talent. Many knowledgeable people, like Mike, will argue that nobody has ever hit a higher percentage of flush shots than Fred.

"That's very difficult for me to tell you about," Arnold said. "Let me think about it some."

I figured it was a topic that, for whatever reason, Arnold didn't want to get into. We moved on to other things. The Ryder Cup. Kit and Arnold's annual trip to watch the Pirates and Cubs play. The Wake Forest–Duke football game. What happens to players when they go to the broadcast booth.

A full fifteen minutes had passed when Arnold said, "I've been thinking about your question." The table went quiet, and I realized almost immediately that Arnold was answering a question that was far different and more interesting than the one I had asked him.

"Tiger was somewhat of a robot golfer," Arnold said. "He was so endeared to his father and what his father had him doing that it is almost difficult to explain. I watched him practice at Isleworth when he was in the midst of it. As long as he stuck to the routine that his father had laid out for him he was going to succeed. Had he continued to do that he probably could have established a record that would never have been broken."

Earl Woods died in May 2006. From Earl's death through the time of our visit, Tiger had won four major titles: the 2006 British Open and PGA Championship, the 2007 PGA Championship, and the 2008 U.S. Open, in the playoff over Rocco Mediate.

"After his father died, and without getting into what happened and why it happened, Tiger got into other things," Arnold said. "He went away from the routine and the work ethic that was so natural for him. It's happened before. It has something to do with the psychological effect of the game. If he doesn't try to go back to where he was five or six years ago, he will get worse instead of better. Could he go back to where he was? He could. Do I think he will? No."

Just so you know, those were Arnold's own questions. It was like he was interviewing himself. It was like Arnold had thought so much about the subject of Tiger and his struggle to win more majors and was just waiting for the opportunity to talk about it. His sentences were so full and precise.

"I'll switch the tables," Arnold said. "If I hadn't won that U.S. Open at Cherry Hills, I could have won at least four other U.S. Opens. I really believe that."

You could almost see him making the list in his head.

"I could have won in '62."

That was the year he lost to Jack Nicklaus in the playoff at Oakmont, in Arnold's backyard.

"Sixty-three."

The playoff at the Country Club.

"Sixty-six."

The one at Olympic.

"Sixty-seven."

Tied with Nicklaus through three rounds at Baltusrol. Nicklaus won.

"Seventy-two."

Arnold shot a Sunday 76 and finished four behind Nicklaus at Pebble.

"Seventy-three."

Tied for the lead through three rounds at Oakmont. Johnny Miller shot 63 on Sunday and won.

"If I had had the same psychological approach I did at Cherry Hills, I could have won all those years," Arnold said. "I lost my edge."

That was some admission and some phrase, those last two words, and I didn't even know what they meant. What I knew was that Arnold was being raw and honest and saying things I had never heard him say.

"Winning that first U.S. Open was an obsession," Arnold said. "The first thing you want to do is win an Open. Then, after you win it, you have to stay aggressive, stay the way you were when you won it. And it's difficult to do."

You might be scratching your head here. After all, Arnold won dozens of tournaments after that 1960 U.S. Open, including two more victories at Augusta and his two British Opens. But what I think Arnold was saying was that after winning the '60 U.S. Open he lost something he was never able to recover. He was never the same, not deep down inside. Mike, in his own way, knew what Arnold was talking about. His golf was never the same after Medinah.

The table was silent for a long moment until Mike said, "It's such a fine edge."

"It *is*," Arnold said. "It's so fine. You have to get in there and you have to stay in there, and once you get out it's very hard to get back in. It's happened to every golfer. Hogan. Nicklaus. Every golfer. It's just a question of when."

Did Arnold have that same obsessive need to practice and improve and win in '65 and '75 that he did in '55, when Winnie would stand with him as he beat balls? No, not with all that endorsement money rolling in and his plane idling on the tarmac and the whole world beckoning for him. *Every golfer*. Tom Watson. Jack Nicklaus. Mike Donald. Tiger Woods. Arnold Palmer. *It's just a question of when.*

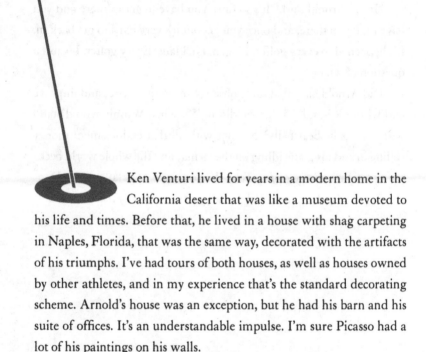

3

Ken Venturi lived for years in a modern home in the California desert that was like a museum devoted to his life and times. Before that, he lived in a house with shag carpeting in Naples, Florida, that was the same way, decorated with the artifacts of his triumphs. I've had tours of both houses, as well as houses owned by other athletes, and in my experience that's the standard decorating scheme. Arnold's house was an exception, but he had his barn and his suite of offices. It's an understandable impulse. I'm sure Picasso had a lot of his paintings on his walls.

Ken's house in Rancho Mirage looked like a curator had been through it. Various shelves displayed his medals, trophies, and notable scorecards. The walls were covered with glass-protected letters and scores of photographs and paintings showing Ken in action as a player, broadcaster, and man-about-town. (One was by LeRoy Neiman, ubiquitous painter of sportsmen.) There were various framed articles and magazine covers, including three of the four times he had appeared on the cover of *Sports Illustrated*, which he did twice in 1964, when he won the U.S. Open and was named Sportsman of the Year. The missing cover was from 1960, when Ken appeared with Dow Finsterwald and Arnold Palmer and the headline GOLF'S YOUNG LIONS. The absence of that cover was not a coincidence. I knew that Ken had a whole, festering thing about Arnold, but that's about all I knew. After seeing Arnold, I knew that Ken—Arnold's nearly exact tour contemporary—had to be my next tour stop. Driving from LAX to Palm Springs, as sparkly and ritzy as Latrobe is muted and down-home, I wondered what Ken would say about Arnold. Maybe he would say nothing. After all, they were both in their eighties. Maybe Ken had decided it was time to finally give it a rest.

We made a date. Dinner for four on a Tuesday night. Ken; his wife, Kathleen; secret weapon Mike Donald, in for Round II; and your tour guide. Mike and I wore sport coats—we knew Ken's code. Ken had made a reservation at one of his regular places, Castelli's in Palm Desert, where the waiters wear ties and speak in low voices and the dining room smells like fried garlic and red wine.

Mike and I got to the restaurant fifteen or twenty minutes early, but Ken and Kathleen, Ken's third wife, were already there, at the bar, having wine. Ken's hair was thick and white and he was slim. His eyes were the same as ever: bright, intense, blue—electric. His manner and his references were Old World Italian, although his mother was Irish and his skin had more pink in it than anything else. He was dressed perfectly and he was chipper. In six months, he'd be going into the World Golf Hall of Fame.

Mike and I ate at a corner table in the back of the back room. Ken faced out, his back to the corner, as the famous and semi-famous frequently prefer. Every now and again a name would elude Ken and he would show a hint of passing frustration, but overall his mind was sharp and he did not tire.

The Masters came up often. Ken told a story, datelined Augusta, in which he gave several posters to a trusted CBS assistant and instructed him to take the posters to Tiger Woods to sign. This is a routine aspect of tour life, done in the name of charity. But Woods would sign only one and the posters came back to Ken. "And I took that one signed poster," Ken told us, "and I ripped it up into little pieces."

Yes, Ken could have made the request himself and maybe the result would have been different. Yes, he could have had at least one signed poster without turning the episode into a confetti show. But the point was that Ken Venturi had his standards, and after this haughty act of disrespect from Tiger Woods they were even more intact.

As Ken concluded the story with those little poster pieces scattered on the ground, his head went into a little north-south shake, like a Friday-night welterweight after delivering a TKO punch. *I showed him.*

He was going through his greatest hits. Ken talked about having Frank Sinatra as a roommate after he broke up with his first wife, Conni Venturi, the mother of his two children. Ken referred to Sinatra as Francis while Sinatra called him Kenneth, Ken explained to us. One night Kenneth and Francis were having dinner with a Mafia don, which Venturi signaled by pushing a finger on his left nostril. Ken then recounted a brief, cryptic exchange in which Francis indicated to this lord of the underworld that Ken was "all right" and that the don could talk freely. Ken—who took pride in being a son of Italian San Francisco, like the DiMaggio brothers and Tony Bennett—wasn't showing any admiration for Mob life, just a familiarity with its customs.

As Ken described his father, Frederico Venturi, the man sounded like a character out of *The Old Man and the Sea*, had it been written by John Steinbeck and set in Northern California in the 1940s. Ken told how his father sold nets and twine to fishermen from San Francisco down to Monterey and how he would drop off Ken at the elite and beautiful Cypress Point Club, where he would caddie.

Years later, in January 1956, Ken returned to Cypress with another fast-track amateur, Harvie Ward, to play two titans of the professional game, Ben Hogan and Byron Nelson, in a money match. Eddie Lowery, the tiny legendary Boston caddie who grew up to become the owner of the largest Lincoln-Mercury dealership in San Francisco, backed the amateurs. George Coleman, a bicoastal industrialist, backed the pros. A popular book—*The Match* by Mark Frost—was written about that day.

Ken talked about a re-creation of the match that was played recently. The day had been a triumphant return for Ken. It was supposed to feature two established pros, Davis Love and his buddy Fred Couples, playing two young stars, Bubba Watson and Rickie Fowler. But Fred withdrew late, and Nick Watney, another young guy, was his last-minute replacement.

In my sense of the day, Fred's absence sort of killed the event. It needed Fred's star power, and the history Fred and Davis represented, to stand in for Hogan and Nelson. But if Ken felt that Fred's absence hurt the event in any way, he didn't share it with us. Without Ken, there was no Match I, let alone its contrived sequel, and Ken didn't need Fred Couples in the house to enjoy the day. In his final CBS broadcast, Ken said, "The greatest gift in life is to be remembered." At Cypress that day, Ken was being remembered.

I asked Ken if the remarkable scores in *The Match* were accurate. The four golfers were said to have made twenty-seven birdies and an eagle between them.

Ken nodded. "I know, because I'm the only one left who was there and I have the card," he said.

He knew the scores and he knew the stories behind the scores. He was the source. He was the man.

•   •   •

Mike and I were under Ken's spell, engulfed in his old-school, fly-straight, DIY values, golfing and otherwise. We were sitting with a man who knew how to dress, swing, eat, drink, swear, tell a story. We were with a man who was a central figure in golf's greatest generation, the gang who made their mark in the prosperity of the 1950s, when a pair of leather golf shoes, hand-sewn in Massachusetts, might weigh six pounds at the end of Saturday's wet round. Ken was taking us wherever he wanted, and it was a pleasure.

By way of his TV work, Ken was a significant presence for me through high school and college. Ken was the doorman to the Masters, always respectful. Later, in my brief stints as a tour caddie, I got a different impression of him, as a man with an unattractive macho streak, a superiority complex, and the best seat at the bar. I got a third version of Ken some years after that, when I spent parts of two days with him for an *SI* story. I remember telling my boss that I was overwhelmed by how wrong my impression of Ken had been. He had charisma and warmth. The way he was connected to his own past was so endearing. Every question triggered a story, and he gave no rote answers. He just slowly sipped his Crown Royals and talked. What struck me most was his devotion to his second wife, Beau, then in the late stages of brain cancer. Her end was coming, and any visitor would have seen the same thing: Ken was heartbroken.

When Ken retired from CBS, I wrote a farewell piece. For that story, I sat in a corner of the broadcast booth at the Kemper Open as Ken worked the final tournament of his long career. One person after another came in to pay tribute. The most telling thing was how moved the players were by his retirement and how much the players meant to Ken. They looked at Ken Venturi and saw their fathers and their boyhoods.

In more recent years, I helped Ken write several first-person pieces for which he instructed that his writer's fee go to a hospital in Loma Linda where he had received treatments for cancer. When he gave lessons, his entire fee, typically five hundred dollars, went to charity. One favorite was for the training of guide dogs. Another was the Stuttering Foundation. (He was a recovering stutterer.) He had the servant heart. Ken had been the host of a charity golf tournament that in a single year raised nearly $1 million for the construction of a sixty-bed shelter for victims of domestic abuse. It bears Beau Venturi's name. Ken gave at the office, at home, in public, in private. Ken gave.

His life, with all its ups and downs—three marriages, money problems and health problems, a publicized DUI arrest late in the day, horrible play and brilliant play—was like an old-time movie, with James Garner playing Ken. You'd need a slightly older man to play the Supportive Parish Priest. In various books and magazine pieces about the '64 Open, there's often a section about Father Murray, from St. Vincent de Paul in San Francisco, and the inspirational letter he wrote to Ken on the eve of the tournament, when Ken was, as they used to say, down on his luck. That letter led Ken to a Catholic church in Washington, D.C., on the eve of the Open, and that visit, as Ken told and retold the story, made all the difference. Ken was a devout Catholic, and redemption as a life theme ran deep with him.

Everything ran deep with him. That's why we, his viewing public, responded to him like we did. That's why total strangers, who knew him only from TV, would call out to him, "Hey, *Kenny!*"

Many of Ken's dinner stories were about Hogan, who came off as a second father figure. (Byron Nelson and Eddie Lowery did, too.) Ken told us about being a pallbearer at Hogan's funeral and about his many practice rounds with Hogan. He told us how Hogan, after being absent from the national open for several years, agreed to play in the 1966 U.S. Open at the Olympic Club in San Francisco if and only if the USGA would pair Hogan with Venturi for the first two rounds. That seemed astounding to me, but that was Ken's story.

In rich detail, Ken told us that on the second hole of the opening round, Hogan got stuck while standing over a putt. Hogan had the yips.

"I can't take it back, Ken," Hogan said.

"Nobody gives a shit, Ben," Ken said back.

That bit of wise-guy humor was evidently all Hogan needed to hear: At age fifty-three and playing barely any tournament golf, he finished twelfth. Venturi finished three shots behind. Palmer was leading by seven with nine holes left and lost to Billy Casper in a playoff.

Ken was on a roll. He talked about the aftermath of his win at Congressional at the '64 Open, how he declined a Sunday-lunch invitation with LBJ at the White House so he could go to New York and appear on *The Ed Sullivan Show*, have drinks with Toots Shor at Toots Shor's, eat at "21," and see Carol Channing in *Hello, Dolly!*, accompanied all the while by his first wife, Conni, who looked like she belonged on a Broadway stage herself. Ken said Carol Channing changed the famous lyric of her show's most famous number to this: "Hello, *Kenny*. Well hello, *Kenny*! It's so nice to have you back where you belong." The reference, in Ken's mind, was not just to his return to the bright lights of the big city but also to his position among the elite players in the game, right there with Arnold and Jack and Gary Player. But the real soundtrack to his life seemed to be *My Way*, as sung by Francis Albert himself.

We were talking about the 1964 U.S. Open when I asked Ken if he had watched the 1990 U.S. Open, Mike's Open. Ken recalled the bomb Irwin made on the last hole of regulation to post a Sunday 67.

"How do you think your life would have been different if you had won?" Ken asked Mike.

"You know what?" Mike said. "I doubt it would have been very different."

Ken shook his head. "It would have been different," he said.

Our conversation turned to Curtis Strange, who had been trying to win his third straight Open that year at Medinah. Ken jumped to the '85 Masters, when Curtis opened with an 80 and still managed to get himself in contention on the back nine on Sunday. During that '85 broadcast, Venturi had been critical of Curtis's play in the final round, when he made bogeys on Augusta's two back-nine par-fives, each time knocking his second shot into a water hazard beside the green. Curtis finished two shots behind the winner, Bernhard Langer. In the broadcast, Ken said Curtis should have laid up short of those water hazards. Later, Ken said, Curtis confronted him about what he had said. "He poked his finger in my chest and said, 'If I had it to do again, I'd play those same shots again.'

"And I said, 'Yeah, Curtis? And you'd be wrong again. Which is why you'll never win the Masters! And if you ever poke me again, I'm gonna *slug* ya.' "

There was another little up-and-down nod. Ken Venturi, winner by unanimous decision.

Ken said he learned all he needed to know about Tiger Woods at the 1997 Masters. That was the tournament Woods won by twelve shots at age twenty-one, playing in his first major as a pro. It was all so unlikely. Woods's father grew up in a segregated country. His mother grew up in Thailand. To say the least, they were not country-clubbers. When Tiger holed out on eighteen on Sunday, it was stirring. I was standing right there.

"He walked right by his mother on that eighteenth green and gave that hug to his father," Ken told us. "He showed no respect for his mother."

In his 2004 book, *Getting Up & Down*, Ken talks about the last of his fourteen tour wins, the '66 Lucky International Open at Harding

Park, the San Francisco city course where he grew up playing. For many years, Ken's parents ran the counter in the Harding pro shop. In the book, Ken gloats about beating Arnold by two and says that when he came off the final green to hug his father, Fred Venturi said, "Your mother is over there." In other words, mother first.

You can see the Earl-Tiger hug at the '97 Masters on various highlight reels. Earl and Tida, separated in their married life, were standing on the back of the green arm in arm when their only child made his putt to win and punched the air with unbridled vigor. When Tiger approached his parents, Earl stepped forward, and father and son, teacher and student, shared a hug that was beamed across the world. Many people found it inspiring. Ken saw a mother being dissed.

Over the years, in many private dinners and eventually in public, Ken maintained that Arnold had broken a rule en route to winning his first major, the 1958 Masters. As far as I know, Ken is the only person ever to question Arnold's fidelity to the rule book. The charge was bad enough, and the implication was worse. Ken was saying that Arnold was a fraudulent winner of that Masters, when Fred Hawkins and Doug Ford finished a shot out of first and Ken finished a shot behind them. "They were robbed," Ken wrote. That sentence was a flat-out attack.

To Ken, the Masters and Augusta National represented everything that was great and possible in the world, but his relationship with the place was complicated. He never won there, and after his final Masters broadcast he never went back. Arnold won four times at Augusta. In 1999 Arnold joined the club, not as an honorary member but as a full-status dues-paying one. He was at the tournament and the member events every year. He was royalty there, a "great man," as a Masters chairman once called Arnold, who looked so comfortable in his green coat. Poor Ken. How did envy get assigned the color green?

Still, when Ken went public with his accusation, a lot of people were surprised. As far as anybody knew, Ken and Arnold had enjoyed a good friendship on tour. In the later Eisenhower years, Ken would sometimes take over a house band's drum kit, Arnold would step in as bandleader, other players would pitch in with other instruments, and they would bring down the house. The wives would hoot and holler, Conni Venturi especially. Arnold and Conni had an easy rapport, but that was not surprising. Conni had an easy rapport with a lot of men. All through their married life, Ken had to deal with the fact that various gents, famous and otherwise, were drawn to his wife. She had Sophia Loren's face and hair and Audrey Hepburn's playful spirit and lithe physique.

Ken, like Arnold, had won one U.S. Open. When Ken made his winning putt at Congressional, he dropped his putter and uttered the words, "My God, I've won the Open." Ever since, that sentence has defined the gritty nobility of the great American championship. That win, and that quote, became Ken's calling card.

Ken played in the Masters fourteen times—Arnold played in fifty—and contended three times. In '56, as an amateur, he would have won had he shot a back-nine Sunday 40 instead of the 42 he did shoot. In '58 and again in '60, he was nipped by Palmer in events that helped sell truckloads of color TVs. (Who, man or woman, wanted to watch Arnold stalk those Augusta greens in black and white?) When Arnold first said farewell to the Masters in 2002, having played in forty-eight straight, Venturi was in the booth, making his final broadcast. Then Arnold decided to play two more.

We got to Arnold late, but Ken went deep. He was telling us things he had already said in his book but with more flourish. No lawyers were watching him now. Out of deference to CBS and the network's relationship with Augusta National, Ken had remained silent for decades on the subject of Arnold and the rule book at the '58 Masters.

But when he retired from CBS, Ken felt free to break his self-imposed omertà. It was obvious that the event was a fog of war that had never lifted for Ken.

The incident happened in the last round, when Palmer and Venturi came to the twelfth hole, the little par-three in the middle of Amen Corner. The hole is famous for its fickle winds and a narrow green fronted by a murky creek. The green sits off by itself in splendid isolation.

Palmer was leading the tournament when they arrived on the twelfth tee. Venturi was trailing by a shot and would be playing first. (He *had the honor*, in a telling piece of golf-speak.) The course was wet from a heavy Saturday-night rain. The hole was cut on the far right of the green, and Venturi hit his tee shot hole-high and twenty feet left.

Palmer followed by hitting his tee shot over the green and near a bunker. About half his ball plugged into the soft turf. Palmer sought to use a local rule, sanctioned by the USGA rule book, which provided a free drop for an embedded ball. But the official on hand, Arthur Lacey, would not give embedded ball relief to Palmer.

Here I will turn the story over to a partial source: Venturi, writing in *Getting Up & Down*:

> Finally, an angry Palmer played the shot. Not surprisingly, he flubbed the chip and the ball did not even reach the putting surface. He hit the next one five feet past the hole but then missed the putt, making a five. The two-shot swing put me in the lead for the first time since early in the third round. Two years after my memorable collapse, I was on my way toward a memorable comeback.
>
> Only Palmer wasn't ready to give up on the twelfth hole just yet.
>
> "I didn't like your ruling," he said, glaring at Lacey. "I'm going to play a provisional ball." (He was really playing what is called a "second ball.")

"You can't do that," I told him. "You have to declare a second before you hit your first one."

Ken agreed with Arnold. He felt that Lacey should have given Arnold embedded ball relief. Regardless, Ken's position was that Arnold broke a rule of golf by not saying right from the start, in a contested rules situation, that he would be playing two balls, with the idea that the rules committee would sort through the issue later. The words he said to Palmer have almost lawyerly precision: "You have to declare a second before you hit your first one."

And Arnold didn't do that. Arnold made a five on the first ball and then, according to Ken, furious at the ruling and his score, returned to his original position, dropped another ball, and made a three with that one. That's why Ken maintained that Ford and Hawkins, the runners-up, were robbed. Ken said, "What would Arnold have done if he had made a three on that first ball? Try it again to see if he could make a two?" Ken's point was that in golf, you don't get to choose which score you like better. I could see that. But I could also see that the situation was confusing, and Arnold likely got stuck with a bad decision and was looking for a fair appeals process.

At the end of that round, Ken and Arnold shook hands and walked off the green together. But moments later, Ken said, he was telling Arnold he was signing a scorecard for a lower score than he actually made. Doing that is an automatic disqualification. But Palmer didn't get disqualified. He won. Doug Ford, the defending champion, held the shoulders and Arnold slipped into his first club coat.

Nineteen years later, Ken told us, he was playing Augusta National's par-three course when he saw Clifford Roberts, the club's chairman and co-founder. This was days before the start of the 1977 Masters. Roberts was old and ill. He approached Ken.

"He apologized," Ken said.

He apologized for allowing Palmer's score of three to stand in 1958. "He *apologized*," Mike said.

Mike knew: Roberts was not the apologizing type. He was the ultimate autocrat.

"He apologized," Ken said. "He said they made the wrong decision. They should never have let Palmer's three stand. And six months later he was dead!"

Roberts took his own life beside Ike's Pond, not far from where he and Ken had that fateful conversation.

We were in a time machine. The names! Spiro Agnew. Carol Channing. Roger Maris and Mickey Mantle. Frank Sinatra. The great DiMaggio. Bobby Jones and Cliff Roberts. Palmer this and Palmer that. Not the Palmer whom Mike and I had just seen in Latrobe, his mind sharp, his body ailing. No. This was the Palmer who left women swooning and men gasping and Venturi so mad he couldn't see straight. Ken was talking about the Palmer who played the final two holes of the 1960 Masters with only six shots. A birdie-birdie finish to win. *Bop, bop, bop; bop, bop, bop.* The birth of the Palmer charge.

In fact, Arnold made three threes to finish that year. On the par-three sixteenth, he had a long downhill birdie putt and left the flagstick in and untended, as the rules then permitted. He hit the putt too hard, his ball clanked off the flagstick and instead of going off the green, as it might have, it stopped two feet from the hole and he made par. On the seventeenth hole, with Venturi watching on TV, Palmer made a cross-country fifty-foot putt for a birdie. When Palmer played eighteen, Venturi could not even watch. The lusty crowd roar told him all he needed to know: Palmer had made a birdie on the last to win.

All through those final two holes, Venturi said he was hoping that he and Palmer would finish in a tie. He wanted a playoff—an eighteen-hole Monday playoff. He wanted to beat the man straight up and right in front of him.

Ken has said many times that he left Augusta that day a defeated and broken man. To anybody watching, Ken left Augusta in '60 as one of the preeminent figures in the game. But he felt otherwise. In his mind, he was in Palmer's wake.

In his book, Ken recounts this exchange with Arnold, from the awards presentation at the 1960 Masters:

PALMER: "I wish it could have been you. I wish you had won."
VENTURI: "It's two years too late."

If Arnold was apologizing, Ken was not accepting.

Ken's book takes you deep inside his head. He concludes his chapter on the '58 Masters by describing a scene from the early 1980s. He was at Augusta and saw Nathaniel "Iron Man" Avery, Arnold's Augusta caddie. Iron Man explains to *Mr. Ken* that he tried to tell Palmer that he was doing the wrong thing back in '58.

Venturi writes:

"Ironman, I am so proud of you," I said. "You did the right thing. You should have no regrets. Your family and you are the most important thing. What counts more to me is that I have you as a friend." I gave him $100.

Ironman walked away, still in tears.

Incredible.

For Ken, the '60 Masters will forever be linked to the '58 Masters, and '58 to '56. Try as I might, I don't think I'll ever really understand the true toll those three tournaments took on him.

Ken did his own psychoanalytic study of the club's '58 ruling in Arnold's favor. In Ken's mind, it was an act of revenge against Ken, for the ungracious things Ken said to reporters at the San Francisco airport after returning home from the '56 Masters. In those interviews, Ken managed to insult the club, their tournament, and his fellow competitors. He told Mike and me the airport story. He had told it many times. I had heard it from him before, almost word for word, years earlier. The amazing thing to me was the level of emotion he still had for it, and how little it had changed.

On the Saturday of the 1956 Masters, Ken was nothing but promise. He was a handsome, self-assured twenty-four-year-old amateur golfer who had a four-shot lead through three rounds in a celebrated tournament. He was an army veteran with a gorgeous wife at home in San Francisco with their healthy infant son. He had a job selling Lincolns for Eddie Lowery at a time when you could make money selling Lincolns and cultivate useful relationships through golf. (Just the *suggestion* of a future game with Ken might help make a sale.) The story of his exciting match at Cypress Point was making the rounds at your better private-club cocktail parties in Northern California.

The Masters that year, its twentieth playing, was on national television for the first time, with a half hour of coverage on Friday, an hour on Saturday, and another on Sunday. Ken's fame was starting to spread beyond San Francisco courtesy of that Saturday telecast. Sunday promised to be bigger yet.

Yes, Arnold Palmer was in the process of making a name for himself. He had won the '54 U.S. Amateur and the '55 Canadian Open. But in April 1956 Ken was ahead of him, with Hogan and Nelson and Lowery in his corner. He had a classic swing, the slender physique of a man who did not do physical labor, a dazzling smile, a tremendous head of hair. And the third-round lead at Augusta. He was an amateur showing the pros how to play the game.

That Saturday night, Ken was the leading man. As Ken told it, Jones and Roberts invited him in for a private conversation. Jones, the great amateur, said he had been hoping an amateur would someday win his tournament. He was rooting for Ken. He hoped that Ken would stay amateur if he won, and that club members would help Ken become an executive with Ford, so he wouldn't have the financial pressure to turn pro. Jones envisioned Ken someday becoming chairman of the club. That was Ken's memory of the meeting. It must have all sounded so grand to him. Ken didn't want to turn pro. Pros were commoners. Ken wanted the elegant life of the career amateur. He wanted the status of club membership. Each member had a specialty. Roberts was a skillful banker. Ike was an accomplished soldier. Ken's special skill would be golf.

Jones and Roberts wanted just one thing from Ken. The previous year, Byron Nelson, with no chance to win, played on Sunday with the third-round leader, Cary Middlecoff, who waltzed to a seven-shot victory. Weekend tee times and pairings were not done by score in that era. It was all sort of hand-stamped. Jones told Ken he could pick his Sunday partner—as long as it wasn't Nelson. Nelson had worked with Ken on his swing. Nelson, pushed by Eddie Lowery, had lobbied his fellow former champions to have Ken at the tournament by way of a special invitation they controlled. A win with Nelson would taint his victory. "Anybody but Byron," Jones told Ken.

"I've played with everybody else," Ken said. "How about Snead?"

And on that basis, Sam Snead was delivered. Sam Snead had the best view of Ken's closing 80 on the Sunday of the 1956 Masters. That score allowed Jackie Burke, a grizzled Texas pro, to win by a shot over Ken.

The next day Ken flew home to San Francisco, and that was when his life changed forever. At the airport, he was greeted by his parents, Conni, and a group of San Francisco newspapermen. Among them was a man named Harry Hayward, the golf writer for the *San Francisco Examiner*.

Ken came home on a Monday, and the writers wrote him up for the Tuesday papers. Each reporter twisted what he said, but the worst offender by far was Harry Hayward. That was Ken's take on it. Hayward had Venturi complaining about how Snead treated him as a playing partner and about his tee time. In Hayward's account, Ken showed no gratitude to the club. He was dismissive of the pros and disrespectful toward Jones and Roberts. Hayward had Venturi claiming that the club would not allow Eddie Lowery anywhere near Ken during the fourth round, when Ken could have used some moral support. It was a hatchet job. They all were, but Harry Hayward's was the worst. Ken despised the man.

After the stories came out, Ken's patron, Eddie Lowery, trying to make things better, made things worse by sending via telegram and over Venturi's name an apology to Roberts and Jones for his remarks, with copies to the newspapers. Damage control. "I never saw that letter," Venturi said.

A letter that had Ken Venturi apologizing for comments he did not make with an apology that was not his.

The high status he had enjoyed that Saturday night in Augusta was vanishing. His dream of living the life of the gentleman amateur, in the tradition of Bob Jones of Atlanta and Chick Evans of Chicago and Francis Ouimet of Boston (for whom Lowery caddied in the 1913 U.S. Open) died that week. Venturi turned pro before the year was out.

Ken finished tenth on the 1957 money list as a rookie. He won five times on tour before the '58 Masters. But Ken was far more focused on what his life would have been had he won the '56 Masters as an amateur—or the feelings of redemption, over Harry Hayward and various others, that he would have enjoyed had he won the '58 Masters as a pro. Or how, had he won in '60, he could have had the last laugh over Palmer and Cliff Roberts and various others for Palmer's favorable ruling. But Venturi didn't win at Augusta in April 1960. It was Palmer who did, by a shot.

It was Palmer who appeared on the cover of *Time* the following month. It was Palmer who had an intimate friendship with Eisenhower through the sixties. It was Palmer who reinvented the British Open, Palmer who piloted himself around the world in his private jet, Palmer who had a line of clothes named for him, Palmer who appeared repeatedly on the *Tonight Show*, Palmer who was the grand marshal of the Tournament of Roses parade.

Only Ken could really understood the scope of the wrong Palmer had committed on that twelfth hole in 1958. The public could not be bothered with it. Not in 1958, when it happened. Not in 2004, when his book came out. Not ever. *Some weird rules thing from a hundred years ago—who cares?*

Ken and Arnold had arrived in Augusta for the '58 Masters with nearly equal status. But by that Sunday night, Arnold had become golf's leading man, while Ken had been reduced to supporting player.

Over a half century later, as Mike and I sat in the back of Castelli's with Ken and his wife, nothing had really changed. There was no way Ken could let go of Harry Hayward or Arnold or that favorable ruling. Ken once told me, "Harry Hayward's long dead, but I still don't forgive him." Forgive and forget was not in Ken's DNA.

The check came, and there was no fight over it. It had been a working dinner, at my behest. But it didn't feel like work. It felt like a journey into a man's head. The dinner group congratulated itself for going four hours without looking at a cell phone. Well, not Ken—that was not even an issue for him—but the rest of us. Ken buttoned his blazer and headed out to the valet.

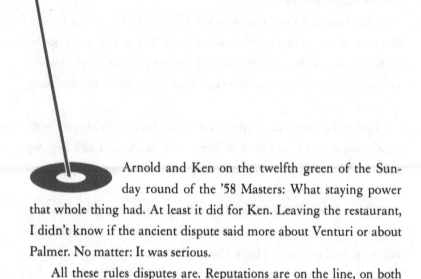

Arnold and Ken on the twelfth green of the Sunday round of the '58 Masters: What staying power that whole thing had. At least it did for Ken. Leaving the restaurant, I didn't know if the ancient dispute said more about Venturi or about Palmer. No matter: It was serious.

All these rules disputes are. Reputations are on the line, on both sides of the accusation. Consider the case of Mark McCumber. At the 1978 Milwaukee Open, playing the second PGA Tour event of his career, McCumber whiffed in the woods on the tenth hole of his Friday round and didn't count it, according to a caddie who was there that week. McCumber made the cut by a shot, but his caddie quit on him before the start of the third round. A whiff is a tricky matter because a player can always say he decided, at some point during the downswing, that he no longer intended to hit the ball. Under the rules, that is not a swing. By custom, the player's word is accepted unless the evidence against him is overwhelming. Still, that '78 event followed McCumber for his entire career. F. Scott Fitzgerald would understand.

Whenever golf is played for keeps, the rule book sees all. It directs all the action. That was true long before Bobby Jones ever played, and it will remain true long after Tiger Woods has holed his final putt.

Every legend on my list, even if he or she has never read the *Rules of Golf*, understands the wisdom of this passage from the first page:

> Golf is played, for the most part, without the supervision of a referee or umpire. The game relies on the integrity of the individual to show consideration for other players and to abide by the rules. All players should conduct themselves in a disciplined manner, demonstrating courtesy and sportsmanship at all times, irrespective of how competitive they may be. This is the spirit of the game of golf.

In any system of belief, an unshakable faith can be instilled at a tender age. There are surely people who accept the importance of golf's rules as an act of blind faith. But it is much more common and much more powerful to find religion on one's own.

In August 1972 Mike played in the fifteen-and-sixteen-year-old division of the Crutchfield Invitational, a junior event in Sebring, Florida. Mike won. He was seventeen. He won his age division and every age division. Had he been honest about his age and played as a seventeen-year-old, another kid could have had the pleasure of being named the fifteen-and-sixteen-year-old champ. Over time, that tournament became a do-the-right-thing wake-up call for Mike. His career has had various moments when he called penalties on himself that only he could see. Don't give him a medal. All he was doing was playing golf by the rules.

In the spring of 1976, 1977, and 1978, I was on my high school golf team at Patchogue-Medford High School on Long Island. (I am still embarrassed about voting for myself for captain.) Our season began in late March, and the courses were raw and unkempt. We played under a local rule by which we were allowed to lift, smooth, and place our balls in sand traps. The purpose of this rule was to get relief from animal dung, hoof prints, rocks, sticks, and the general detritus of winter. One raw day, I was playing in a nine-hole match at Timber Point, a beautiful old bay-front public course. On the eighth hole of a close nine-hole match, I was in a greenside trap. I lifted, smoothed with my foot, and placed. However, I placed my ball not in the smooth pathway I had created but on a little ledge just *above* the path. In other words, I had teed my ball up to make my bunker shot easier. I cheated. Man, is that hard to write.

In 1986, when I was caddying for Mike at the Colonial in Fort Worth, he was grinding it out in the second round, trying to make the cut. On the par-three eighth hole, Mike hit his tee shot in a greenside bunker. I got to the bunker ahead of him and saw there was a rake in it, some distance in front of Mike's ball but in his line of sight. On tour, rakes are typically left outside bunkers. I picked up the rake. The sand was soft and the rake left an indentation. I smoothed it out with the rake.

Mike started yelling, "You're testing, you're testing!" His face was red. One of his caddie-yard nicknames was Mad Dog.

The caddie, by the rules, is an extension of his player. A player cannot "test" the surface from which he is about to play. Raking a bunker before playing a shot was testing. Mike called for a rules official. I went into a hole.

Mike Shea, a PGA Tour rules official and a former player, arrived by cart. Mike told Shea exactly what I had done. Shea had a reputation for being a stickler, for going out of his way to call penalties on players. But without hesitating, he said there was no problem with my action. I didn't know why, and Mike didn't, either, but he was in the clear.

Shea's ruling gnawed at me for decades: Was it fair? Had Mike Shea, for reasons I could not fathom, given us a break? That prospect was troubling. The rules cannot allow for a break. Mike made the cut on the number. It was a quiet weekend all the way around.

Years later, I asked David Fay, by then the retired executive director of the USGA, about the ruling Shea had given Mike. When he was running the USGA, David spent many hours during U.S. Opens sitting in the NBC broadcast booth, ready to answer any rules question that might arise. David's presence, sitting in those elevated green plywood boxes with Johnny Miller and Dan Hicks, had the effect of putting a human face on the USGA, not an easy thing to accomplish. David's presence, even if it was subliminal, helped make the rules a central character in the story unfolding below, as they must be.

David knows golf's rules like you know the route home. His first instinctive answer was that Mike should have received a two-shot penalty that day at Colonial for my bunker-raking with Mike's ball in it. That was his second answer, too, after checking in with a fellow rulesman.

Several days later, I heard from David again, by e-mail. He wrote that he had been troubled by the whole thing and dug out a copy of the 1984 rulebook, the one in use in '86. He found something called Exception 3 to Rule 13-4. It reads: "The player after playing the stroke, or his caddie at any time without the authority of the player, may smooth sand or soil in the hazard, provided that, if the ball still lies in the hazard, nothing is done which improves the lie of the ball or assists the player in his subsequent play of the hole."

I was that caddie, smoothing sand without the authority of the player. Nothing I did improved Mike's lie or assisted him in his play. Shea knew what Mike and I did not: Exception 3 to Rule 13-4 from the 1984 rule book. My raking was fine.

"That destroys the mercy-on-the-hapless-caddie angle," David wrote. "If Shea had determined that your action had improved Mike's lie, he would have nailed Mike with two shots and you probably would have been sacked at the conclusion of the round, if not right on the spot. Ain't the rules of golf entertaining?"

In the space of eight months in 2013, Tiger Woods incurred penalties on four different occasions. The first one was in Abu Dhabi in January, where he took embedded ball relief in a sandy area covered with vegetation, with the approval of his playing partner. But you can't take embedded ball relief from any sandy lie, and he was given a two-shot penalty, which caused him to miss the cut. The second was at Augusta, when he dropped incorrectly after his third shot on the fifteenth hole in the second round hit the flagstick and ricocheted into a pond. That resulted—after the most torturous half-day in the history of golfing jurisprudence—in another two-shot penalty. The third episode came at the Players Championship in May. On the fourteenth hole in the final round, Woods drove it into a pond that runs down the left side of the fairway. Under the rule option he chose to use, Woods was required to drop within two club lengths of where the ball last crossed that water hazard. With the ball in the air, Mark Rolfing, an NBC reporter who was standing on the tee, indicated that Woods's ball last crossed the hazard about seventy yards in front of the tee. Footage of the shot from a blimp seemed to confirm that. Immediately after hitting his shot, Woods looked away in disgust, his head spinning left, typical body language for a shot that is, as the players say, *dead*. A ball that has a chance to stay dry you typically watch. But in consultation with his playing partner, Casey Wittenberg, Woods dropped about 230 yards in front of the tee, not seventy. Woods's drop had Wittenberg's stamp of approval, which absolved Woods of any wrongdoing, at least on a technical level. But it looked to me (and others) like an outrageously bad drop.

Four months later, Woods was playing in an event called the BMW Championship in Lake Forest, Illinois. On the first hole in his Friday round, Woods hit his ball over the green, and it came to rest in a wooded area. Nobody was around except his caddie, Joe LaCava, and a cameraman from PGA Tour Productions. About one third of Woods's ball was submerged in forest dirt. The ball was leaning against a cigar-shaped twig. You can see this clearly if you're looking at the footage shot by the cameraman, but only with the benefit of super magnification. In other words, only when you see it as Woods saw it, with his head about two feet above his ball as he started to attempt to remove that twig.

There's an old tour player who likes to say that your ball is like a bomb in those situations. If your ball moves, you have detonated it. Every serious player watches his ball like a hawk when removing what the rule book calls *loose impediments*. That week the field took 20,646 strokes, and the slim volume called the *Rules of Golf* was riding herd on every last one of them. It has to be that way.

When Woods came in from his round, a veteran PGA Tour rules official, Slugger White, who is married to Joe LaCava's cousin, added two shots to Woods's card. The first one was assessed because Woods caused his ball to move, and the rules require a golfer to play a ball as it lies. (That's the starting point of the rule book; the rest is commentary.) The second shot was for not moving his ball back to its original position. When a player causes his ball to move inadvertently, the rules require him to move it back.

Woods argued that the ball did not move. He said the ball "oscillated," a word found in the rules to allow for situations in which the ball moves and returns to its original position.

White could have chosen to accept Woods's explanation. He didn't. And that, I think, has proven to be far more damning to Woods than anything the *New York Post* ever said about him at the height of the stiletto-parade craziness.

It does not matter that the ball barely moved and that its new position would have no impact on the chip-out Woods was about to play. It does not matter that it would be nearly impossible to move the ball back exactly where it had been. As Woods likes to say, "Rules are rules." Without strict adherence to them, tournament golf would be chaos.

When Slugger White added the two shots, he was doing for Woods what Woods would not do for himself. That is beyond rare.

Woods, hot, didn't talk to reporters that day. But he did the next. He had this exchange with Doug Ferguson, the AP's ubiquitous golf writer:

FERGUSON: It looked like on the video that it dipped down, but I didn't see it dip back up.

WOODS: As I said, from my vantage point I thought it just oscillated and that was it.

FERGUSON: On the video you didn't see any difference?

WOODS: They replayed it again and again and again, and I felt the same way.

FERGUSON: It's kind of weird when Slugger would say one thing and you would say another, and doesn't it usually fall on the side of the player?

WOODS: I don't know, but I went from five back to seven back real quick.

Ferguson dug into the heart of the matter with that third question, and Woods's evasive answer is revealing. Broadly speaking, yes, by tradition the player's word is the final word. (The phrase *honest judgment*, in another context, appears in the rule book.) The assumption is that the player will fill in the squares of his scorecard with complete accuracy, which is to say with complete integrity. In this case, Slugger White stepped in for the player.

These are subtle things. We're talking about a ball perched on a twig in the woods and how Tiger Woods handled it. I know Tiger does the grand gestures of his public life well, and that he does a lot of good for many people. For whatever reason, I am far more interested in a person's littlest gestures, the ones that we don't readily see. My view is that Tiger got it wrong when he was over his ball, got it wrong in the scorer's trailer, got it wrong when he discussed it later. He put himself ahead of the game and his fellow competitors. Maybe it was just a bad day. We all have them. But what I fear is that Tiger Woods, the man who carries the mantle of the game, wrote a book that day.

What the rules do is make every golfer equal under the law. By being slavishly devoted to the rules, a golfer shows both respect for the game and consideration for his or her opponent. That's the fundamental reason why the game remains civilized when much of the world is not.

When the Venturi-Palmer dispute first emerged, I paid barely any attention to it. Like many others, I figured the statute of limitations had expired on the case (1958!) and that there was no way to sort through the actual facts from such an old crime scene. But after our dinner with Ken, I saw it in a different light. I saw it just like I saw the incident with Woods and his ball in the trees, as a moment when there's a weird confluence of events and true character gets revealed. Whose character, in the case of Arnold and Ken, I could not then know.

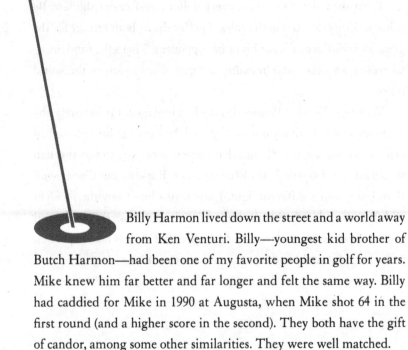

Billy Harmon lived down the street and a world away
from Ken Venturi. Billy—youngest kid brother of
Butch Harmon—had been one of my favorite people in golf for years.
Mike knew him far better and far longer and felt the same way. Billy
had caddied for Mike in 1990 at Augusta, when Mike shot 64 in the
first round (and a higher score in the second). They both have the gift
of candor, among some other similarities. They were well matched.

Billy's father, Claude Harmon, had been the longtime pro at
Thunderbird, the oldest of the California desert country clubs. Going
back to the fifties, Ken used to hang out at Thunderbird, and he never
got along with Claude. Ken once said to me with bizarre pride, "I got
Claude Harmon fired at Thunderbird." When Billy heard that, he
said, "Ken thinks he got my father fired at Thunderbird? My father
got himself fired at Thunderbird." He was saying that his father was a

drinker who never quit. Billy was a drinker who did. In his sober state, he enjoyed shocking people with his candor.

Mike and I went to see Billy, a teaching pro, the day after our night with Ken. After the intensity of that evening, seeing Billy felt like poolside lounging. Mike and Billy were like long-lost brothers, each in command of subjects an outsider could never know. The double-speak being perfected by tour bureaucrat X. The utter bullshit being espoused by swing guru Y. The unplayable greens on a new course designed by architect Z. I've never been around two people who collapsed time more efficiently.

Twenty minutes into their reunion, they were revisiting the eighteenth hole of the second round of the '90 Masters, when Mike's drive went dead left, bounced off a restroom roof, and into a cement flood-control drain. Spectators saw Mike's ball disappear. Mike called for an official.

"So here comes P. J. and he's got David Eger with him, riding up in a cart," Billy said.

Two rules officials. Not ordinary. The officers of the law were P. J. Boatwright, Jr., an officious, well-pressed USGA rulesman, and David Eger, an unsuccessful tour player who had become a golf administrator.

"And the first thing Mike does is look at Eger and say, 'What the *fuck* are you doing here?' "

Mike actually likes David Eger. (It's a short list.) But Mike, as was his wont, had the red-ass, and for no logical reason he felt that Eger would make his life harder at that moment.

Boatwright assessed the situation and decided that Mike's ball was in a hazard, no different from being in, say, a pond. That meant he would get a one-shot penalty.

"And Mike says to him, 'A hazard? How the fuck can it be a hazard? It's not even marked!' "

Mike wanted a free drop, not a one-shot penalty. After all, it wasn't his fault that the course had a cement drain as a secret obstacle. It wasn't like the drain was part of Alister MacKenzie's brilliant strategic design. They were playing the eighteenth at Augusta National, not the final hole at a putt-putt course featuring a clown's nose.

Mike got nowhere. Boatwright had all the cards and all the power. And if he needed backup, Eger was right there.

I first met Billy in 1985, when he was a real tour caddie and I was having a fling. That same year Billy met his wife, Robin, at the Pleasant Valley Country Club outside Boston when the tour touched down there in September. Robin was a Tufts grad and a Rhode Islander, and her father was a golf nut and a doctor. Billy was working for the veteran tour player Jay Haas, likely best-known then for being Curtis Strange's college roommate. The apex of their short and irregular courtship came when Billy and Robin left Providence and drove west for about two thousand miles. They hit Tucumcari, New Mexico, found a motel, got some sleep, and then carried on, bound for California. For a long while, Billy's life was right out of a certain Lowell George song, Robin riding shotgun and playing the drums.

I've been from Tucson to Tucumcari
Tehachapi to Tonapah
Driven every kind of rig
That's ever been made
Driven the back roads
So I wouldn't get weighed
And if you give me
Weed, whites, and wine
Then you show me a sign
I'll be willin' to be movin'

Anyone who saw Billy in those days, regardless of whether he was drunk or high or both—or sober, for that matter—will tell you the same thing: There was an elfin spirit about him, and he never lost it.

Billy was lucky. He never got in a car wreck. He never got his face smashed in a barroom brawl. When he quit drinking, he called as many of his former girlfriends as he could find and apologized for any ungentlemanly behavior he may have committed under the influence. The response was always the same: *You were a nice drunk, Billy.*

I recall seeing him early one morning at a diner near Endicott, New York, during the '85 B. C. Open. Jay Haas, his boss, was at that same counter, as was another caddie, "Gypsy" Joe Grillo. Everybody was laughing about something. Wherever Billy was, it seemed like a party was about to break out.

Tiger's near-perfect swing and extraordinary record under Butch Harmon, circa 2000, are points of brotherly pride for Billy, but the oldest and the youngest of the brothers could not be more different. There's a lot of posturing with Butch, and he takes himself very seriously. Nobody would accuse Billy of doing that. As a caddie, he had the innate and necessary ability to roll with the punches. He loved to hang out and talk. The game was in his bones and probably his soul, although he was dismissive of anybody who tried to turn playing golf into any sort of religious experience.

In Billy's adult life, a term used loosely here, a certain type of golf student has sought him out because what he teaches is tried and true and what he says is not sugarcoated. He follows in the tradition of Hogan, who famously said, "The secret's in the dirt." Hogan meant lighted driving ranges, empty fairways at dusk, high school football fields early on Sunday mornings. People really did teach themselves golf at such places once. Not today's titanium-headed game. Yesterday's persimmon game, the one that lives on in Arnold's barn.

In Hogan's day, a guy had a better chance of fixing himself when things were going wrong because, to borrow a phrase, *he owned his swing*. I'm sure this sounds comically quaint to any youngsters who have made it this far, but this is what Billy believes. You want to get better? Billy will give you the fundamentals. His brothers will, too. The rest is up to you. The flight of your shots will tell you what you need to know. I asked Billy once what he liked best about golf. He said, "The ball in the air."

That Billy is a member of a clan known as the Harmon Brothers is a meaningless designation in most places, but in certain golf circles it is like saying you're golf royalty. There were four Harmon brothers, all golf pros: Butch, Craig, Dick, and Billy. (And two sisters, not in the biz.) Their father was the winner of the 1948 Masters and the last club pro to win a major tournament. Claude Harmon could flat-out play. For pure talent, of the four sons, Billy was the closest to him.

Claude won his Masters when he stopped off in Augusta while driving from what was then his winter job, at Seminole in South Florida, to his main job, at Winged Foot in Westchester, New York. Later Claude was lured west to Thunderbird, which, like the other clubs where he worked, was an enclave of the rich and the super-rich. The Harmon kids were always surrounded by wealth, even though it stopped at their front door.

Butch taught Greg Norman in his prime, which was why Earl brought Tiger to Butch in '93, when Tiger was seventeen. Butch and Tiger worked together through 2004, when their relationship suffocated under the weight of their collective egos. The breakup did not serve either man well, but you can imagine how thin the air was on their mountaintop.

Craig Harmon, the second oldest of the four sons, was the head pro at Oak Hill, site of various major events, for decades. The third brother, the late Dick Harmon, was a beloved club pro in Houston. Billy, batting cleanup, was for years the ne'er-do-well son, a born golfer who, in his early twenties, lost his desire to beat his opponents. It was the early 1970s, he was at San Jose State, and smoking weed just seemed like so much more fun. Butch had made it to the show as a player. Billy got there as a caddie.

He was available to work for Mike at the 1990 Masters because Jay Haas wasn't in the tournament. It was a week when Mike actually allowed a caddie to advise him, which was remarkable, because few players in the history of professional golf could have wanted less from a caddie than Mike.

But Billy was different. He was steeped in the game and its people. He knew Augusta. He had played it. He had caddied for Jay there. He had been in groups with Jay's uncle, Bob Goalby, who won the '68 Masters when De Vicenzo did not. He had heard Craig Wood, the '41 Masters winner and Claude's predecessor at Winged Foot, talk about the course. And his father. And Hogan himself. Mike had reasons to trust Billy.

Reading a twenty-foot birdie putt on the fifth hole in the first round of their Masters, Billy said to Mike, "I know it looks like it goes left, but it actually goes right." Mike didn't see it but he took Billy's insight on faith. You can guess the outcome.

Later, Mike stood over his ball on the par-three twelfth hole with a 7-iron in his hands. He was already six under par.

"Is it a big one?" Mike said as he made a final waggle.

"Not really," Billy said as Mike made his backswing.

It's insane for a player and caddie to be discussing a shot *during a swing*. But they were oddly in synch. Mike's shot on twelve finished about a foot from the hole and he kicked it in for his third two of the round.

That put him at seven under. After twelve holes, he had made seven birdies and five pars. He made pars on thirteen and fourteen and a birdie on fifteen and three pars to finish.

His card:

454 232 443
342 544 344

That score, 64, was one short of tying the course record and came on a day when there were only four scores under 70. Mike, in his first round at his first Masters, was the first-round leader by two shots. In his post-round interviews, he praised and thanked Billy. When he shot a second-round 82, with a triple on the last, he answered every question from reporters and put it all on himself.

Billy has caddied in dozens of majors, in Ryder Cups, on many Sunday afternoons with funny-money riches up for grabs. He's been in team rooms and scoring trailers and locker rooms all over the world. He's hung out with Tiger, Shark, Phil, Fred. He once ate dinner with Hogan at his parents' house. (His father asked, "How do you want your steak, Ben?" Hogan said, "I'll grill it myself.") But it was obvious that his week with Mike was one of his best ever. Sixty-four, eighty-two, whatever. They were partners.

Billy loved Goalby. Jay Haas's Uncle Bob. Golf does not produce men like Bob Goalby anymore. He was a central figure when the players broke away from the PGA of America in 1968 and formed the PGA Tour. The breakup was made formal by a vote at the Atlantic City Country Club. Arnold once told me how he was a proud supporter of player emancipation, but Bob had a different take on Arnold in this period, telling me once that Arnold was "sitting on the fence" on the whole question of the split. In Goalby's version, as the years passed and the independent PGA Tour became a thriving entity, Arnold had turned himself into one of the ringleaders, along with Goalby, Doug Ford, Tommy Jacobs, and Gardner Dickinson. Old men and their war stories.

On the eighteenth hole of the Sunday round of the '68 Masters, Goalby found himself standing over the most significant four-foot putt of his life. If he made it, he would be in at eleven under par for the tournament, which would tie him with the leader in the clubhouse, De Vicenzo. A tie would mean an eighteen-hole Monday playoff. Billy told us about the little pep talk Bob gave himself before attempting that four-footer: "Step up there like a man, you choking son of a bitch, and knock this motherfucker in the hole." In it went.

As it turned out, there was no Monday playoff. Shortly after Goalby holed out, it was revealed that De Vicenzo had signed for a 66 instead of the 65 he actually shot. Cliff Roberts and Bobby Jones conferred in Jones's cabin. The rule book was clear. When a player signs for a score higher than he actually makes, he is required to take that higher score. Rule 38, Paragraph 3. The 66 De Vicenzo signed for left him at ten under. Goalby's four-footer turned out to be for the win.

Mike repeated Goalby's choking-dog quote, savoring each word.

Billy said, "What do you think the golf therapists would say about *that*?"

The golf therapists would not have been able to handle Mike at any point in his career. Scores of 64 followed by 82 in your first Masters are not business as usual, and something beyond the phrases *peak performance* and *comfort zone* must explain them. Mike had done something similar in his first U.S. Open, in '84 at Winged Foot, Claude Harmon still around as pro emeritus. His opening-round score was 68, which tied him for the lead with Jim Thorpe, Hubert Green, and Hale Irwin. He followed with a 78. Not as dramatic as 64-82. Still. In his first U.S. Open and his first Masters, after one round, nobody shot a score lower than Mike.

Mike used only one ball during his 64, which was rare in those days because the ball that pros played then, with its balata cover, was soft and scuffed easily. Balata balls actually went out of round. But Mike's ball was on a hot streak, he was catching it squarely, and he was not hitting it very often. Billy suggested he stay with it, and he did. When Mike came off the final green, he gave his mother a hug and his game ball and invited her to join him in the press building.

Mike was the first-day story. Everybody wrote him up. In the Friday papers, one story described Mike's mother, Pearle, who had worked for years as a waitress, taking a cigarette break as Mike climbed the hill to the eighteenth green. Another had a quote from Mike's father, Bill, a mechanic, from somewhere during the back nine: "Let's hope he doesn't wake up." There was a story with a reference to Mike's brother, Pete, wearing a yellow hat marked with the words MIKE's MOB. In *USA Today*, Steve Hershey described Mike as "a grinder, but one of the most personable guys on Tour." In his story for Friday's paper, Hershey led with Mike giving his Titleist to his mother. He quoted Mike with expert precision: " 'This was the round of my life,' Donald, 34, said, his voice catching. 'I played a lot of rounds when I was a kid pretending I was at Augusta, but I never shot this good.' " You have to admire how Hershey faithfully recorded Mike's grammar and the unobtrusive way he captured Mike's emotion.

There was a little box at the bottom of the story, giving basic biographical information about Mike, like you might see on the back of a baseball card. His height, his weight, his tour earnings, other factoids: "Has lived with parents in Hollywood, Fla., since age 3. Got his own apartment three months ago." Later, when they played together on Sunday, Lee Trevino said to Mike, "Your parents must be so proud." Thirty-four, with a place of his own.

Pearle was the source for that homeboy bit. She had enjoyed her own powwow with the writers after the round. That was when she let out that Mike had lived at home through age thirty-four. It wasn't any sort of secret on tour. Mike was on the road about forty weeks a year, he wasn't married, and the other twelve weeks he lived at home. It was part of his financial success, a big part. More to the point, it allowed him to lead his arrested-development, golf-bum life. One day he counted sixty-two golf shirts on the floor of his bedroom.

The personal information in the *USA Today* sports section would have had no impact except that it also appeared on the front page of the paper, in a big story with a big picture: the lunch-bucket pro, age thirty-four, who was leading the Masters and still living with Mom and Dad. Mike's life had been defined for the world to see.

That Page 1 story included telling quotes from Pearle, including "Mike will never get married. He's married to golf." There were other nuggets that Mike's girlfriend, at home in Mississippi, was not keen to read. This was before Golf Channel, before the Internet, at a time when a front-page story in *USA Today* had a wide, wide reach. That morning Mike went from being a largely anonymous touring pro, winner of one tour event that had concluded on a Monday, to public property.

His Friday-afternoon tee time was 2:21, the last of the day. He was paired with John Huston, another journeyman. That morning Mike went to a department store in a mall on the outskirts of Augusta and bought a pair of new pants so he would look "half decent" (his phrase) for a round that would surely get on TV. He drove to the golf course with his parents in a tournament-issued Cadillac. Mike was embarrassed by the *USA Today* front-page story. His girlfriend was, too. How did that story look to her friends?

Mike and his parents drove down Magnolia Lane, the grand driveway that leads from the commercial sprawl of Augusta's Washington Road to the genteel calm of the Augusta National clubhouse. When they arrived in the players' parking lot, Mike took his white Wilson Staff tour bag out of the cavernous trunk and said to his mother, "If I play good again today, and they want to do more interviews, I would appreciate it if you wouldn't talk about my personal life."

Mike's mother said, "What do you mean by that?"

Mike said, "Well, you didn't have to tell them about me living at home and being married to golf."

That was what had set off Mike's girlfriend in Mississippi. Pearle wasn't worried about that. She didn't approve of her. She didn't approve of any of her three sons' girlfriends, except for the one Pete had married. Mike was her pride and joy, and that day when Mike shot 64 had been one of the great days of her life.

"You know what? I'll just go home," she said. "I can't do anything right. I shouldn't have come in the first place." She was close to hysterical.

This is Mike's memory of a Friday in April 1990. He revisits it often. His mother died nine months later, and Mike regretted what he had said. Pearle Donald's Thursday had been out of a dream. Mike wishes he had left it alone.

The session in the parking lot was not the ideal warm-up for his second round. Mike missed a thirty-inch par putt on the crusty first green. On the second, Mike was looking at a downhill six-footer for birdie, and Billy's advice was to lag it, so fast was the putt. Mike needed three putts from two yards.

Mike was one of the top sixty players in the world at that point, easily. A bad second-day score, with nerves clanging and all the rest, might have been 75. Not 82. His new status as public person, and all that it entailed, had to figure in that second-round blowup. Fame, in a fifteen-minute dosage or otherwise, is a funny thing.

As for the 64, something has to explain that, too. A round when everything went right. Mike had raised his game to the circumstance, and that's not the norm. On that Thursday in Augusta, aided and abetted by Billy Harmon, Mike "built a score," as he likes to say. He had a partner (Billy Harmon). He was playing for others (Mike's Mob). The day was right there to be seized. You could say that every day is there to be seized, but the truth is that most days just come and go. This day was different. "It was magical," Mike said. Not a sentence you'll hear often from him.

Nick Faldo won that year in a playoff over Raymond Floyd. Ken Venturi called it for CBS. Mike's good friend Bill Britton finished in a tie for seventh. Mike was near the bottom of the finishers. He made $3,900 for the week. He spent nearly $6,000, including his Sunday-night tab at the Holiday Inn-Augusta bar.

Billy and Mike swapped stories that Sunday night in Augusta. They laughed and cried and closed the bar. Billy's father, the 1948 Masters champ, had died the previous summer. Mike knew his own mother's end was coming. That week they had seen all that golf can give.

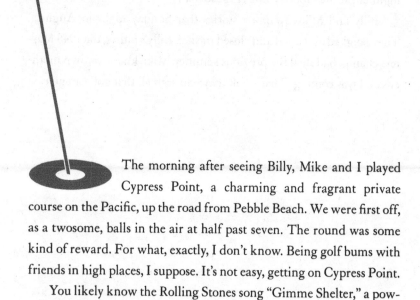

The morning after seeing Billy, Mike and I played Cypress Point, a charming and fragrant private course on the Pacific, up the road from Pebble Beach. We were first off, as a twosome, balls in the air at half past seven. The round was some kind of reward. For what, exactly, I don't know. Being golf bums with friends in high places, I suppose. It's not easy, getting on Cypress Point.

You likely know the Rolling Stones song "Gimme Shelter," a powerful anthem that practically airlifts you to some distant street riot. It couldn't be less golfy. But there's a moment in it that captures for me the critical nanosecond when clubface and ball connect. That is, when they connect properly. About three minutes in, backup singer Merry Clayton, in a pleading soprano, belts out, "Ra-a-ape, *murderyeah*," and Mick Jagger is so overwhelmed by the raw power of her high note that he blurts out a single "*Woo!*" That's it. That *woo*. That's the strike.

Mike pured his first shot of the day, and then it was my turn. I tried to inhale on the backswing and exhale on the downswing. (Easier said than done.) Then came the click, and off my ball went into the morning gray. As you only get one chance to make a first impression, you only get one chance to start your round. My ball was in the air. If it was any good, I did not know.

Back when drivers were made of persimmon, you could feel your most solid shots. On the best ones, you felt nothing. And you knew. With the modern titanium driver, you can miss the sweet spot by a half inch and be blissfully unaware. My ball was still rising when Mike broke the silence: "Michael! That's *beautiful*." There may have been a small measure of surprise in his tone.

We marched out. Golf is a simple game, really. You hit a little ball, chase after it, advance it toward and finally into a distant hole using an odd set of tools, pick it out, move on. Our spectators that morning were deer so tame they seemed more like backyard pets. Mike and I got to the fifteenth tee, an itty-bitty par-three, and stood by a rail fence that keeps you from falling down a cliff and into the ocean.

"Come on in here; I know it's hard for you," Mike said as he put his arm around my shoulder as posing golfers playing bucket-list rounds have done for a hundred years.

I can't stand it when people have more insight into me than I have into myself.

I put my arm around Mike, and our caddie snapped a keeper.

The morning after our Cypress game, Mike and I said thank you in person to the man who had set it up, Sandy Tatum, a lion of the San Francisco bar, a thoroughly erect man in his early nineties who still played golf and paid club dues. Sandy is the golfiest person I know, but as Mike and I settled into his sleek, modern, book-lined law office in Palo Alto, I was surprised to see that it held very few nods to his avocation.

Like Venturi, Sandy was one of the celebrated figures of San

Francisco golf and, nationally, a symbol of establishment amateurism, a breed that is close to extinct. He won the NCAA individual golf title while at Stanford in 1942 and served the USGA for thirty-six years before becoming its president. In the decades after his presidency he had been a USGA adviser and counselor. For the past several decades he has been one of the game's grand old men.

In 1966 he was a middle-aged member at Olympic, in San Francisco, when the U.S. Open was played there. He brought his family to the opening round. The Tatums were an eightsome that morning: Sandy, with his noble nose and patrician manner; Barbara, his spirited and lovely wife; and their six children. Yes, the Tatums were practicing Catholics then. Over time, Sandy gave up the practicing part.

"We mobilized the children, but there were the expected delays, and we arrived as Hogan was teeing off the second hole," Sandy told us. There was a High Mass formality to his speech. "He was playing with Ken Venturi."

Mike and I looked at each other. With no prompting of any sort, Tatum was laying a track right on top of one of Ken's greatest hits: Venturi playing with Hogan at Olympic in '66. I was eager to hear how they would match.

"Hogan's tee shot on two practically landed where we were standing, on the left side of the fairway. He lines up that second shot, takes a final drag from his cigarette, and throws down the butt. Barbara picks it up, and later we tacked that cigarette butt on a bulletin board in our kitchen, where it remained for years until it fell apart.

"Hogan proceeded to hit a most magnificent iron shot to the second green, and we followed him to it. He was approximately twelve feet from the hole. Hogan stood over that putt for quite a considerable time and then he walked away from it. He conferred with Venturi. What they said I could not hear, but later Venturi shared with me their interaction. Hogan had told him that he could not bring the putter head back, to which Venturi said, 'Ben, nobody gives a shit!' "

Tatum laughed his throaty laugh, a laugh that sometimes ends in a worrisome cough. He had told the story just as Venturi had told the story. As the TV detectives say, it *checked out*.

Tatum had mixed feelings about Venturi. He described how much he loved Venturi's swing, which was almost immodest in its beauty. Some golf swings draw looks just as surely as some sweaters do.

"He had that childhood stammer, and it was terribly difficult," Tatum said. "It left a hole in his personality, made him very inward. It impaired his socialization as a young man because communication was such an ordeal for him. The solitary nature of golf was his salvation, but it also impeded his growth. There's always been a quality of self-absorption with Ken, no question. But he has also, as a grown man, plugged that hole, quite effectively and admirably. The '64 Open was one of the great moments in the game, to win like that, after his game had nearly deserted him. And then the second career at CBS? Given what he had to overcome, it was nothing less than astonishing."

What a powerful phrase, *given what he had to overcome*. Sandy's speech was often rich in meaning. It's hard to imagine any other ninety-something man analyzing another old man's life with such insight and empathy.

Harding Park, the bucolic San Francisco public course that Ken had grown up playing, was one of Sandy's hangouts, too. The Harding clubhouse, where Venturi's parents worked behind the pro shop counter, had morphed into the Frank "Sandy" Tatum Clubhouse. In the early 2000s, Sandy oversaw the restoration of the course to its circa-1954 glory.

Sandy was already a veteran of marriage, fatherhood, and the law when Venturi played in that famous four-ball match at Cypress Point in '56. Tatum knew all four players and the two men, George Coleman and Eddie Lowery, who had set it up. He knew Sam Snead, Bobby Jones. Tom Watson. He knew Tiger Woods, his fellow Stanford Cardinal, although that relationship, to the degree that there was one, started to deteriorate after Tatum urged Woods to stay at Stanford and graduate before turning pro. (Woods quit school after two years.) Between what Sandy saw firsthand and what he gleaned from Bobby Jones and Jones's contemporaries, Sandy could account for nearly the entire 125-year history of American golf.

Sandy set up the course for the USGA at the 1974 U.S. Open, the first one Hale Irwin won. That tournament became known as the "Massacre at Winged Foot." Palmer didn't even put '74 on his could-have-won-it list, but had he shot a final-round 70, even par, he would have finished in a tie for first. His closing 76 dropped him all the way to fifth. Usually, if you start Sunday in contention and shoot 76, you will finish in oblivion. The joke was that caddies looking for balls in the rough went missing themselves. The greens were dying of thirst.

There were columnists and players who thought that the USGA had created such misanthropic conditions in response to the final-round 63 Johnny Miller had shot the previous year in the Open at Oakmont, one of the hardest courses in the world. That sounds like human nature, but Sandy told us it was not the case. To paraphrase the Hebrew National hot dog ads that were popular then, Sandy was answering to a higher authority. That is, par.

Sandy was asked during that '74 Open if he and his USGA committeemen were trying to humiliate the best golfers in the world.

"No," Sandy said. "We're trying to identify them."

They succeeded. Among the top-ten finishers that year were Arnold Palmer, Tom Watson, Jack Nicklaus, Gary Player, Tom Kite, Lou Graham, and Hale Irwin, who won with a score of seven over par. Some gang.

In 1979 Irwin won his second U.S. Open and Tatum was presiding over it as USGA president. In the opening round that year at Inverness, in Toledo, one of the pros, Lon Hinkle, decided to play the par-five eighth hole by hitting a 1-iron into the seventeenth fairway and a 2-iron second shot to the eighth green from there. He two-putted for an easy birdie.

Tatum admired the ingenuity but not the bastardization of a true unreachable-in-two par-five, to say nothing of the resulting disruptions to play on the seventeenth. Early Friday morning, Tatum oversaw the planting of a giant spruce in an attempt to stop Hinkle from taking his shortcut.

"The players complained," Sandy said. "'You're changing the course, you're changing the course!' I said, 'We're rectifying a problem.'"

Tatum spent that Friday on the eighth tee to quash any possible revolt. He watched as Hinkle teed his ball on a scorecard pencil and launched a shot over what was already being called the Hinkle Tree. It was such a delicious little contretemps and an insight into the mindset of the pro. Whatever the course will yield, the pro wants it to yield more. The players often have a love-hate relationship with courses and their designers, and also the inept, ignorant bureaucrats—you've already seen P. J. Boatwright and Cliff Roberts and now Sandy Tatum in action—who attempt to administer and regulate play. Somehow Tatum rose above this lowly status to become an admired figure in the game.

Frank D. Tatum, Jr., wasn't really a blueblood, not in the Boston Brahmin sense of the word. Sandy grew up in the 1920s and 1930s in the Los Angeles of *Chinatown*. He went to public school, and his father was a real estate broker. But there's something about a USGA affiliation. It imposes formality on a person. Maybe it's the blazer.

One of Sandy's brothers, an actor who worked under the name Warde Donovan, was married for a time to Phyllis Diller. (No, he was not Fang, the ineffectual manager-husband who was a gag in her act.) Tatum had his own brushes with Hollywood. He told us how as a teenager he saw Howard Hughes and Katharine Hepburn playing furtive golf at the Wilshire Country Club in Los Angeles, where his father was a member. Those sightings gave Sandy a secret bond with the great screen beauty. He never forgot her red lipstick. It was more than he could stand.

Sandy fell just as hard for golf. As a boy he would bike to Wilshire after school with his clubs on his back. When he played two balls (with hickory-shafted clubs), one ball would represent Bobby Jones and the other Walter Hagen. The great amateur and the great professional. He loved their dress, their manners, their play. (He saw them in newsreels at his local movie house.) Then, in 1931, Bobby Jones played an informal exhibition match at Wilshire with two pros and Charlie Seaver, a noted amateur. (His son Tom enjoyed a career in sports, too.) Bobby Jones in person was overwhelming to young Sandy. Seeing Jones that day sent him down a path he followed for the rest of his life.

In the early 1970s, Tatum was visiting Augusta National when a subtle conversation began to unfold amid a small group of well-placed members. Tatum knew where it was going: He was rising in the USGA hierarchy and he was a good golfer with an attractive wife. He was deemed club material, and the men were gauging his interest in joining. Tatum demurred. He offered the most irrefutable of excuses: He couldn't afford it, with six children to feed and clothe and educate. Plus the club was far from home. Everything he said was true. But it wasn't the whole truth.

Sandy knew about the intraclub power struggle at Augusta National during the final years of Bobby Jones's life. Bobby Jones wanted his son, Bob Jones III, to succeed him as club president. Cliff Roberts, the club's chairman, was opposed. With Jones physically incapacitated by his spinal disease, though mentally unimpaired, Roberts took over the reins at Augusta National. He somehow rendered Jones powerless at the club he had cofounded. That was Sandy's sense of it. Jones was his hero, and thinking about his final years left Sandy feeling queasy. Jones died in December 1971. Bob Jones III, his namesake son, died two years later at forty-seven. Roberts was not invited to either funeral, which Sandy described as the "ultimate expression" of how the Jones family viewed Clifford Roberts.

"I saw how Roberts treated Jones and his son and I found it troubling," Tatum said. "It was singularly unattractive, the way Roberts managed the club. I knew I would never want to be a member of a club over which Roberts was presiding."

In Sandy's Mount Rushmore of golf, he has busts of Jones, Hogan, Palmer, and Nicklaus. When I asked Sandy about Arnold, he said, "What Palmer conveyed to me, and doubtless to millions of others, was that there was more to life than being the greatest golfer of all time."

Palmer was not the greatest golfer of all time, even though he looked like he might be when he won all seven of his major championships in quick succession between 1958 and 1964. But he had the longest, most successful afterlife in the history of sports. Tatum offered an insight into how that happened. "Palmer had a sexual charisma that was really quite remarkable, and I say that looking at him from a masculine, heterosexual point of view. But boy was it ever impressive. And the affection that women had for him was nothing less than astonishing.

"Many years ago, a friend of mine won a two-week trip with Palmer and two others as part of some sort of contest. It was a major advertising campaign underwritten by one of Arnold's sponsors. The trip was to result in a promotional film of some kind. They went to Asia and Australia. They had a great time. When my friend returned, he remarked that it was just incredible how the men, wherever Palmer went, were drawn to him, and how the women *swooned* in his presence. Quite attractive women, I might add."

In 2012, when the U.S. Open was being held at Olympic, Sandy was asked to write a piece for the USGA program. He analyzed an imaginary field for the 2045 U.S. Open. He predicted that half of the 156 players would be black, thirty players would be from China, and twenty would be from India. In his crystal ball he saw twenty female players competing, maybe a half-dozen openly gay players, and one or two transgender players. The USGA killed the piece.

I once said to Sandy, "Wasn't I lucky to come of golf age in the seventies?"

You know the drill: Watson, Nicklaus, and Trevino at the height of their powers; Palmer hanging on; Curtis and Crenshaw and Seve rising. The plaid bell-bottoms giving way to Sansabelt. The tour wives in their crazy hats and headbands. Some guy in a Budweiser T-shirt yelling *freeee-BIRD* while a long putt rolled on, hell-bound for the hole. That decade was Tatum's decade, too. He was at the epicenter of the game then.

"Yes, you were," Tatum said. "But the fifties were better."

I asked why.

"Hogan, Nelson, Snead." The American triumvirate.

"What was it about them?" I asked.

Without pausing Sandy said, "They came out of the caddie yard."

Viewed through that light, it's interesting that Sandy had such an affinity for Tom Watson, who grew up at the Kansas City Country Club and not in its caddie yard. But Watson also has a toughness and a directness about him that made you forget about his privileged background. His attitude has always been *Tell me the bad news now*. There is a lot about him to admire, but Sandy loved him, which is something, because I wouldn't describe Watson as obviously lovable. When he was yipping late in his tour career, Watson once asked Davis Love how he gripped the putter. Davis told him what he did. Watson said, "That's wrong." There are a thousand other examples. But Sandy never saw that side of him. Or if he did, he ignored it.

Tatum and Watson met in 1968, when Watson was in his brief hippie phase and a member of the Stanford golf team. There was a match against an alumni team, and Tatum played for the old guys. Later, and for twenty consecutive years, Tatum and Watson played together in the Pebble Beach Pro-Am, either as partners or in the same foursome. They played together all over the United States and in Ireland and Scotland, often wearing rain suits.

Part of the appeal for Tatum was Watson's Scottish approach to golf, including his walking speed and his decisiveness over the ball. In Watson's decade or more of superior golf, starting in 1975, he was golf's one obvious stoic, the closest thing the seventies and eighties had to a Hogan. He was almost painfully forthright. Watson's attitude, as Sandy and Herb Wind and many others saw it, was that the game owed him nothing, and whatever the golf course gave him, good or bad, he took it without complaint.

Consider Watson's response to the second shot he hit on seventeen in the fourth round of the '84 British Open. He was a shot off the lead. He was trying to win his sixth Open and third straight. He was trying to do it at St. Andrews. The stakes were high. Watson hit too much club, approaching that seventeenth green, and he hit it too hard and too far right. His ball finished about a yard from a rock wall where there is no free relief. All realistic hope for victory ended with that shoved 2-iron. I have long suspected that his caddie, Alfie Fyles, urged that club on Watson, though Watson has told me that was not the case. With his ball in the air, Watson showed his disgust by taking two steps to his left. You could see nothing on his face. He always hid hurt well.

For years, it was an open secret on tour that Watson had a drinking problem. Stories would go around depicting Watson at dinner, drinking too much and becoming belligerent and even more of a political and golfing know-it-all. One of his tour nicknames was Carnac II, a play off a Johnny Carson character who had an answer for everything.

Any addiction, of course, is a personal and tender matter, even when the disease falls to the famous. Tatum would not have discussed

Watson's drinking with me, with my notebook out, and I would not be writing about it here, if Watson had not been public about it first. Some months before Mike and I went to see Sandy, Watson did a Golf Channel interview with David Feherty in which he spoke about his drinking problem. Feherty has talked about how Watson helped him get sober.

Feherty and Watson were at a golf event one year in Canada when Watson said, "You're not well, are you?"

"How do you know?" Feherty said.

"I can see it in your eyes," Watson said.

"What do you see?"

"My reflection."

Alcohol runs through golf like spit tobacco runs through baseball. Watson's father, Ray, a good amateur golfer himself, quit drinking late in life. Tatum knew Ray Watson long before he knew Tom. "I had been asked to come to Watson's home in Kansas City," Tatum said. "It was a gathering of friends and family members who were concerned about Tom's well-being. The goal was to get Tom to deal with his drinking, which was pervasive, to put it mildly.

"This intervention was orchestrated by a professional who had been to jail twenty-one times because of his drinking. And this man was remarkably effective. As he began a dialogue, Watson broke down in tears. He acknowledged then the magnitude of his problem. He saw that there were people who could help him find a way out of it. He saw the love for him from the people in that room.

"There was a vehicle waiting for him. That was part of the program. You didn't pack or have long good-byes. It called for the participant to get into an automobile and go to a treatment facility, where you do the real work. And that is what Watson did. When I think about it, it is the most remarkable thing I have ever seen him do."

•   •   •

When I was falling under the spell of the game, Watson seemed always to be on TV. He was the leader through three rounds in that '74 U.S. Open at Winged Foot, the first I can recall following. He won the '75 British Open by a shot in an eighteen-hole playoff, wearing a plaid woolen British racing hat. Two years later he was the star of the Duel in the Sun, the pen name for his one-shot win over Big Jack at the '77 British Open at Turnberry. That's the most fun I ever had watching TV, and I'm including all those Saturday nights in the seventies when Mary Tyler Moore and Bob Newhart and Carol Burnett batted first, second, and third. In '79 Watson lost at Augusta in a three-man playoff.

Watson wasn't like other golfers. I imagine that was part of the attraction for Sandy, and I know it was for me. In 1990 Watson resigned his membership at the Kansas City Country Club because a prominent businessman, Henry Bloch, a founder of H&R Block, had been rejected for membership, and Watson felt there was only one biographical fact that had kept Bloch out: He was Jewish, as was Watson's wife, Linda Watson, née Rubin. Watson's son and daughter were Jewish, too. So was Watson's manager, Chuck Rubin, Linda's brother. In a pinch, you could count Watson for your minyan.

You could also count on him to take principled stances. In the 1983 Skins Game, Watson accused Gary Player of violating a rule by removing a small part of a live weed that was behind his ball. Player maintained that Watson could not see what he was doing from thirty feet away. Player also said that he was just trying to determine whether the plant matter was attached or unattached. (The issue became public only because Dave Anderson of the *New York Times* heard them arguing about it.) Watson could be difficult, impatient, and abrupt. Once, when I was caddying in Watson's group in the Masters, he asked Dow Finsterwald, an honorary marshal, if there was a backup on the first tee. When Dow couldn't immediately tell him, Watson said, "You should know." (To which Finsterwald said, "Okay, *Tommy*.") But on matters related to the rule book, on anything related to the spirit of the game and how it should be played, Watson was beyond reproach. Sandy Tatum had been sending out that message from a high place for years.

A few weeks after our visit with Sandy in his office, Tom Watson was introduced, at a stagy press conference in the Empire State Building, as the new Ryder Cup captain. Watson was asked about his relationship with Tiger Woods. He said, "My relationship with Tiger is fine. Whatever has been said before is water under the bridge. No issues." It was such a political answer. That wasn't the Watson I knew and admired. The real Watson—Sandy's Watson—was the one who came into the press tent after losing that four-hole playoff for the 2009 British Open at the astonishing age of fifty-nine. Watson saw the bummed-out reporters assembled before him and said, "This ain't a funeral, you know."

Watson at that Ryder Cup announcement was saying what he needed to say in order to live another day. Watson in defeat at Turnberry was exposed and real. The sun and the wind had left his voice dry and scratchy, and he dropped in that casual *ain't* like he knew what real pain was all about. He was saying the events at Turnberry did not qualify. What a sense of balance. Watson had lost, and he was handling it better than we were.

I asked Sandy once if he ever discussed that Open with Watson.

"No," Sandy said. "The subject's too painful. For me."

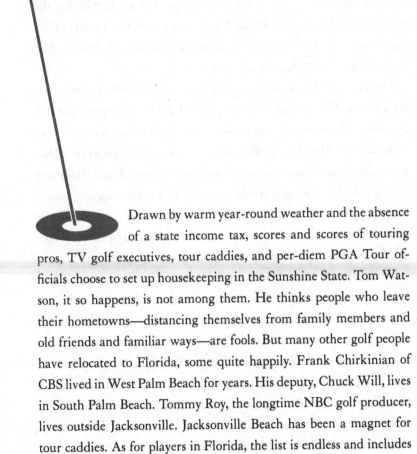

Drawn by warm year-round weather and the absence of a state income tax, scores and scores of touring pros, TV golf executives, tour caddies, and per-diem PGA Tour officials choose to set up housekeeping in the Sunshine State. Tom Watson, it so happens, is not among them. He thinks people who leave their hometowns—distancing themselves from family members and old friends and familiar ways—are fools. But many other golf people have relocated to Florida, some quite happily. Frank Chirkinian of CBS lived in West Palm Beach for years. His deputy, Chuck Will, lives in South Palm Beach. Tommy Roy, the longtime NBC golf producer, lives outside Jacksonville. Jacksonville Beach has been a magnet for tour caddies. As for players in Florida, the list is endless and includes Woods, Nicklaus, and Palmer. The center of Arnold's universe may be Latrobe, but his official residence is a modest townhouse in Bay Hill, an Orlando golf community (no gate!) that he helped create. His office is above the pro shop.

If you know the name Chuck Will at all, it's likely from seeing it scroll by in the production credits at the end of hundreds of CBS golf telecasts over the course of twenty years, beginning in 1968. Chuck knew all about Venturi, Palmer, Tatum, the Harmon brothers and their father. But none of those people would have known Chuck, not in a meaningful way. Of all my Secret Legends, Chuck Will was the most secret. His work, as Frank Chirkinian's right-hand man at CBS Sports, had kept him in trailers and broadcast trucks. He wasn't often in the sunlight. Still, he seemed to know everybody.

Mike seemed to be having a good time, working the legends beat with me, and he was on board to go see Chuck. The appointed day for our rendezvous was spectacular, nothing but blue skies in every direction, but Mike was willing to take the day off from work. (That is, checking on his investment portfolio and playing Eagle Trace and hitting balls on its range.) We drove to Chuck's condo together, southbound on A1A through South Palm Beach and along a collection of oceanfront high-rises where you could stop in the lobby and readily get a golf game, a gin game, or the name of a good osteopath.

I met Chuck at the '85 Players Championship in the manner that many unemployed caddies met him. I was looking for work, and Chuck hired caddies as casual laborers for weeklong stints at CBS tournaments. When I moved to Philadelphia in 1986 to work for the *Inquirer*, we would talk regularly and play occasionally, always at Bala Golf Club, a cozy old club for the city's pols and fixers. The Bala course, in the city limits and near the intersection of City Avenue and Golf Road, is a tiny little thing. But it's old, and the golf vibe there is deep. Chuck and Frank, who met in Philadelphia in '48, contributed significantly to the club's culture. Chuck once told me that Frank's game was driver in the rough, Ginty 7-wood recovery shot. In other words, not very good. But he did have a fabulous selection of golf sweaters. Chuck was a former club champ at Bala and he played competitive golf. One time he shot 65 in a local tournament when he was supposed to be working at his job as a cardboard-box salesman. Joe Greenday of the *Philadelphia Daily News* wanted to write him up. Chuck said, "Talk to somebody else." A golf bum with a conscience.

Chuck and I were once partners in a money match at Bala, and I found myself apologizing to him for my play. Chuck said, "Are you trying your hardest?" He knew I was. Too hard, if anything. "Then you have nothing to apologize for."

We had a good friendship. Then I wrote a story for *SI* in 1995 that Chuck thought I should not have written, and our friendship went into a deep freeze. The story resulted in the firing of Ben Wright, an English newspaperman whom Chirkinian had turned into a CBS golf commentator. Wright had made a series of inane, sexist, and homophobic comments about the LPGA to a reporter named Valerie Helmbreck from the *Wilmington News-Journal*. Wright said women's breasts interfere with their swing. Another of his pearls: "They're going to a butch game, and that furthers the bad image of the game." When Helmbreck's story came out—which she wrote absolutely straight— the *New York Post* had a field day and a perfect front-page head: THE BOOB ON THE TUBE.

It was a passing storm until Wright went on TV and trashed Helmbreck's reputation in an effort to save his own job. Our story in *SI* was able to show that Wright had made the comments he'd claimed on national TV he did not make. That's why he got fired. My friendship with Chuck was another casualty of the bombastic interview Wright gave Helmbreck. On that Monday in early March my barren years with Chuck were about to come to an end.

Chuck still had a home on the Main Line but spent his winters in a first-floor condominium in short, boxy building that fronted Lake Worth. He was at an open door when we arrived.

Mike said, "You're looking good, Chuck!"

It was a statement of fact. Chuck was wearing flip-flops, loose shorts rendered baggier by his stick-figure legs, a golf shirt, and a black sweater vest. His hair was long and his glasses had a purplish tint. He looked like a retired concert promoter. He liked to say that he was never young, but to me he had always been of indeterminate age. It was good to see him. He greeted me not as a long-lost son but something like that.

Chuck and Mike knew all the same people. Chuck told us about a youthful romance he had with one of the Bauer sisters way back when, and Mike knew exactly what that meant. He knew the Bauer sisters were the LPGA's original glamour girls in the 1950s, and that Marlene had married Alice's ex-husband, and that there was a whole weird thing there, and that if you had ever even sipped cocktails with one of the Bauer sisters, as Chuck surely had, you must have had a lot of game. Mike and Chuck both knew the Fred (Couples) you and I do not, the one who no-showed here and no-showed there but would charm you to death effortlessly the next time he saw you. They were both lifers, Chuck and Mike, and they had dug their own trenches. No bullshit could pass in Chuck's condo on that perfect winter day in South Florida. They both knew too much.

Chuck had a thousand players in his memory bank. He knew their swings and their divorces and their IRS audits. He knew Palmer and Venturi in ways I never would. He had a name for everybody. He called Ben Wright "Bentley," Earl Woods "Colonel," his own father "Admiral," Cliff Roberts "The Old Man," Ray Floyd "Junior," Gene Sarazen "Squire." (Not "The Squire." That was common.) He knew Mike as "Statman." He knew that Mike hung with Lance Ten Broeck ("Last Call"), Bill Britton ("Toy Cannon"), Jim Boros ("Truck"). Chuck knew that Truck, when his tour days were over, had become the pro at the city course in Allentown. Chuck knew close to all. Who was broke, who was stepping out, who was on the first tee Saturday morning with Friday night on his breath. He heard everything the caddies said, stored it all away, and seldom, if ever, used it. But it was there, in reserve. He was Frank Chirkinian's eyes and especially his ears, which is saying something, because Chuck liked to say that Frank "could hear twice as well as any other person I knew."

Over the years I had learned from Chuck that Chirkinian's general view was that televised golf was part of the network's entertainment division. Frank, aided and abetted by Chuck, treated the golfers like they were stars in the old Hollywood studio system. Maybe it was a better way. Frank understood that a well-framed single moment could define a player for the rest of his life. Hubert Green, for instance, at the '78 Masters, Sunday night creeping in, the last man on the last green in his shiny green Sansabelt slacks, looking at a four-foot birdie putt to tie Gary Player and force a playoff. Chirkinian cleared the stage.

Frank saw sport as theater and the Masters as a play in three acts, with Thursday and Friday as Act I, Saturday as Act II, and Sunday as Act III. The course was his stage and the players were his actors. Frank stage-managed Hubert's putt to tie as if it were a scene of improvisational theater. In actual fact, he did that hundreds of times per broadcast. Hubert missed, by the way. *CUT TO: Gary Player reaction shot.*

Golf, under Frank and Chuck, was special on CBS, and the Masters particularly so. By saying less, Frank's commentators said more. He hired drinkers, newspapermen, Englishmen, voices, understaters, and one U.S. Open winner, Kenny Venturi, for whom the Masters represented unrequited love. Somehow we picked up on that, and that added urgency to the proceedings. The message from CBS, from Frank and Chuck and Kenny and Pat and young Jim Nantz and Ben Wright, was that Augusta was a place to celebrate tradition and to practice discretion, manners, and class. Frank understood TV. Chuck understood golf. They were good for each other.

Chuck and Mike and I sat at a table just off the kitchen in the small apartment Chuck shared with his wife, Kathleen, twenty-eight years younger than he. She put out a big plate of shrimp for us. No matter where the conversation went, it returned to Frank, like those old Central Park rental horses returning to their stable as if on autopilot. We talked about Fred Couples and Venturi getting into the Hall of Fame, and Chuck talked about Frank's path in.

"Frank called me when he got the news that he was going into the Hall of Fame," Chuck said. "He was dying. He said, 'Charlie, isn't it a little late?'"

Chirkinian's induction ceremony came about ten weeks after he died in March 2011. The next month, a lot of the old CBS golf group got together to celebrate Frank's life and times, but Chuck did not go. It was still too raw for him.

"I fell in love with Frank, I really did," Chuck said, "and I worked hard for him, even when I was drinking. I'd have the dry heaves. And then I'd go to work and do the job." Chirkinian wasn't going to fire him. Chuck did his job well. He was Frank's homeboy.

Chuck described various sodden CBS dinners, commentators half-smashed while on the air, unable to climb the ladder to the broadcast booth without an assist, rehearsals that were a total mess, with Frank's screaming as the soundtrack. Then four P.M. would come, the red light would go on, and nobody would miss a beat.

The whole gang was comically profane. As *horseshit* is part of the lingua franca of big-league baseball, Frank and Chuck and the CBS golf crew of their era kept the word *asshole* in constant circulation. Chuck told Mike and me the distinction he made between regular assholes, flaming assholes, and gaping assholes. In the week I worked for him, Chuck had called me *asshole*, no modifier, like it was my name, and I took it as a sort of welcoming. "The one you don't want to be is a gaper," Chuck told us. He kept lists of gapers and he kept lists of caddies who owed him money. There was a lot of overlap.

Chuck knew all the drinkers at CBS and cited them, but Chirkinian and Jim Nantz, both connoisseurs of fine wines, were not among them, even if Chirkinian did buy many bottles of Opus One over the years on his CBS credit card.

"Live television is a chancy thing," Chuck said. "Everybody's on edge. The job is to keep mistakes off the air. So there are things people do to relieve the pressure, and drinking is one of them." He wasn't making excuses. Hardly. He was just explaining life on his show.

Chuck had the highest regard for Nicklaus, in victory and especially in defeat. He liked Palmer. He had many ups and downs with Venturi. He said that when Ken was in a good mood, nobody could be more fun, but he was often cranky and self-centered. "I played golf with Kenny a number of times," Chuck said. "He talked about himself."

He marveled at Palmer's charisma. He saw people throw themselves at Arnold, a recipe to develop egomania if ever there was one, and to a remarkable degree, Chuck said, Arnold stayed on the ground. His gifts were almost inexplicable.

"There was a time we needed Arnold to read something for us off a piece of paper," Chuck said. "He couldn't do it. It was lifeless. We put it on a teleprompter. He couldn't read it off that, either. He was like a wood soldier. We did take after take. It was devoid of personality.

"But then there was Arnold on the course. That was entirely different. You had all these other pros, they'd make a putt and they would maybe tilt their head. Right? And then Arnold Palmer comes along, and this guy was just so expressive. He was the very figure of a man. He exuded sex."

Chuck half-cackled at his own observation, surprised by where it had concluded. I was struck that it was so similar to what Sandy Tatum had said about Arnold's appeal. Chuck didn't use Sandy's phrase—*sexual charisma*—but he could have. Its absence or presence can make or break a TV show. If you ever watched *Charlie's Angels* or the NBA finals in the Michael Jordan era or *Mad Men*, you know what I'm talking about.

"Augusta made Arnold and Arnold made Augusta, and they both made Frank," Chuck said. "But Frank would also tell you that he helped make Arnold. He used to say, 'I put his name up in lights.' " Frank invented golf on TV. Chuck wasn't there at the start, but he was there when it got good. Over time, for good and for bad, golf on TV *became* golf.

Chuck told the story of Seve Ballesteros winning the Masters in 1983 and being interviewed by the club chairman, Hord Hardin, in Butler Cabin. On live TV, at the conclusion of another artful Frank Chirkinian telecast, Hardin asked, "Seve, let me ask you—a lot of people have asked me." He paused. "How tall are you?' "

"And Frank started screaming, 'He did not just fucking ask that!' "

In the CBS/Augusta National relationship, the club had all the power. Augusta National officials did a lot of dictating and CBS executives did a lot of note-taking. But on this occasion the club had gone too far. Chirkinian later said to Hardin, "Do you want us to continue doing this tournament?" In his threat, Frank was looking for one thing: He wanted the Butler Cabin winner's interview to be handled by one of his trained professionals, and from that point on it was.

"I could sit here and cry like a baby, talking about Frank," Chuck said.

He turned the calendar back to the Monday after the 1981 Danny Thomas Memphis Classic. Jerry Pate won. Mike had missed the cut.

"I was hungover," Chuck said. "I saw Frank. He said, 'It can't go on like this.' He didn't tell me to stop drinking. He just said the truth: It can't go on like this. That's how he changed my life."

That was Chuck's one-man intervention. Chuck figured out there were things he loved more than drinking. Chuck quit the next day, June 30, 1981. The Tuesday after Memphis.

When we were close to leaving, Chuck addressed Mike and his U.S. Open. He said, "You didn't win. But you were memorable." He then said something to me about the fallout from the Ben Wright story. My heart was racing so I'm not sure precisely what he said, but it was something close to this: "Just because we drifted there for a while didn't mean we didn't love each other." It was a mighty thing for him to say.

Out we went, the three of us, into the fading sunshine of a winter afternoon in South Florida. Chuck stood in his condo's parking lot in flip-flops, the lenses on his purplish glasses growing darker. I had been struck by Chuck's ability to talk about friendship, regret, good times and lost chances, love in its different forms. There was something so modern and healthy about it. He had told us that he was eighty-seven. I hadn't thought of his age, and the number took me by surprise. It had been eighteen years since I had last seen him. Too long, and the years went too fast. Golf on TV. That was his baby. Chuck had seen it grow into advanced middle age. He had seen me do the same.

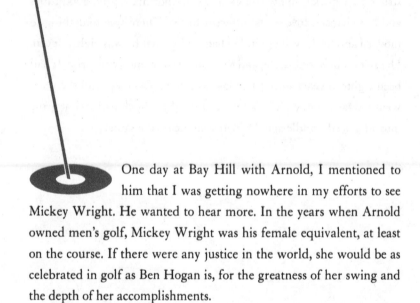

One day at Bay Hill with Arnold, I mentioned to him that I was getting nowhere in my efforts to see Mickey Wright. He wanted to hear more. In the years when Arnold owned men's golf, Mickey Wright was his female equivalent, at least on the course. If there were any justice in the world, she would be as celebrated in golf as Ben Hogan is, for the greatness of her swing and the depth of her accomplishments.

Between 1956 and 1973, she won eighty-two LPGA events. At her best, she was as dominant as Tiger Woods was at his best. She won four U.S. Opens between '58 and '64 and four LPGA Championships between '58 and '63. All the while, she was the ultimate soul golfer (to bastardize a term of surfing). Hogan once said of her, "She had the finest swing I ever saw—man or woman."

I was not surprised to be rebuffed by Mickey, politely but firmly, through the good offices of Rhonda Glenn, a longtime USGA media official, historian of women's golf, and friend of Mickey's. Even in 2000, for an *SI* story, Mickey wouldn't let me see her in person. At least then she was willing to talk by phone. In the intervening years she had made herself less public. She was leading the life she wanted. She and Peggy Wilson, a former LPGA player, lived together in a modest house in Port St. Lucie, on the east coast of Florida, between West Palm Beach and Vero Beach. Mickey read the *Wall Street Journal*, smoked, played cards, cooked, shared jokes with close friends via e-mail. There was nothing in the world beyond Port St. Lucie that she wanted. She repeatedly declined invitations to do a this-is-your-life studio interview on Golf Channel. She didn't go to a gala at The Breakers in Palm Beach, an hour by car from her house, to celebrate the LPGA turning fifty. She didn't go to the USGA Museum in Far Hills, New Jersey, for the opening of its Mickey Wright Room (adjoining the Arnold Palmer Room). My request fell into the black hole of her former life. Others called her a recluse, but I don't think that's the right word. She had just moved on.

My rejection made me realize how lucky I was to talk to her at all in 2000, the year she turned sixty-five. At that point, Mickey had not played in any sort of tournament in seven years and was already leading her own version of Hogan's final quarter century. Mickey and Peggy's home was on the Sinners' Course at the Club Med Sandpiper, and often, in the still of early morning, Mickey would hit forty or fifty balls with a 7-iron off a mat in her backyard into an empty fairway. A course worker—a keen golfer, the father of a club pro—sometimes watched her, awed by her swing and the flight of her ball.

The LPGA player Patty Sheehan was at Mickey's last event, a senior tournament in 1993. Sheehan had never met her fellow Hall of Famer. "Everybody knew Mickey didn't want pictures taken, so I just watched by myself, trying to take it all in," Sheehan told me. "I had seen old film clips of her swing. It looked the same: very fluid, very powerful—flawless. You could see she was in love with golf and dedicated to hitting a golf ball purely. She had these old clubs, old as dirt, and it was clear they were her best friends." They were '63 Wilson Staffs, basically the same clubs Palmer took on the road in the winter of '55.

You could sub in Hogan for Mickey in Sheehan's observation and those sentences would still make sense. But Mickey was even more of an enigma than Hogan. Hogan had his golf company. He was at Shady Oaks in Fort Worth every weekday, hitting balls and eating lunch. (Mickey joined Shady in the 1960s in part because she wanted to observe Hogan at close range without being obtrusive. He returned the compliment by watching her.) In 1983 Hogan gave a revealing seven-minute coat-and-tie TV interview with Ken Venturi that has been mined for its many pearls, including this one: "I feel sorry for the rich kids now. I really do. Because they're never going to have the opportunity I had."

Mickey Wright didn't pursue a life in business when she was done playing, as Hogan had done. She didn't do corporate outings. She gave few interviews. She never married; she never had children. Her private life was private. Were it not for Rhonda's efforts and a 1983 story she wrote for the USGA's late, great *Golf Journal*, Mickey might have faded into complete obscurity. Of course Arnold was interested. They were exact contemporaries and didn't even know each other.

"She doesn't want to talk about golf," I said. I should have added *with me.*

"Isn't that something," Arnold said. He was baffled.

"She doesn't play at all," I said.

"I can't believe that," Arnold said.

With Mickey's rejection, my legends tour had reached its first impassable road. As your bus driver, I would like you to know that

I never considered taking Mickey off my Living Legends list. If anything, I was thinking of adding her to my Secret Legends list.

Once in St. Andrews, I found myself trying to learn more about Old Tom Morris, the longtime custodian of the Old Course. I went to visit a golf historian and actor named David Joy, who gave me Old Tom in full regalia. He had the accent, the beard, the woolly clothes. Most significantly, he understood Old Tom's heartbreak over the death of his namesake son. In not quite the same way, I asked Rhonda Glenn if she could discuss Mickey's life and times with Mike and me, and she was willing.

On that basis, my reporting partner and I saddled up and headed to the North Florida horse country where Rhonda lived, in the town of Summerfield. We went there on a mission, to learn more about the woman who was one part Palmer, two parts Hogan, and, alongside Jack Nicklaus, Bobby Jones, and Tiger Woods, in the foursome of the most dominant golfers ever.

As we approached Summerfield, Mike told me about being at the Hollywood Lakes Country Club, near his home, on a December Sunday in 1968, at age thirteen, when Peggy Wilson won what turned out to be her only LPGA tournament. In the next tournament, Mike remembered that Peggy was playing well until a tee popped up and struck her in the eye. The things Mike remembers.

We arrived at the front door of a tidy, comfortable development home in a gated golf community and met the ladies of the house: Rhonda Glenn, unofficial historian of Mary Kathryn "Mickey" Wright, and Barbara Romack, winner of the 1954 U.S. Amateur over "Miss Wright," as the papers had it back then. Barb won her Amateur the same year Palmer won his, in 1954. She looked like a woman who knew a lot.

She was wearing a bright pink cashmere sweater over her slender shoulders. Rhonda's blond hair was just splendid. These were women who did not wing it. They both were loaded with energy and charm. Rhonda was in her mid-sixties and Barb was—she'll hate this—done pushing eighty. Mike and I had never met either of our hosts, but we settled into a comfortable conversation almost immediately. They knew my typing and Mike's playing career. We weren't strangers.

Before long, Rhonda was showing us an *SI* dated April 16, 1956. The cover girl, a golfer, had her hair up and braided. Her hands, high above her left shoulder in follow-through, were on a leather grip. She was wearing bright red lipstick and a lively patterned blouse. The headline was barely a whisper:

BARBARA ROMACK,
CURTIS CUP STAR

The brief story mentions that Romack, as a member of the amateur U.S. Curtis Cup team, would soon sail—*sail!*—to England for the May matches. On page 28 of that same issue is Herbert Warren Wind's account of the '56 Masters. "A cool and careful golfer, the slim young man seemed a certain winner when he arrived at the sixty-third tee with a six-shot lead over Middlecoff," Wind writes midstory.

Wind's cool leader is Ken Venturi. You and I both know how that story ends. Or how it doesn't.

Before long, Rhonda, author of *The Illustrated History of Women's Golf*, was showing us a collection of film clips that documented Mickey's swing through the years. Her swing had changed over time. All of the swings were athletic, but some from the mid-1950s were out of balance and saved by her strength and athleticism. At her peak, Mickey looked like Iron Byron—the USGA ball-hitting machine—if it had soul, style, and a cardigan. Her best swings looked like ones that could repeat forever. There wasn't a moment of inefficiency or eccentricity in them. In the clips Mickey is tall and slender—not skinny—with a wide stance, a low take-away, and a full turn. Her backswing had the rhythm of a cresting wave. Her follow-through was so full that some of the swings endangered her schoolteacher glasses.

Hearing Rhonda talk about Mickey was like hearing Billy Harmon talk about Hogan. In both cases, the admiration was deep and sincere. The initial attraction for Rhonda might have been Mickey's golf, but it went far beyond that. She appreciated Mickey's standards, her nonconformist view of the world, her intelligence, humor, and loyalty. If Mickey was a complex personality—as her unwillingness to attend the opening of her own room at the USGA Museum might suggest—Rhonda wasn't going to discuss that with me. She accepted Mickey as she was. Rhonda once wrote of her, "She viewed golf as a form of self-expression rather than a contest between people." What a sentence. Rhonda didn't need to god her up. Mickey was on another level all on her own.

Rhonda graduated from Lake Worth High in 1964 and played often at the Palm Beach Par-3, just up A1A from Chuck Will's condo. Her mother worked at that course for thirty years, and Rhonda had all the free-range balls a girl could want to hit. She was an excellent junior player. She first met Barb as a teenager, when Barb was giving lessons on the range there.

"Did Mickey ever tell you what she was thinking at the start of the backswing?" Mike asked Rhonda after we had viewed the Mickey Wright highlight reel. He was an ideal guest, asking questions, offering opinions, grateful for the chance to learn something new.

Rhonda picked up a club in her office and gripped it. Certain hands just look like they belong on a golf club, and that was the case with Rhonda. By way of answering Mike's question, she showed us an old-fashioned hands-first lag takeaway. Just a split second where the right wrist moves before anything else does. That move is the opposite of the up-and-in move Mike was working on daily at the range at Eagle Trace. Mike didn't say a word to Rhonda about what he was doing. We were at the Glenn-Romack ranch in search of Mickey.

In 1966, when Rhonda was nineteen and a student at Palm Beach Junior College, she was invited to play in the St. Petersburg Women's Open. She was paired with Mickey, and they've been friends ever since.

"When I called Mickey to tell her about the USGA's decision to open a Mickey Wright Room, she cried," Rhonda told us. "I told her we would need some of her memorabilia. She said, 'It's all moldy.' "

Rhonda described Mickey as a wonderful cook. She remembered the hearty Southern food that Mickey made in her Port St. Lucie kitchen when Rhonda visited. When Rhonda was talking while the chef was over her stove, Mickey said, "If you don't mind, I can't talk while I'm cooking."

"She wasn't meek," Rhonda said. "She visited me once when I was living in Dallas. She drove there from Florida because she liked her dentist there."

Mickey was in a rush for nothing. She liked driving and didn't like flying. "I had a sports car then, a two-door Mazda RX-7. White. It was a beautiful car. Mickey said, 'Do you mind if I give it a test drive?' She *squealed* out of my driveway. I'm in a suburban development, and she practically left rubber."

I asked Rhonda why, after Mickey's competitive career was over, she stopped playing golf entirely.

"Maybe this will explain it," Rhonda said. "I used to play quite a bit. Mickey was always interested in how I played, and I did play pretty good golf for a long time. Then one day a couple of years ago, she asked me how I was playing. She had not asked for a while. And I said, 'I'm done. I've quit. I just can't play the way I used to.' And Mickey said, 'I understand completely.' "

In 2010 Mickey received the USGA's highest honor, the Bob Jones Award. She did not go to the dinner at Pinehurst to receive it. Rhonda was chosen to accept it on her behalf. We watched a tape of the occasion, Rhonda in her blue USGA blazer.

Later, I read Rhonda's 1983 *Golf Journal* piece about Mickey. She and Mickey were on the Southern Methodist University campus. Mickey was visiting one of her old golf instructors. The USGA had invited Mickey to play in the '83 U.S. Open on a special exemption. It would have been something like when Hogan, late in the day, played in the U.S. Open at Olympic in '66 and Sandy Tatum's wife nabbed his cigarette butt.

At SMU that day, Rhonda asked Mickey, "Are you going to play in the Open?"

This is from Rhonda's piece: " 'I haven't decided,' she said sharply. There was a sudden bite to her voice and her face clouded. For a moment I sincerely wished that I had not asked."

Just the question was like a flashback for Mickey. I felt for them both.

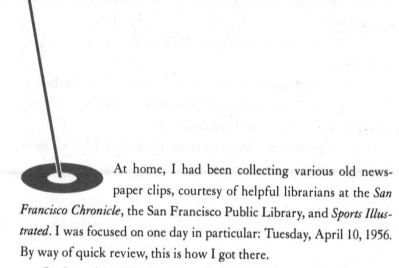

9

At home, I had been collecting various old newspaper clips, courtesy of helpful librarians at the *San Francisco Chronicle*, the San Francisco Public Library, and *Sports Illustrated*. I was focused on one day in particular: Tuesday, April 10, 1956. By way of quick review, this is how I got there.

On Saturday night, April 7, 1956, Ken Venturi—then an amateur golfer from San Francisco with a four-shot lead in the Masters—had a private meeting with the two men who ran the club and the tournament, Bobby Jones and Cliff Roberts. It was there that Ken's vision of his future, as the gentleman amateur with a green coat in his closet, fully took form. On Sunday, April 8, Ken shot a final-round 80, a score that left him a shot behind the winner, Jackie Burke. On Monday, April 9, Venturi flew home, accompanied by Eddie Lowery, to San Francisco. At the airport, Harry Hayward of the *San Francisco Examiner*, along with other reporters, awaited Ken's arrival. On Tuesday,

April 10, their stories were published in various newspapers. These were the stories that changed the course of Ken Venturi's life. They poisoned his relationship with Jones, with Roberts, with Augusta National. They were part of a fast sequence of events that forced Ken to abandon the life Bob Jones had prophesied for him on that magical Saturday night in Augusta.

On Sunday, while Ken was trying to win that Masters, Harry Hayward went to Harding Park to see Ken's father and write up the scene there. His story in Monday's *Examiner* could not have been more empathetic. His lede: "Papa Fred was brave—and proud, too—as the final returns were in."

Hayward's story in the next day's paper begins with four brief setup paragraphs followed by a long series of quotes from Venturi without a single interjection from Hayward. I'll cite here the quotes from the front page of the *Examiner* sports section on Tuesday, April 10, 1956, before the reader was asked to jump to page 8. This is exactly as it ran except the quotes in the paper were in bold:

"They wouldn't let my pal Harvie Ward talk to me when I reached the seventeenth. A tournament official stopped him, said he might be accused of helping me if he made the friendly gesture.

"They took care of Mr. Lowery, too, sent him to referee the Byron Nelson–Ben Hogan twosome so he couldn't be close to me.

"They also switched the pairings. In the first round I was paired with Billy Joe Patton, the second Jimmy Demaret, the third Jackie Burke. And I was supposed to go out with Byron Nelson in the fourth and final round. But, oh, no, they switched and put me in with Sam Snead, instead.

"They were afraid that Nelson might give me some help. They knew of our long friendship and that he had helped me build my game.

"Snead hardly said a word to me all the way around. That's OK.

He can't be accused of helping me. But have you noticed that the pictures prove that Mike Souchak was helping Jackie Burke all the way around the course?

"All I heard back there was it would be great for an amateur to win the Masters for once. Well, if they wanted an amateur to win all they had to do was let my original pairing with Nelson stand and send us out at 12 o'clock noon, instead of 2:06 P.M.

"I would have won by five strokes if that had happened.

"They started me on the first day at 9 A.M. I took the lead with my 66. So they started me after 2 P.M., when the wind had dried the greens to lightning fast texture on each of the following three days.

"Give me a decent starting time and I would have been OK.

"It's a pro league.

"Turn pro? Hell, no, I'll never turn pro."

It is unlikely that Harry Hayward recorded that session; the quotes don't read as if they're verbatim. (Many of the quotes in this book are not verbatim, either.) The quotes in the stories by Hayward's competitors are not identical. But how is he going to make up all *that*? Or really, *any* of it? With the other reporters there? And why would he? He was a guy who obviously cared about his beat. He was his paper's main golf writer, not the off-season football writer. He knew he would be covering Ken for years to come. He would have no reason to want to bury him.

Maybe I'm showing my prejudice here, but I have to believe that what Hayward wrote is very close to what Venturi said and even closer to what Venturi meant.

Ken spent the next half century saying he was misquoted, that his words were twisted and taken out of context, that he would never forgive Harry Hayward, even though the man was dead.

Taken out of context? Reading Hayward's story, and the others, the context is obvious: Young, annoyed amateur golfer comes home after shooting an 80 that costs him the Masters, sees a bunch of familiar faces at the airport, and spouts off. I feel duty-bound, as your tour guide, to offer an opinion here: I think Ken was blaming the wrong guy for his troubles. And it made me wonder about other things. Or, more accurately, wonder more.

I sent another e-mail to David Fay, my retired friend who ran the USGA, asking if we could talk about the Palmer-Venturi rules dispute from 1958.

After that, I settled in with Google and tried to find Conni Venturi. I clicked here and there, not knowing if she was dead or alive. A Conni MacLean Venturi of Napa, California, had written a recent letter to the editor of the *Napa Valley Register* to praise the local theater scene. Of one local actor, she wrote, "I think he could go to Hollywood and light up that mecca." That had to be her: Conni, no *e*. A phone number was proving elusive. I had a possible address. Her former husband's Hall of Fame induction was coming up. I wondered what that meant to her, if anything at all.

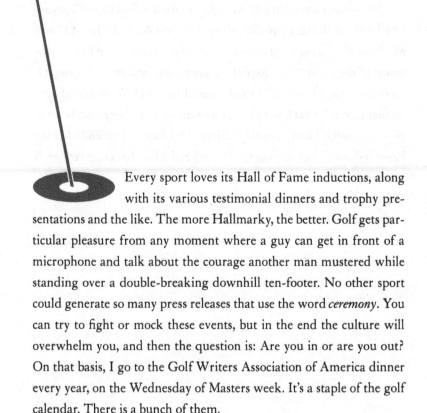

Every sport loves its Hall of Fame inductions, along with its various testimonial dinners and trophy presentations and the like. The more Hallmarky, the better. Golf gets particular pleasure from any moment where a guy can get in front of a microphone and talk about the courage another man mustered while standing over a double-breaking downhill ten-footer. No other sport could generate so many press releases that use the word *ceremony*. You can try to fight or mock these events, but in the end the culture will overwhelm you, and then the question is: Are you in or are you out? On that basis, I go to the Golf Writers Association of America dinner every year, on the Wednesday of Masters week. It's a staple of the golf calendar. There is a bunch of them.

The best of these annual rites in golf is the Sunday-night Green Jacket Ceremony in Butler Cabin, at the conclusion of the Masters, Jim

Nantz of CBS presiding. Jim does similar events in other sports and always adds a certain solemnity and gravitas. That's because he is missing the gene for sarcasm and cynicism. He makes those Butler Cabin sessions feel like papal inaugurations.

Over the years, glimpsing the inside of the great cottage became a Holy Grail for a small group of us, and one year my *SI* colleague Alan Shipnuck did it. He slipped into Butler Cabin on a Sunday night while Bubba Watson and family, celebrating a second Masters victory, were in it. When Alan was spotted by a club official, he made a beeline for the loo and turned it into a hideout. For the crime of overzealous reporting, Alan was banned by the club for the next year's tournament. Was his act *so* outrageous? Yes, but I admire it anyhow. Another Sunday-night tradition at Augusta has the new winner attending a members' dinner in the clubhouse. I fully expect Alan to show up some year in a waiter's jacket.

The looming World Golf Hall of Fame induction, where Fred Couples and Ken Venturi would get enshrined, promised to be a particularly important night for Nantz, as he had been tapped to make introductory remarks for both of them. Ken was his CBS tower-mate and golfing mentor, and Fred was his University of Houston roommate. One man introducing two inductees: In the history of the World Golf Hall of Fame that had never happened before!

About a month before the induction date, I went to see Nantz in Hilton Head, where he was renting a house when the tour was there. Jim had agreed to write a first-person piece for *SI* about Ken, and I was going to help with it.

Jim greeted me wearing blue jeans and a dress shirt. He had been doing waist-up tapings for the induction ceremony. He asked about the lag time between finishing the *SI* piece and its publication. I told him what I knew. Jim said slowly, "Kenny's very ill. Right now, whether he can make it to the ceremony or not, it's touch and go."

Life will really throw curves, won't it? Ken had waited for decades to be elected to the Hall of Fame, but a spinal cord infection had shown up seemingly overnight and he could not shake it. Jim said the PGA Tour would make its private jet available to Ken if that was what he needed to get to his date with destiny.

He opened up a bottle of wine, one from his own label. He had not stamped his line of wines with his own surname, as celebrity vintners typically do, but dubbed it The Calling. "Have you unlocked yours?" asks the company motto.

I've helped many people write first-person pieces over the years, but I have never worked with anybody who paid closer attention to what he was writing. There was one rewrite after another. In the end, his piece took the form of a letter to Ken. It was tinged with good-bye.

The World Golf Hall of Fame is the centerpiece of the World Golf Village, located off I-95 in northern Florida. The hall is about thirty miles south of Jacksonville's downtown high-rises and surrounded by a housing development and cart-only golf courses. There's also a Murray Bros. Caddyshack restaurant and a Renaissance hotel. The induction ceremonies are held in the hotel's Legends Ballroom. One year Peter Alliss, the English golfer and broadcaster, started and finished by thanking his parents, followed by a quick nod to a Mrs. Weymouth, a boyhood teacher who said in a report, "I fear for his future." By way of farewell, Peter raised his middle finger high in the air in salute to Mrs. Weymouth and walked off to a standing ovation.

The day before Ken's induction, there was an afternoon discussion group amid the new class of inductees, with one notable exception. Ken was in a hospital in Palm Springs. He would not be attending his own induction. What a bummer for him and his family.

His absence left three living inductees in the house: Fred, Colin Montgomerie, and Ken Schofield, the retired executive director of the

European Tour. I had been invited to moderate that warm-up-act discussion group. The inductees waited in a back room, and when showtime came I followed the honorees into a ballroom with maybe two hundred friends and family members, plus Hall of Fame employees and volunteers. The three Hall of Famers and I were on a stage, and right there in the first row, in loafers with no socks, was Ben Wright, the old CBS golf commentator. The man Chuck Will called Bentley. I hadn't seen him in the flesh in years and years.

I opened the session by telling blips of stories about the three inductees. For Fred, I stole one of Mike's stories, going back to 1982, Fred's second year on Tour.

Fred and Mike were driving from the Westchester Classic, in suburban New York, to the Buick Classic, in Flint, Michigan. They were heading west across Ohio on I-80 and pulled in to a motel for the night. A sign in the parking lot posted room prices as a filling station does for gas by the gallon: $32 for a single, $36 for a double.

"Pull 'round back," Fred said. "Tell 'em you're a single."

Mike pulled around to the back. Fred hid in the car. Mike checked in as a single, even though there would be two guys in the one room. The move saved Mike and Fred two dollars each.

Fred nodded sheepishly and said, "It's true."

He had signed on for a couple of days of this-is-your-life. Not his kind of thing—he despises attention—but he was being a good sport about it.

Every inductee at the Hall of Fame has a locker. In the locker reserved for the writer Dan Jenkins are an electric typewriter and copies of his books. Arnold's is stuffed with golf clubs, shoes, a bottle of wine, sport coats—enough stuff for a yard sale. Hale Irwin's has his first set of clubs. Mickey Wright's locker is empty except for a copy of her book, *Play Golf the Wright Way*.

Months before the event, two Hall of Fame curators had been

assigned to go to Fred's house on a memorabilia scavenger hunt. They went to Fred's with low expectations, and understandably so. Fred had put them off for months, and nothing in his personality suggested he was a saver. On the day of their visit, Fred conveniently arranged to have an all-day dental appointment. He turned the matter over, as he has various other personal matters in his life, to his agent, Lynn Roach.

But when Roach let the Hall of Fame men in, they were stunned. Fred had stuff that evidently had survived his many moves. He had saved a circa-1979 bright red University of Houston golf shirt with a collar so big it looked like the fins of a skate fish. A classic. You could imagine Fred wearing it well.

I had caddied in his groups and had seen him in press conferences but had never been around Fred very much. Just here and there. I would say I got one real glimpse of him. On the Sunday night of the 1999 PGA Championship, after Woods won at Medinah, I was flying from O'Hare to LAX. I was frequent-flyered to first class and happened to be sitting beside Fred (we each had an aisle seat in the same row). I was going to visit Christine's family in suburban Los Angeles. Fred was living near Santa Barbara at the time. We chatted. An hour or so into the flight, Fred said, "Could you wake me up in like an hour? I'm supposed to call Crenshaw."

He needed to make a call to the U.S. Ryder Cup captain to find out if he had been picked for that year's Ryder Cup team. Ben Crenshaw would be announcing his two picks the following morning. Fred had been on the previous five teams.

In that period, if there'd been something in his public life known to be important to him, it would have been Ryder Cup golf. Fred loved any sport with a roster, and his Ryder Cup experiences allowed him to be on a team, in a uniform, with guys on his side. For some players, it is a welcome break from the solitary nature of tournament golf. It can remind a guy of playing in college, when golf was fun.

Fred woke up from his nap without any help and released the whitish plastic rectangular phone from the seat back in front of him. I went to the head to give him space.

Fred is Italian on his father's side—he'd be Fred Coppola, had there never been a name change—and his skin is dark, especially by the Sunday night of a tournament week. But when I came back, Fred's complexion resembled skimmed milk.

"You got bad news," I said.

Fred made a solemn nod. Ben had chosen somebody else. You could see Fred's surprise and hurt and how much he cared.

The induction ceremony was held on a Monday night in the Legends Ballroom. Dan Hicks of NBC Sports introduced Jim Nantz of CBS Sports, and Nantz talked about the evening's absent star, Mr. Kenneth Paul Venturi, "son of Fred and Ethyl." Nantz spoke in fully formed sentences and without notes. He said, "Audiences considered Ken their trusted friend." If you knew Ken only from his work on TV, and that was how millions knew him, he really was like a friend. For thirty-five years, he was always there.

A taped tribute showed something I had never focused on before: Venturi's well-oiled swing. There were clips from the '64 U.S. Open and black-and-white Masters clips.

Nantz introduced Venturi's two grown sons, noting that the Hall of Fame crystal "needs the fingerprints" of the Venturi family. Out came Matt and Tim. They were both well into their fifties and spoke movingly. Nantz stood beside them, almost as a third brother.

Nantz talked about Ken the way he liked to talk about himself, as a character in a 1950s movie. Venturi, like Arnold and Gary Player and various other legends, came out of the final days of golf's studio system.

There were men on high, at the networks and in magazine offices and sitting in press boxes, who created the heroes we needed, and we all went to sleep feeling better. Along the way, the players did their job to keep the whole operation going.

Ken was maybe the last of those stars. He played the part perfectly. *My God, I've won the Open.* Lines don't get better than that. I once made the mistake of asking Ken how that quote got off the final green at Congressional and into the world at large. Did his playing partner, Raymond Floyd, hear it? Did Ken tell the writers? Ken said he did not know, and that was when I realized something: *My God* was the most important sentence in the script, and it did not matter how it got there.

Nantz created a powerful image that night: a triumphant Kenny, healthy and beaming, returning to the Legends Ballroom in twelve months to accept the trophy in person. "The prognosis is still good," he said. He dropped his voice. Suddenly there was a hint of Texas in it. "He can get through this."

The broadcaster owned the room. Total silence.

"I really believe that in my heart."

Mahart.

It was a wild night, by the tame standards of these velvet-rope affairs. Fred's induction speech was the grand finale. I sat behind Joe LaCava, who caddied for Fred for twenty years before signing up with Woods. Joe lasted because he was more than a caddie, and Fred didn't need a caddie anyhow. With the ball at his feet, he always knew what to do with it. But what Fred did need was a minder, a driver, and a road buddy who shared his interest in fast 40-yard dash times at the NFL Combine. Joe was perfect for all of that. He looked after Fred.

Standing at a lectern with a plant at its base, Fred gave Joe a nice shout-out in a long series. He talked about "Mr. Venturi" and the memorable dinners he had with him and how he would wake up the next morning "so jacked to play golf." Fred mentioned a few of his mentors, noting especially Raymond Floyd, Tom Watson, and Lee Trevino, who called him Freddie Cupcakes. (Couples quoted Trevino this way: "Cupcakes, Cupcakes, what the hell are you doing?") Fred tripped for a moment on Trevino's name, a moment of unscripted emotion, and looked away. He seemed a little embarrassed when people started applauding. The applause, when you get right down to it, was part of the TV show. All Hall of Fame inductions are TV shows. But Fred was going way beyond that. He was remembering the clinic Trevino conducted in Seattle when Fred was fourteen, and how they got paired in the Saturday round of the 1979 U.S. Open five years later. Two events that defined his life.

Fred mentioned a few of his contemporaries: Jay Haas and John Cook, who were in the room, and Phil Mickelson and Davis Love, who were not. The first player he mentioned was Mike. "Mike Donald," Fred said, "who I grew up playing the tour with—we all know Mike."

Fred had notes on a piece of paper, but his remarks were mostly unprepared. Near the end he said, "I was told to finish with a bang." He was doing just fine with his kicker until he got to its last sentence. "Thanks for taking a kid from Seattle and putting him in the Hall of Fame." Then, overwhelmed by the moment and gasping for air, he said, "This is the coolest night of my life."

He exited stage left with his fists high.

I called Mike after the ceremony and told him what Fred had said. I thought he might be moved by it.

"That's nice," Mike said.

Yes, Fred had singled him out, but that wasn't going to undo the past twenty years. It wasn't going to change the fact that when Mike's father died in 1996, Mike never heard from Fred. "No call," Mike once told me. "No card. No flowers. No nothing."

To Mike, Fred was stuck in adolescence. Mike would tell you he was qualified to make that assessment on the old it-takes-one-to-know-one basis. Mike avoided all the standard long-term commitments that most American men sign on for. Being a husband and a father, owning a house and a dog, anything that might intrude on his golf-first existence. But Mike knew what he was doing. His choices were willful.

Sometime after the Hall of Fame induction ceremony, I asked Mike to explain the essence of his friendship (1981–1993) with Fred.

"We were the same," Mike said. Working parents, hourly wages, public courses, foam pillows. They had the same view of the world. "We're in a clubhouse, this one time. Sometime in the early eighties. We're watching Curtis get interviewed on TV. Curtis says, 'That's as good as Curtis Strange can play.' And Fred goes, 'Could you *ever* in your life say that?'" People referring to themselves in the third person—Mike and Fred didn't get that.

There were many good times. They may not translate here. In '86, in New Orleans, the Thursday round got rained out, and Mike and Fred hopped on a Southwest flight to Houston, watched both games of the regional doubleheader in the NCAA basketball tournament, and flew back to New Orleans that night. (Louisville over Carolina in the late show—Never Nervous Pervis!) Their decade-plus together was a litany of ballgames in person, basketball games on large-screen TVs, Tuesday practice rounds, salad-bar steak houses, episodes that defy close inspection. You know: the night Fred hid under the bed while the girl's enraged boyfriend climbed through the second-floor window, Mike out front, waiting in a Buick Open courtesy car. That sort of thing.

In March 1992, when Fred was on his way to winning Bay Hill, Mike was invited to go into the NBC broadcast booth to talk about him. Johnny Miller said Fred's game was not well suited to Augusta National because he liked to fade the ball and so many tee shots and

Sunday pin positions at Augusta are designed for draws. Mike told Johnny and the vast NBC audience that he disagreed, that Fred could hit the ball any way he wanted, and that he could win on any course he played, including Augusta National. Fred never said a thing to Mike about his unpaid stint in the network tower, but Mike wishes he hadn't done it. Mike knew that Fred didn't like attention, and here was Mike, bringing more to him.

The next month Mike was leading the second-city event in Hattiesburg, Mississippi, through three rounds. On that same night Fred was the third-round leader at the Masters. Fred won and Mike did not. Fred finished first on the 1992 money list. Mike finished 117th. Fred was moving on up. Mike was trending down.

In 1993 Fred and Mike were seldom in the same tournaments or in the same outings. Fred had a new girlfriend. His life was changing. Mike was part of his old life.

"I was struggling," Mike said. "Fred could have called and said, 'Let's play a practice round. Let's go to the range and look at your swing.' He never did. The last time he called me was in August of '93. He wanted to know if I could be a witness in his divorce from Deborah."

As I left the Legends Ballroom on the night of Fred's induction I had the fleeting idea that I might get Mike and Fred and me together in a room, just as Chuck Will and Mike and I had gathered in one and Arnold and Mike and I had gathered in another. That was not going to happen. I once asked Mike if he had any desire to talk to Fred about what had happened to their friendship.

"No," Mike said. "Let me rephrase that. I would. I would love to have that conversation if I thought Fred was capable of having it. But I don't think he is."

It wasn't like one was dead to the other. They saw each other from time to time, on this driving range or that one, and had little chats about inconsequential things. For Mike, their friendship was a good memory frozen in time, like Ted Williams's once impressive head in that freezer in Arizona.

On another occasion, I asked Mike what he would want to ask Fred if we ever did a sit-down interview with him.

"I'd ask him, 'Fred, who filled out your application for that '79 U.S. Open? Who wrote the entry check? Because I *know* you didn't do that yourself.'"

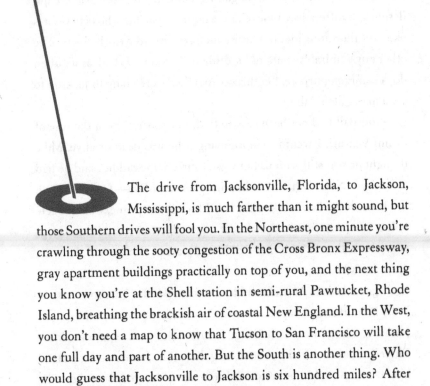

The drive from Jacksonville, Florida, to Jackson, Mississippi, is much farther than it might sound, but those Southern drives will fool you. In the Northeast, one minute you're crawling through the sooty congestion of the Cross Bronx Expressway, gray apartment buildings practically on top of you, and the next thing you know you're at the Shell station in semi-rural Pawtucket, Rhode Island, breathing the brackish air of coastal New England. In the West, you don't need a map to know that Tucson to San Francisco will take one full day and part of another. But the South is another thing. Who would guess that Jacksonville to Jackson is six hundred miles? After that Hall of Fame induction, Mike and I made the drive.

A couple of hours into the trip, I called Jaime Diaz, my writer friend and secret legend, and he reminded me of "Jackson," the dueling duet Johnny Cash used to play with his missus. (Johnny: "I'm

going to Jackson, I'm gonna mess around." June: "See if I care.") I had
that song in my head for five hundred miles (no, not quite) of the first
stretch of the drive, a long straight shot west on I-10. I had done the
drive before and Mike had done it many times. The tour in his day was
more Southern than anything else. Our plan was to spend the night
in Mobile, hometown of New York Mets Hall of Famer Cleon Jones.
That was my plan, I should say. Mike got in the car not knowing or
caring where we would spend the night. He is a ridiculously accommodating travel partner. We were getting along fine on our various trips,
despite our differences. One of us is a no-meat pacifist who believes it is
okay for the authorities to require motorcyclists to wear helmets. The
other guy admirably contains his disdain. Anyway, we had, as we often
do, a common purpose. On this occasion, we were going to Jackson to
see a man called Ball.

Golf Ball had not been easy to find. For starters, as in the case of
Conni Venturi, I went in not knowing if he was dead or alive. Mike
thought he was still with us but wasn't sure. Some caddies said he had
to be dead. Nobody had seen him in years. Golf Ball—Dolphus Hull,
to his mother—had worked for Ray Floyd in his prime, Calvin Peete
in his, Lee Elder in his. Bunches of others. He was a caddie-yard legend who had won with many different players. But he had done the
ultimate fade-away.

I got a break. At a charity tournament on the Trump course in
West Palm Beach, I happened to sit down at breakfast next to Arthur
Johnson, a large man in a Coogi sweater who once represented Lee
Elder and other African-American golfers. Mr. Johnson—he seemed
like a mister—told me he wanted to make a documentary about the
black experience in professional golf and had been looking for Golf
Ball himself. What he knew for sure was that Golf Ball was alive, liv-
ing in Mississippi, and in failing health. I wasn't looking for a ghost.
Johnson thought that Calvin Peete, Golf Ball's boss for years, might
know how to find him.

A couple of months later, I saw Calvin Peete walking around the press building at the Players Championship. Calvin had won the '85 Players with Golf Ball on his bag. I was working for Chuck Will as a CBS spotter in the booth at fourteen. Ben Wright called the 8-iron Calvin stiffed on the seventeenth hole on Sunday, over the pond and to a back right pin on the famous island green. Ken Venturi was working the tower over the eighteenth green. When Calvin, a slender and dark man in a Kangol hat, holed out on eighteen, his playing partner, Hale Irwin, gave him a warm hug and a planted a palm on his chest. Irwin then turned around to find Golf Ball and shake *his* hand, a rare player-to-caddie gesture in those days. Venturi, Chuck, Hale Irwin, Golf Ball: four of my legends, right there. By the way, nobody doffed his cap to shake. What an overdone thing that has become.

That week can play like a movie on my eyelids. Golf Ball was even skinnier and darker than Calvin. He was a piece of wire, really, with ropy veins protruding up and down his arms, along his neck, and across his forehead. He carried the bag on his left shoulder and had a cocky strut, with his right arm swinging across his belt buckle with every step. He was often bearded or unshaven, and the whites of his eyes were a grayish yellow. He wore porkpie hats, brim up all the way around. When his man was unsure what to do, he got right in there, standing almost over the ball. He made a strong impression in every way. The man was wired, amped up. I figured he had to be on something. I once told Mike that I found Golf Ball scary. Mike said, "*I* found him scary." All that made him more of a legend.

I approached Calvin and asked about Golf Ball. He had his own name for Dolphus Hull: "Hully could read a green," Calvin said. "He really could. I couldn't, but Hully could."

You almost never hear a player give that kind of credit to a caddie. The typical touring pro needs to think *he* has the magic. But Calvin wasn't a typical player, and Golf Ball was not a typical caddie. For one thing, Calvin didn't turn pro until he was thirty-one. Before that he sold Florida farmworkers whatever they needed from the back of his car, diamond studs in his front teeth, adding a little uptown-Saturday-night glamour to the proceedings. Calvin refined his swing under the lights of a Fort Lauderdale softball field. He was Hogan's ideal, and he won millions with Golf Ball caddying for him.

We spoke for a few minutes. Calvin said he talked to Golf Ball only occasionally but that Raymond Floyd talked to him often. Raymond would know how to find him.

I reached Raymond by phone the same day. I told him about my Secret Legends list and Golf Ball's place on it. Raymond, like Calvin, seemed happy to talk about him. Raymond Floyd, the man who pulled Ken Venturi's golf ball out of the last hole of the 1964 U.S. Open. Golf Ball was already working for Raymond then, though not at that Open. In summer, in the Northeast, the players were required to take a club caddie. Raymond was sending a regular check to Golf Ball, although not likely made out to that name. Raymond could not have been more unassuming about his loyalty and generosity.

Golf Ball had turned seventy on his last birthday. Raymond said he had given the anniversary the attention it deserved. But when Raymond turned seventy soon after, he didn't receive a call from Golf Ball, let alone a gift or a card. He called and said, "Golf Ball? How come I remember your birthday *every* year and you never remember mine?"

Raymond grew up in North Carolina, in Fayetteville and Fort Bragg, where his father was the pro at the army golf courses. Raymond grew up playing integrated baseball and integrated golf. On tour he had an easy, natural rapport with many black players and caddies. When Raymond got on tour in the early 1960s, nearly all the touring caddies were black, many of them from Augusta, Dallas, Houston, and, like Golf Ball, Jackson. Floyd painted a vivid picture of his caddie as a man who was often in debt, sometimes in jail, intoxicated now and again, and occasionally just *gone*. That is, missing. He also described Golf Ball as a caddie and man who had an immense capacity for saying the right thing in the right way at the right time. Golf Ball had the ability to adjust Raymond's swing or mood with a single comment. That's why Raymond always paid him more than the going rate. When Floyd won his green coat in 1976, Hop Harris caddied for him, in the era when the players were required to use Augusta National caddies. But Floyd won tour events with Golf Ball before that and after that.

"I fired him six times," Floyd said. "Maria hired him seven."

Maria was Floyd's late wife. She was a no-nonsense Italian girl from Rocky's neighborhood whose family owned a well-known South Philadelphia watering hole called the Triangle Tavern. She was a force in her husband's professional life, and when she died she was written up lovingly in the Southampton and Palm Beach newspapers. The Floyds had traveled far. Golf Ball didn't just carry the bag. He helped pave the way. "He was the best caddie in the world," Raymond said.

"Look what Calvin was able to do with very limited experience in tournament golf," Raymond said. "I give a lot of credit to Golf Ball. For every time he was wrong about what club to pull, I was wrong ten times. He had an extra sense. A perception."

Raymond had intense relationships with his caddies. Steve Williams worked for him and later won thirteen majors with Tiger Woods. "Steve Williams was the most professional caddie I ever had," Raymond said. "But Golf Ball was the best."

Golf Ball would drive Raymond's car between tour stops, and Raymond told me that he lost one of them, a '66 Lincoln. Those were big cars, presumably hard to lose. On at least one occasion, Raymond bailed him out of jail.

"Golf Ball and I were in the heat of competition a lot, and people change in that heat," Raymond said. "That heat gave Golf Ball clarity." He described an exchange they had on the eleventh hole of the final round of the 1982 Memorial.

"Golf Ball, how far to lay up?"

"It's 232 hole."

"Golf Ball, how far to lay up?"

"I'm telling ya, 232 hole."

"The layup, Golf Ball."

"Man, you want to win the tournament? Take the damn 3-wood and knock it on the green."

What Golf Ball told Raymond on the eleventh fairway didn't help him only on that hole. Floyd said it gave him the necessary feeling of aggressiveness—on a Sunday with a crowded leaderboard, on a demanding course, with a fat winner's check hanging in the balance—that carried him all the way to the house.

Raymond won that tournament by two. His check was for sixty-three thousand dollars. Raymond's check to Golf Ball was for about six thousand. He was flush.

Raymond looked up Golf Ball's number. The area code, 601, once covered all of Mississippi. He told me not to call on a Monday, Wednesday, or Friday. Those were his days for dialysis. A bad fall, Raymond said, had confined him to bed. "He's a ward of the state," Raymond said. It seemed unfitting. In his prime, Golf Ball was a man at-large if ever there was one.

Mike and I stayed at a stately old hotel in downtown Mobile, courtesy of my lavish supply of Marriott points. As we were checking in, so were several Korean LPGA players. The women's tour had a stop in Mobile that week. Mickey Wright had carried that tour on her back for years. I wondered if those young players knew her name.

The next morning, Mike and I headed north and west to Jackson. It was May and the drive was spectacular, Alabama crossing into Mississippi, fields and creeks and forests untouched by time. Alongside U.S. 49, north of Hattiesburg, I had never seen so many wildflowers. We drove by a sprawling clearing with pale grass, and Mike said, "That's all I'd need." That would replace his Eagle Trace driving range. Mike's paternal grandfather was a North Carolina sharecropper who could not read or write. He drank and chewed and lived to be 105.

When I'd asked Golf Ball if we could bring anything, he asked for seedless red grapes. The farm stands did not have them. They all had grapes, but not seedless ones. There was some kind of blight, we were told, and the prices had become outrageous. Finally, at a supermarket in Jackson, we found them. I bought two big bunches and worried that I was overdoing it.

"Ball!" Mike said as we entered his room.

"Man," Dolphus Hull said, "you got heavy."

The man lying in that second-floor nursing home bed would not be sugarcoating anything.

Ball was as skinny as ever—120 pounds in his sweatsuit—but the jumpiness was gone. There was a calm to him now, and he wasn't scary in the slightest. He was sitting up. He spent most of his life in that bed.

There was no preamble. Ball and Mike picked up right where they left off, sometime around 1992, when Ball's body started to betray him. They both had the gift for observation and recall. Ball knew Mike's road family and Mike knew Ball's.

"I got a trivia question for you, Ball," Mike said.

Ball was ready.

"Name the three black golfers who won Anheuser-Busch." That was the event Mike won.

"Calvin, Lee Elder," Ball said. "Jim Thorpe?"

They were the three most prominent black golfers of the 1980s, along with Jim Dent. I once asked Thorpe about Ball, and he said, "Golf Ball had a better chance of showing up for a seven-thirty time than one-thirty."

Mike provided Ball with the answer: "Calvin Peete, Lee Elder—and Ronnie Black."

"Ronnie Black," Ball said. He started giggling. Ronnie Black is black in name only.

Ball started telling us about his start in golf in Jackson in the 1950s. He caddied and played. Pete Brown was a long-hitting black golfer from Jackson, about seven years older than Ball. Ball was telling us about Pete Brown's win at the 1970 Andy Williams San Diego Open. Ball caddied for Brown that week. I asked why that win didn't get Pete an invitation to the '70 Masters.

"I never could figure that out," Ball said.

Win-you're-in wasn't the rule at the Masters then, as it became later. Still, Pete Brown could have been invited.

In '75, Lee Elder became the first black player to play in the Masters. In '84, the club allowed the players to bring their own caddies for the first time. Augusta National is not a place where change comes quickly. Ball finally got to see it with his own eyes. The caddies from Augusta had been bragging about it for years.

Ball told Mike and me about his start on tour in 1963. "Eight guys," Ball said. "Two cars."

"You just told your parents that you were going to go out and try to caddie on tour," Mike said.

"I told my mother, 'They make more money out there than they do here.' She said, 'Don't forget to send me back some of that money.' "

He talked about Smiley—black Smiley, not white Smiley—the brothers Swordfish and Catfish, Killer, Bebop, various others. One winter on the West Coast, Ball and his boys gave Arnold Palmer the nickname "Bull," for the steam that came out of his powerful nose in the early-morning cool. I loved that: Ball called him Bull. Ball told us about recruiting a young caddie called Froggie to the tour. He said, "C'mon, Froggie, gonna learn you how to caddie." Years later, when the white traveling caddies started to come out, Ball was welcoming. He told a white caddie named Disco, "I'm gonna learn you how to read a green, but I ain't giving you *everything*."

There was a lot of that in his stories, caddies looking out for one another. Using beautiful, poetic, regional English, he revealed a sort of giving nature. (He could take, too.) Ball's friend Killer (Sam Foy) was the same way. Killer caddied for Hale Irwin for years, won the '79 U.S. Open with him, and ended most sentences with the word *babe*. I will always remember Bill Britton, when I caddied for him in New Orleans, asking Killer about my prospects for finding work in Las Vegas the following week. Killer, who sensibly caddied in knickers on dewy mornings (that is, with his pant bottoms stuffed into his socks), told me about the ninety-nine-cent all-you-can-eat breakfasts in Vegas. There was nothing I could do for Killer. He didn't care. Killer, a black ex-boxer from Houston, was sounding the same note the folkies do during group sings: *all together now*. I thanked him. Killer said, "Okay, babe."

Maybe this is a weird sort of stereotyping, but from what I have seen, black people often have less and give more. I am remembering now a moment late in Christine's first pregnancy. Her water broke, and she was keeping it together as we made the urgent late-night drive to the hospital. We got to the maternity ward, the double doors opened, and Christine burst into tears. An enormous black woman working the overnight shift spread her arms and said, "Come here, baby." Christine wept in her massive bosom. It's the quality of knowing exactly what a person needs, particularly when the chips are down. Killer had that gift. Golf Ball had it, at least with Raymond. The immense Herman Mitchell, who caddied for Lee Trevino for years, had it, too. It goes beyond empathy.

In 1987 Davis Love was playing Hilton Head. Herman was working for Davis that week. Davis was shaking as he stood the eighteenth tee on Sunday, trying to win his first event. He was fingering a 1-iron.

Herman said, "Ain't nothing but a driver." With the ball in the air, you could hear Herman say, "That-away to drive it, babe." Jaime Diaz once told me about visiting Lee Trevino at his home in Dallas, where a guest bedroom was reserved for Herman. Beside the bed, on a nightstand, was a framed childhood picture of Herman. There can be a lot of love between a player and his caddie.

Herman and Ball were good friends. Herman could break par, and Ball played well, too. They played a lot of money matches together on public courses all over the country. Ball told Mike and me how he had twice finished second to Herman in the caddie championship played each year on the Monday after the B. C. Open.

Ball's road life was his life. An old car in need of a new timing belt. A motel room with three guys in it. A caddie-yard card game for more money than he had in his pocket. It was rough-and-tumble and a good time. In those days, a player could use the same caddie for three consecutive weeks but not more. Tour officials were afraid if the caddie-player partnership became too strong it would encourage cheating. Ball and Raymond had a strong partnership. They'd go three, switch off for a week, and come back together. They were both in their early twenties when they started, and Raymond was cashing good checks right away. When the player does well, the caddie does, too.

"Now you were making some money, and some of your buddies weren't doing as good," Mike said. "How'd you handle that?"

"That wasn't no problem," Ball said. "I just be like, 'What you need, man?' I'd give 'em some money to get down the road. They would do the same."

One day, Raymond told Ball to come by the hotel to get paid. Ball knocked on the door. Raymond opened it wearing nothing but his golf visor. As Ball was telling the story, you could almost smell the perfume from Raymond's guest under the sheets. Ball told Raymond, "Man, you just wanted me to come here so I could see you're getting some pussy."

Raymond probably hates that story. Over the years, Raymond morphed into one of golf's elder statesmen, and it's almost like his runaround twenties—when he played his ass off, closed bars, flew with Arnold, and shot a bunch of 68s—never happened. Ball is here to tell you: Ray Floyd was once a bachelor.

We started talking about the drinking and the drugging on tour in Ball's day. When cocaine was everywhere in the seventies, it was on tour, too. Ball said he stayed clear. "I just liked the pot and the drink. Billy Harmon, man. He'd say, 'Let's go smoke a joint, Ball. If I don't got one, I know you do.'"

He told about returning to his hotel room one night and finding it occupied by a fellow caddie and two women. "Them girls was as wide as this bed," Ball said. "They said, 'Come on in here, Ball, join the fun.'"

"'Nah—that ain't my style.'"

"You always had those sexy girls with the boots and the short skirts," Mike said.

"You remember Jackie, she be out with me in that yellow Grand Prix I had?" Ball asked.

Mike said yes.

"She was my girl. We went to this club this one night. We're seeing Marvin Gaye. I come back with the drinks and her head's on the table. And she looked up and laughed. And it was the wrong laugh. I took her back to the room and I turned her pocketbook over and four of them little packets came out. It was the shit. I slapped her upside her head and told her I was taking her to her daddy.

"She says, 'Don't do that.'

"But I did. I told him. And he says, 'You should have killed the bitch.'

"I says, 'No, I can't do that. I love her too much.'"

Ball told it all in such a matter-of-fact way, but his voice was soft. The memory was so vivid you knew the hurt survived her. Jackie's death sounded like a suicide, but one way or another there was a needle in it. She was found in Ball's car, near a hospital, "her head hanging right out the door," Ball said.

The yellow Grand Prix. Ball could never drive that car again.

Mike and I were transported. The TV above Ball droned on. He had a private room with almost nothing in it. No books or pictures or cards. It was all in his mind. He was taking us to a faraway place, the old vagabond tour. Mike had caught the tail end of it. Ball had lived it.

Ball worked whenever he could, wherever he could, for anybody he could. He worked every week. He told us about the first time he saw Ben Crenshaw, during the '73 tour qualifying school. Ball said he was working for a rookie named Randy Watkins who was playing okay, but all the while he had an eye on Crenshaw. The qualifying tournament was an endurance test—144 holes, eight rounds, two locations—and it was mental torture, too. Crenshaw won by twelve. The only way you could win by twelve was if you just played and didn't think, and that's what Ben did. Ball had never seen a more natural talent. Every year in that era there was a new nominee as the next Nicklaus, but Crenshaw was the most viable of them. There were guys Ball wanted to caddie for and never did. Bull and Big Jack were at the top of the list. Ben Crenshaw, who learned the game from the legendary Harvey Penick at the Austin Country Club, was right there with them. They were never player and caddie but they had developed a friendship.

"Crenshaw says to me, 'Ball, what do you do if you love a girl but she don't love you?'"

Crenshaw was talking about his first wife, Polly, from Westchester County, in suburban New York City. That marriage ended in 1984, the year Crenshaw won his first Masters.

I remembered Polly Crenshaw from the mid-1970s, when she and Ben were newlyweds. She was spectacular, with long blond hair and big white teeth. Golf's Farrah Fawcett. I figured she came from great wealth. How else did she get into the clubhouse of the Westchester Country Club, where Ben Crenshaw was lucky enough to meet her? Polly Crenshaw. She was from another world.

"If she don't love you, you gotta let her go," Ball told Crenshaw.

"I believe you're right," Crenshaw said, in Ball's recounting of it.

"I know I'm right."

Mike said, "Did you know Polly's in Austin?"

Crenshaw had spent his life in the Texas capital.

"*What?*" Ball said.

He knew, immediately and instinctively, what Polly Crenshaw's presence in Austin would mean for Ben. What empathy. Why wasn't she in New York? She was a New Yorker. Ball was in Jackson and Mike was in South Florida. What the hell was Polly Crenshaw doing in Austin thirty years after she split on Ben? But that's where she was.

"Well I'll be goddamned," Ball said.

Ball had a plain intelligence and an uncommon dignity.

"Excuse me," he said at one point in our visit, responding to sounds that you could not readily ignore. "My colostomy bag."

As a man, he was credible. As a storyteller, I couldn't say. Was Raymond really wearing nothing but his visor when he showed up at that hotel door? Not likely. We were visiting a man in his stuffy second-floor bedroom in the Hinds County Nursing and Rehabilitation Center. We were hearing the stories of his life.

"Raymond was like a brother to me," Ball said. "I called Maria 'Sis.' " Once, when Ball had gone a record time without getting fired, he said to Raymond, "You and me is *married* now."

Ball was like Arnold. Both men were so comfortable talking about their true loves and high times. Arnold and Winnie had ventured out together. Raymond and Ball had done the same.

Ball once said to Raymond, "See you got yourself a white boy caddying for you now."

Raymond said, "He can't caddie your shoes."

Ball would never drive another yellow Pontiac, just as Arnold would never fly another Citation X. Ball had accepted with grace the things he could not change. He said, "I'm in the best place for me." The gospel according to Ball.

Near the end of our visit, I asked Ball if he still had golf clubs.

"Yeah," he said. "I got 'em in my house here."

"You have a house here?"

"Yeah."

"Anybody living in it?"

"Yeah, the girl who took care of me when I got sick. She's living in it."

"That's awfully nice of you," Mike said.

"She saved my life," Ball said quietly.

I asked Ball when he was last in that house.

"Last year," Ball said. "I went home for a night. They had a party for me. Raymond was there. He came up for it. I don't even know how he knew they was having a party."

"Raymond was in your house?" I asked.

Ball's house was on Lyndon B. Johnson Drive, in a poor black section of Jackson grandly called Presidential Hills.

"Yeah," Ball said. "He was playing these little gambling games. He was kind of handing out money. He stayed overnight."

Mike and I were both amazed. How often does a rich white guy, accustomed to the finest *everything*, stay as an overnight guest at a black friend's house in a neighborhood with forty-five-thousand-dollar fore-closure homes? If Golf Ball's story was true, it was incredible. If it was not true but Ball believed it was, that was something, too.

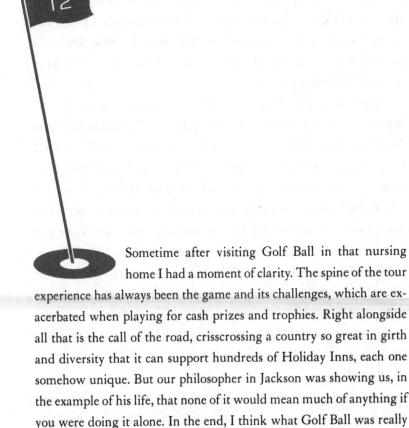

12

Sometime after visiting Golf Ball in that nursing home I had a moment of clarity. The spine of the tour experience has always been the game and its challenges, which are exacerbated when playing for cash prizes and trophies. Right alongside all that is the call of the road, crisscrossing a country so great in girth and diversity that it can support hundreds of Holiday Inns, each one somehow unique. But our philosopher in Jackson was showing us, in the example of his life, that none of it would mean much of anything if you were doing it alone. In the end, I think what Golf Ball was really doing, in that visit Mike and I had with him, was making a serious nod to the institution of marriage, tour-style. And when I say marriage, I mean a committed relationship between two people in which each person, motivated by love, tries to improve the other person's life on an ongoing basis. I know, I know: very idealistic.

How sex figures into the whole gestalt of tour life, I don't know. It's there because it must be. Whenever you have winners and losers—in sports, in the arts, in business, in politics—isn't an undercurrent of the whole thing that the winners enjoy more and better sex? The reason Tiger Woods was so effective selling Buicks for years is because he was playing against type. Here was an incredibly successful athlete—a light-skinned black man with a welterweight's body playing Bobby Jones's old game—who could be using his exalted status to get anything he wanted. And all he wanted was to drive a brand of safe, sexless family cars.

My writing hero, Roger Angell, revisiting his life at age ninety-three in a *New Yorker* essay called "This Old Man," unearthed this gem from Laurence Olivier: "Inside, we're all seventeen, with red lips." Well, the golf tour will keep you young like little else, and careers on it can endure for decades. (Then you hit fifty and start all over again.) The Ponte Vedra promotional department tried its best to paper over man's baser instincts with a painfully bland marketing line: *These guys are good.* The truth is that the PGA Tour is closer to the NBA than any of us would realize. In other words, loud music, various drugs, sex in all the usual forms: straight and gay, consensual and forced, committed and casual, purchased and proffered, consummated and unconsummated. Golf requires restraint, and for some players its discipline will show up in their sex lives, one way or the other.

I'm not going crazy with this whole carnal theme, and you shouldn't, either. When Ball said to Raymond, "You and me is *married* now," that was a comment devoid of sexual innuendo. Ball was expressing friendship, happiness, security, love. Mike and I both felt what made our visit with Golf Ball such a rich experience was the reservoir of appreciation he showed for the life he had lived and what it had given him. He loved the caddies, the players, the action, Jackie in her short shorts, that yellow Pontiac Grand Prix, the game itself, the road and its twists, his caddie-yard status, Raymond.

•   •   •

After seeing Ball, I felt compelled to write to Mickey Wright. I knew she didn't want to talk about golf, but I wondered if she might want to talk about friendship. I wrote her a short letter and sent it off by U.S. mail. I heard back by e-mail within days. Here, just slightly edited, is what Mickey wrote. Note her precision and her avoidance of the first-person pronoun. That is, *I*.

Hi Michael,

Nice to hear from you. I never was much into networking, so didn't really have many relationships outside of the golfers. They were like family, though never spent a whole lot of time with them off the course.

A few friendships have lasted down through the years. Girls whom I consider close friends and talk with quite often are Peggy Wilson, Kathy Whitworth, Pam Higgins, Mary Bea Porter, Betsy Rawls, Sandra Spuzich, and others occasionally, such as Sherri Steinhauer and Marilynn Smith.

It's interesting; never talk with non-golfers about golf. Only other pros who have been there seem to know what it's all about.

My dearest friends outside of golf are a couple, Max and Gertie White, from Angola, Indiana. They lived across the fairway from us for twenty years and they were the only people I ever gave golf lessons to on an extended basis. They've now moved back to Indiana and we miss them very much.

Went out and hit a few wedges the other morning for the first time in years. The 78-year-old muscles hollered at me but it was fun, as is always the case. Was working on my grip and ball placement. Some things never change in golf. Seems strange looking at those big faces and having the long shafts hit you in the stomach. The new 6-iron is the length and loft of my old 4-iron. New game out there.

If you still have any questions that you think would be helpful to you, please feel free to send them along.

Hope this finds you well and enjoying life one shot . . . oooops, meant one day at a time.

Mickey

Later, Mickey and I had a long phone conversation. She told me about her father, who had played football at Michigan. He graduated in 1908 and from Michigan's law school two years later. He then moved to Southern California. *By horse.* "My father told me, 'You'd pass someone on the road, you'd tip your hat and move on.' It was still the Wild West."

Arthur Wright became a prominent lawyer in San Diego, a gambler, a man-about-town. "Every time he got married, he asked me for permission," Mickey said, not counting the marriage to her mother. "I never said no." Even when she didn't like the new gal, and that was every time.

Mickey's father had custody of her every weekend, and he would take her to horse races, prizefights, card games. A youth well spent. She adored him. Mickey went to Stanford for a year and left to play the brand-new LPGA tour. Her father staked her with a thousand dollars. It was all she needed.

Mickey seemed equally fond of her mother, Kathryn, a Georgia belle with an independent streak who followed her first husband, a newspaperman, to California. (Mickey's father was Kathryn's second husband.) For two years, mother drove daughter, a promising junior golfer in an era when there was no such thing as professional women's golf, from San Diego to Los Angeles for a weekly golf lesson. One hundred twenty-five miles and three hours to get there. Half-hour lesson. Then back. The teacher was Harry Pressler from the San Gabriel

Country Club. The *instructor*, I should say. Pressler told his students what to do. He believed the swing was a series of correct positions, and young Mickey followed his instructions precisely.

She talked about golf in San Diego in the late 1940s and early 1950s, studying Gene Littler's swing and watching Billy Casper make greenside shots "that make Phil Mickelson's short game look like a child's."

She had a crush on Tom Watson. She talked about him following her at an LPGA event when he was a young player and she was an old one. "He shook my hand and said how much he liked my golf," Mickey told me. "He gives me goose bumps."

Mickey never knew Venturi, never even met him. I could guess what she thought of him as a TV commentator, because she had no use for pretty much anybody who talked about golf on TV. She watched a lot of golf but always with the volume off, unless the commentator was Renton Laidlaw, an Englishman who worked European Tour events. She preferred the European Tour.

She loved Hogan. She admired Nicklaus. Her indifference to Arnold was obvious, though she never said anything explicit. She had met him a couple of times and didn't feel like he made much effort.

Mickey told me about a made-for-TV event where Palmer and Dow Finsterwald played Mickey and Barbara Romack in an eighteen-hole match on the Desert Inn course in Las Vegas, with each hole playing as a par-three.

"It took all day to film," Mickey said, still annoyed a half century later. "Barb and I won, and CBS never aired it."

Peggy Wilson's golf mentor, Harvey Penick, of the Austin Country Club and author of *The Little Red Book*, was the opposite of Harry Pressler. Harvey's approach to teaching golf was to work with the clay. His adjustments were never wholesale. His emphasis was on the short game, the power of positive thinking, and reducing golf to its essence.

His pet phrase—*take dead aim*—is a swing thought for the ages, but it means nothing if you don't have sound fundamentals.

Mickey first met Peggy in 1957, when Peggy attended an exhibition Mickey was giving in Vicksburg, Mississippi. Peggy grew up on its outskirts, in the country. Several years later, Mickey was visiting Betsy Rawls in Austin when Betsy was getting a lesson from Harvey. At that point, Peggy was divorced, teaching physical education at the University of Texas, working for Harvey and taking lessons from him, too. A divorced woman in Mississippi had few options back then, Mickey said. That's why Peggy moved to Texas. Mississippi represented the rural life. Peggy wanted something different. She wanted the golfing life.

In 1962 Peggy made it to the tour. Mickey was already a legend, and Peggy, though the same age, was just starting out. None of that impeded their friendship. They became practice-round partners and traveling partners. The drives were often long and usually fun. "We were helping each other out," Mickey told me.

Mickey described how Peggy shared important qualities with Mickey's mother: independence, humor, an excellent family recipe for fried chicken. Mickey appreciated how Peggy had grown up: "They were poor and didn't know it." That's because Peggy's family always had a productive garden, a fat pig, ample firewood, and water in the well.

Mickey and Peggy had been living in the house in Port St. Lucie on the Sinners' Course since 1974. They used to do a lot of fishing, but that stopped a long time ago. They were both in their late seventies. They played cards, cooked, watched golf with the sound off, read their novels and newspapers, managed their investments, e-mailed their golf jokes to friends. They led quiet lives, and time unfolded for them without the intruding rush of the modern world. "She takes care of me in my illnesses and I take care of her in hers," Mickey said.

Life in their house likely wasn't very different from the lives un-folding in a thousand other houses in Port St. Lucie, except in this house the occupants were two older women who had won eighty-three LPGA events between them.

"We're best friends," Mickey said. "Best friends forever."

I wondered if Mickey even knew that it was a phrase of modern culture. Either way, what a nice choice of words.

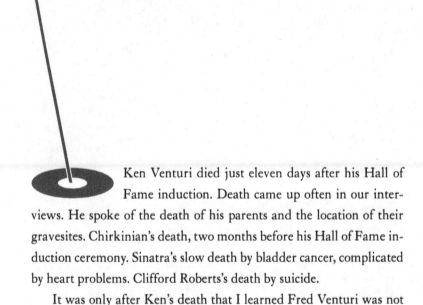

Ken Venturi died just eleven days after his Hall of Fame induction. Death came up often in our interviews. He spoke of the death of his parents and the location of their gravesites. Chirkinian's death, two months before his Hall of Fame induction ceremony. Sinatra's slow death by bladder cancer, complicated by heart problems. Clifford Roberts's death by suicide.

It was only after Ken's death that I learned Fred Venturi was not Ken's biological father. His biological father, as described to me, was a San Francisco Irishman with a drinking problem whom Ken never knew. Fred married Ken's mother, Ethyl, and raised Ken as his own. By DNA, Ken was Irish-American through and through, but by identity he was an Italian-American of the old school. I don't think his place in the Italian American Sports Hall of Fame will be in any sort of jeopardy from this revelation. Frederico Venturi was Ken's father. That was how Ken treated him, and that was how he treated Ken.

Jim Nantz spoke at Ken's funeral, tapping the coffin on his way to the pulpit. He told a Ken-at-dinner story.

"An unsuspecting waitress comes to the table and says, 'Can I get you guys a cocktail?'

"Ken looks at her straight-faced. 'I'll have a Diet Dr Pepper.'

" 'Sir, we don't have Diet Dr Pepper.'

" 'Then I'll have a Crown Royal on the rocks.' "

On the punch line, Nantz signaled in the air like a first-base umpire making an out call. It was a telling bit of imitation. All his life, Ken used his arms and his hands in conversation like a conductor to help combat his stutter.

A few weeks later, when the U.S. Open was at Merion, there was a dinner of former champions. Glasses were raised to Ken. Many of the people at that dinner—Arnold, Jack, Watson, Lee Trevino, Curtis Strange—knew something about the man. They didn't know all the details, but they broadly knew there were difficult, dark things that Ken Venturi had carried right to his final resting place. They knew that Ken was a man who could not let go.

That champions dinner—Mike was one stroke away from attending—was described by various people as a disaster. From what I heard, the USGA president, Glen Nager, overdid everything, including his own role. Arnold was overserved. Someone thought it would be a good idea to seat Watson and Woods next to each other. The logic was that Tom Watson would soon be captaining a Ryder Cup team that Woods would be anchoring. But they had nothing to say to each other and sat there like underwater boulders.

In the Open itself, Woods finished twelve shots behind the winner, Justin Rose, who shot one over par for the week. The U.S. Open was played ten miles from my house on a course I have played many times, but it didn't feel like a home game. With all the people and commotion and through pouring rain I could barely recognize the place. A highlight of the week was reading Rick Reilly's column about the private house that got turned into player hospitality and how the owner's son held the TV remote hostage. Our son, Ian, made some college spending money collecting trash at Merion, biking to work in the predawn dark. When I brought him a slicker in the first morning's driving rain he barely acknowledged me. A statement of independence if ever there was one.

A couple of days after that Open, there was an ALS fund-raiser at an old Philadelphia course, Whitemarsh Valley, where a tour event used to be played. Bruce Edwards, Tom Watson's longtime caddie, died from ALS in 2004, and Watson has been devoted to the cause of finding a cure. He has raised millions of dollars in Bruce's name and immersed himself in the science of the disease. He knows the doctors who have devoted their careers to researching it. Bruce was by his side for the best times of his life. He could lift Watson's mood. You know what it's like: You're driving along and suddenly "God Only Knows" is on the car radio and everything, courtesy of Brian Wilson, seems better. Bruce was like that for Watson. He was his balm.

Sandy Tatum flew to Philadelphia from San Francisco for the event. He was nearly ninety-three, and he sat on a plane all day to attend. Secret legend Neil Oxman, one of the event's organizers, paired me with Tatum and Watson. (I half begged him not to, but likely didn't mean it.) The fourth was our friend Jay Hass. (Not Jay Haas the pro golfer; Jay Hass the amateur distance runner.) Johnny Hass, Jay's son and my godson, was our one-man cheering section. On the first tee, shaking like a toddler in a June ocean, I hit about the worst push in history, a shot that went farther right than it did out. "Little quick there," Watson said, trying to be helpful.

From the start he could not have been more accommodating, to me and everybody else. Part of it was professionalism. The bigger thing was that he cared. The day and the cause mattered to him.

Sandy's first shot was what you might expect from the 1942 NCAA golf champion, seventy-one years after the fact. A fine shot. Jay stepped up and drilled one, 260 yards and right down Broadway, slight draw. Some people are just good in a crisis.

I was calmer by the time I played my second shot from the middle of the fairway on the second hole. I had 153 yards, uphill, into a slight breeze. I had my ninety-nine-dollar mail-order 5-hybrid in hand. I took it slightly outside and hit (pretension alert) a sort of hold cut that started about four yards left of the flagstick and faded about two yards. The ball finished about six feet from the hole. Watson said, "See what happens when you slow down a little?"

A siren sounded as we stood on the second green—a summer thunderstorm was moving in fast—and our perfect day of golf was over. Tom Watson had seen me hit a good shot.

The day got better. The group retired into a clubhouse ballroom. There was lunch, an auction, a Q&A, storytelling. Watson sat on a dais with Tatum and others. They were singing the praises of golf. "We're all here for golf," Watson said. "It gives us all more than we give it. It is a describer of the human condition. At times we hate it. At times we get so close to that Holy Grail we think we're going to almost touch it. And if we ever think we're going to grab it, it's going to bite us in the ass."

There was appreciative laughter, and I felt myself falling for Watson all over again. This was Mickey Wright's Watson. This was Tom Watson at the height of his powers, expressing with exquisite plainness an essential part of golf's appeal. Any of us who have attempted to play golf for keeps have experienced what Watson was talking about. All golfers endure the same basic emotional responses. You can take that too far, but as a starting point it's true.

Watson then addressed Sandy and said, "I wouldn't call you a golf nut. I would call you a man who will never give up."

Tatum ran with that. He spoke of a system, a mental trick he had developed to get through his appointed rounds. "Every time I get over the shot, I have the hope that I'm going to make the shot and the illusion that I will," he said. "And regardless of the outcome, I use that for the rest of the round. I suggest you work on that. Hope and illusion."

Then Sandy talked about the most memorable sporting event he had ever attended. He had many from which to choose: Watson's victory over Nicklaus at the U.S. Open at Pebble Beach in '82. Tatum's own '79 U.S. Open, when he planted that tree. Hogan at Olympic in '66. Bobby Jones at his home club in '31. But for his answer Tatum strayed far from golf. He started talking about the 1936 Olympics at Berlin, which he attended as a sixteen-year-old during a summer vacation.

Sandy spoke of the American Olympic team as being "dominated by African-Americans for the first time." His audience was several dozen middle-aged white men. He spoke of what Jesse Owens did there and the greatness of his feats. He cited the specifics as if he'd read about them in the paper just that morning. He remembered how Hitler offered the Nazi salute "and eighty thousand Germans went absolutely nuts. Even though I was only sixteen years old, I thought to myself, *What is going on here?*" He remembered how Hitler ignored the black American athletes and the "awful whistling" that filled the stadium as German fans expressed their displeasure in the face of Owens's greatness. Sandy talked about Owens's final broad jump, an event that brought another gold medal to the United States and caused more humiliation for Hitler. "Jesse Owens was the greatest athlete I have ever, ever, ever seen," Sandy said.

He then described Owens's final broad jump: "He hit that board, and I had the feeling he would never come down." Sandy's boyhood pride in the man, already mighty, swelled wildly during that jump. Watson stared right at his friend's rheumy blue eyes, transfixed.

When we were done, I gave Sandy a ride back to his hotel, the

Ritz-Carlton on Broad Street, in the old Girard Trust Building, a likely hangout for the Duke brothers. If you don't know the reference, play is suspended until you watch *Trading Places*.

On the way into town, we stopped at one of my regular pizza places, where they know me as the guy who mixes the regular iced tea with their fruity iced tea and pomegranate lemonade in equal portions. Better, even, than an Arnold Palmer. Sandy was game for trying it and seemed to like it. We talked about this and that. I wondered morbidly if those two holes at Whitemarsh would turn out to be the last time Watson and Tatum played golf together. After all, Tatum would soon be ninety-three, and Watson doesn't play much recreational golf.

But not much later Tatum and Watson played together in Los Angeles. Sandy flew down from San Francisco for the game. They played all eighteen, and Watson told me Tatum got every shot up in the air. Who needs hope and illusion when you have talent?

Jaime Diaz, the only scribe on my Secret Legends list, was in Philadelphia for the U.S. Open at Merion in his role as the editor of *Golf World* and its back-page columnist. Later in the summer he made a second visit to Philadelphia. Who could blame him? My adopted city is one of the great American golf centers. Jaime lives in one, too, in the Sandhills of North Carolina. Mike—with a reserved seat on my legends bus at this point—and I would have been happy to road-trip to North Carolina to see Jaime there. But in the end Philadelphia proved irresistible for him.

So Jaime came to Philadelphia and Mike did, too, and we played twenty-seven holes on the first day, followed by a neighborhood dinner, a plastic-booth breakfast, and more golf the next. This is Mike's everyday life, but for Jaime it was a little break, and for me it was a staycation of the highest order. Golf with friends. Philadelphia could be a prized destination for visiting golfers, though the private clubs would have to be more open to outside play, something the British clubs do as a matter of course and private American clubs seldom do.

In 1989, when I was at the *Inquirer*, I wrote a story identifying the best ten courses in and around Philadelphia. For that story I talked to three experts on American golf: Ben Crenshaw, Herbert Warren Wind, and the course architect Robert Trent Jones, Sr. Among American cities, Crenshaw said that only metropolitan New York had more stand-the-test-of-time courses than Philadelphia. (I *loved* talking architecture with Ben Crenshaw, one of the reasons he's on my legends list.) Herb Wind said only Chicago did. And Trent Jones said no city did.

I haven't played in Chicago and have been to only a few courses there. In my Patchogue youth I got glimpses of some of the classic New York courses, sometimes on a sneak-on basis. But in Philadelphia I know most of our great and near-great courses. We have a half-dozen courses that could host a national open tomorrow.

One of them, according to Mike, is Rolling Green, where Jaime and Mike and I played on our first day together. Our fourth and host was my old friend Fred Anton. Fred knows all the Philadelphia courses, too. He won the 1952 caddie championship at Merion on the club's short, quirky, and excellent West Course, about a mile from the East Course, where so many national championships have been played. Please don't ask me which one I prefer. I have enough trouble as it is.

Jaime swung the club beautifully at Rolling Green and enjoyed being with Mike and Fred. He's an excellent golfer with a fluid, upright swing and a delightful this-is-fun manner, even though deadline tortures him as it does few others. The first time we played together, years earlier, at the Hacienda Golf Club in Southern California, Jaime shot even par.

For a few years, Jaime and I were both on the *SI* masthead, until he left for *Golf Digest* and its sister publication, *Golf World*. Part of the draw for him was the chance for total golf immersion. His departure was a loss for our readers, because there is no one who writes about golf with more insight and passion than Jaime. He is a unique and wonderful presence in the game.

One of my favorite moments from his life and times came during a cab ride he took to Augusta National to report a pre-tournament story. The cabdriver quickly established his passenger's name, residence, and (as it was then) place of employment.

"HI-mee *DEE-as*," the cabbie said with an Augusta burr. "*New York Times*." A pause. "Hymie—you a Jew?"

That's how most people pronounce his name, HI-mee, just like the robot agent on *Get Smart* who struggled with everyday human life. (When Chief says to Hymie, "Give me a hand," Hymie detaches his.) I prefer *HI-may*, stealing the pseudo-Castilian pronunciation favored by our friend Jack McCallum, *SI*'s Hall of Fame basketball writer.

Jaime's father was born in Spain and his mother in Mexico, and Jaime grew up in San Francisco, where he was born in 1953. A first-generation American. There's nothing about our culture that Jaime takes for granted: movies, books, music, the NBA, city living, the country life—the whole great American smorgasbord.

Sometimes when I see Jaime that opening bit from "Don't You Worry 'Bout a Thing" comes to mind: "I been to, you know, Paris, Peru. You know. I mean Iraq, Iran, Eurasia. I speak very, very, fluent Spanish. *Todo 'stá bien chévere*. CHEV-er-A. CHEV-er-A." (Stevie Wonder was years ahead of the curve, mixing cultures and erasing borders, wasn't he?) I mentioned "Don't You Worry" to Jaime once and wasn't surprised to learn that he had an inexplicable attachment to it, too. Some weeks we will, by coincidence, write the same story.

Jaime has a wandering mind. He's like Lieutenant Columbo on the old TV show, always scratching his head and trying to figure out some new thing. He's always asking somebody something. At a tournament in Hawaii one year, Jaime was talking to Jim Thorpe, then the most prominent black player on tour. This was about 1995, when Thorpe was playing a lot of practice-round golf with Vijay Singh, the big dark Fijian. Jaime had picked up on the fact that Thorpe was teaching Singh his own choice vocabulary. Singh has a high, playful voice, and when he used any of Thorpe's preferred phrases— *youthinkyoubadmuddafukkah?*—Jaime had to contain his laughter.

"Jim," Jaime asked Thorpe, "you might think this is kind of a dumb question, but do you consider Vijay to be black?"

"Damn," Thorpe said. "I've been trying to figure out the exact same thing!"

Jaime's interest in golf is broad. He knows rules officials, LPGA caddies, college coaches, players at every level. I love it that he once heard, remembered, and shared with me something Ken Venturi had said to Ed Sneed: "I admire how you mark your ball, Ed." Nobody but Jaime would immediately identify the odd excellence of that sentence.

Mike Donald likes golf. It is part of him. But he once said to me, "No matter how much I think I like golf, Billy Britton loves it so much more it's a joke." That's how I feel about Jaime. He loves golf as much as any person I know. That's why everything he writes about the game and the people who play it is good to its core. He writes about the game from deep inside it. He is forever trying to figure out a golfer's head, and for the most part his subjects welcome it.

Jaime lives in Carthage, near Pinehurst. He's a full sixty miles from the Raleigh airport, but on the positive side of the ledger there are two dozen good courses in his backyard. Jaime and his wife, Stephanie, don't have children but they do have a collection of animals, including some old horses in the backyard. For a while, Jaime was traveling to events with a basset hound named Max. Max, like his master, came by his charm naturally.

Tiger Woods and Jaime met when Tiger was fourteen years old and Jaime was thirty-six. When Tiger was a teenager, Jaime spent many hours with Earl and nearly as many with Sam, as Earl called Tiger. Jaime has played half a dozen rounds with Tiger and more with Earl. Earl would sometimes refer to Jaime as "Stud," which Jaime found odd. Even in the seventies, he was never the guy in the leather vest.

Tiger, as a junior golfer, enjoyed hearing Jaime talk about life on tour. He was curious to learn about "the media" and how it worked. He was fourteen when he asked Jaime, "Why do they have to know everything?" In that same year, Tiger did a TV interview with Trans World Sport, a division of IMG, for whom Earl worked when Woods was an amateur. (Tiger was represented by IMG when he turned pro and remained with the company until he and Mark Steinberg left in 2011.) In that Trans World Sport interview, easy to find on the Internet, Tiger speaks with remarkable poise and little outward emotion about the racism he felt playing country-club golf, particularly in Florida and Texas. "People staring at you," he tells his interviewer while sitting in a golf cart. " 'Why are you here? You aren't supposed to be here.' " He shows no discomfort with the topic. Listening to Tiger's replies, you cannot tell if he's answering as himself or on behalf of his father.

Jaime spent a lot of time in Tiger's rental house in Augusta in 1997, the year Woods won his first Masters. Woods had several of his college friends there and they logged hours playing Mortal Kombat, a video game. Raymond Floyd and his kids, who were staying next door, dropped in a couple of times. Tiger and Jaime played a lot of Ping-Pong, and if Tiger played well, he could get fifteen points off Jaime, an excellent player, in games that went to twenty-one. Jaime did not find Tiger particularly clever or witty: To the better returns for winners, Tiger's most common comeback line was "Fuck you." But in between his losses, Tiger wanted to know how Jaime played certain shots.

For a long time, Jaime would get at least one meaningful interview with Woods per year, usually in December. But that custom came to an end when Jaime helped Hank Haney, Woods's former golf instructor, with a book called *The Big Miss*. It is by far the most insightful book into how Woods thinks and works, and much of the credit for that must go to its ghostwriter. In the book, Haney tells how Woods arranged for tickets to the Masters for two men he met at the addiction center in Mississippi where he was treated. It's the most human thing I have ever heard about Woods doing. Good for Haney for remembering it, and so typical of Jaime to pick up on its meaning.

On our second day, Jaime, Mike, and I, along with Neil Oxman—tour caddie/political consultant/secret legend—played the new course at the Philadelphia Cricket Club. The Cricket Club also has an old-gal A. W. Tillinghast course from 1922 (then closed for remodeling) and a short, delightful nine-hole course called St. Martins. Late on our second day, Jaime and I went out for an emergency nine at St. Martins, and it was during that round, courtesy of Jaime, that I had an epiphany. Golfers, as Tom Watson noted that day at Whitemarsh, are always having epiphanies, the feeling that the grail is within reach. But not all epiphanies are created equal.

I have already burdened you with the revelation that I've suffered for years from the yips, which has seriously diminished my ability to play competitive golf. Though I've tried various remedies, my case has been persistent and severe.

Then came Jaime. As we played St. Martins, he told me about Johnny Miller winning the Pebble Beach tournament in 1994 at age forty-six. At Pebble that year, Miller looked like he might go into spasms on many of his shorter putts. But he putted well enough to win by a shot. It was seven years after his previous win and twenty-three years after his first win. Tom Watson was among the runners-up, yipping his way home on Sunday. To win you have to putt well.

"Johnny told me he never used the same technique twice," Jaime said. On some strokes he looked at the hole. Sometimes he looked at a little dot on the putter head as he took it back. Sometimes he putted with his eyes closed. On some putts he imagined he was his son over the ball. He sliced some putts and hooked in others. One of the points Jaime was making is that the path of the putter head doesn't have to be perfect for the ball to go in. A good path is good enough. The hole, after all, is much bigger than the ball.

I felt like I could breathe. No method as a method! From that day on I have been using the Malcolm X Putting System. ("By whatever means necessary.") It is not foolproof. I still have yippy days. But I have improved enough to where I can play a real match again. I have an admission to make. I haven't even told this to Mike. In fact, until now, the only person I have shared this with is my regular St. Martins playing partner, David Morse, the least judgmental person I know: My go-to move on short putts now is to make the stroke with my eyes closed. I open them when I hear the happy sound of a hard plastic ball settling in for the night. Thank you, Jaime, for that lesson. A shout-out to you, too, Johnny Miller. For whatever it's worth, you were so close to making my legends list.

Mike and I were amazed to learn from Jaime that he remembered Fred Venturi as the counterman at Harding Park. That whole scene seemed so long ago that I couldn't imagine I had a friend and contemporary who knew it. Jaime's father, the senior Jaime, started taking his sports-loving son to watch the Lucky International tournament at Harding Park in the early 1960s. About that same time, Jaime started playing the short nine-hole Fleming course there. Jaime was at the 1966 U.S. Open at Olympic. He knew Sandy Tatum and Ken Venturi, among various others on my legends list. That's the nature of golf, if you hang around it the way Jaime does. More than that. It's Jaime's nature.

Neil, Jaime, Mike, and I had an outside lunch after our round at the Cricket Club at which Mike told a series of life-on-tour stories. He has a thousand of them. The obese groupie he had for a while who brought him nothing but bad luck and missed cuts. The eightieth birthday party he attended for the ornery tour caddie Lee Lynch, only to find out later that Lynch was sixty-four. The time Mike played in a twosome with Bob Gilder and Gilder walked to the next tee while Mike was standing over a three-footer for par.

"You make it?" Gilder asked on that next tee.

The etiquette—the responsibility, really—is to stay put and watch the other player finish.

"If you had fucking stuck around to see, you'd know!" Mike said.

Mike was taking us to a faraway place, the tour when it was still rough-and-tumble, and Jaime was grateful for it. He has an appreciation for travel in all its forms. His Mexican-born mother, Theresa, left high school without graduating, but she learned a lot about American culture by watching *On the Waterfront*, *The Hustler*, and *Requiem for a Heavyweight*, among other classics. (At fifty, she received a college degree.) Jaime would watch with her, absorbing language.

Jaime has a superb ear for quotes. Johnny Miller once told him: "It's not what you accomplish in life that matters; it is what you overcome." Jaime could relate. He used it, remembered it, and shared it with Tiger. Jaime had no reason to think the quote made any particular impression on him. But a couple of years later, when Woods was delivering his post-scandal live-on-CNN mea culpa, Jaime was surprised to hear Woods use that quote. Standing before somber blue curtains in a ballroom at the Stadium Course clubhouse, Woods said, "I once heard—and I believe it is true—it's not what you achieve in life that matters, it is what you overcome." Woods, in a dark place, was seeing the wisdom in something that Johnny Miller had told Jaime and Jaime had told him. It speaks well for Woods.

At our after-golf lunch, Jaime didn't do much talking. Or any, really. Neither did I. Neither did Neil, and that's saying something, because

Neil can take over *any* meal. At one point Jaime was about to say something in response to Mike, but he never got the chance. Mike sort of ran over him. I couldn't put my finger on it, but something wasn't right. Mike had played poorly that day. He has rounds where he's counting down the holes left to play, and that had to be one of them. He knows what it's like to play golf at the highest level.

As he left, Mike mentioned that he had left a pair of shoes in Fred's locker at Rolling Green. I said I could get them back to him.

"No, just have them throw 'em out, okay?" Mike said.

That was typical of Mike—he never wants to inconvenience another person. But the way he said it was curt. Something definitely was not right.

Curtis Strange was next up next. I wondered if Mike was still on the bus.

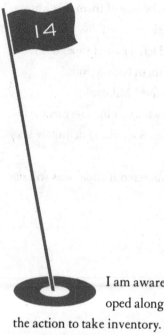

I am aware that several golfing mysteries have developed along the way. I'm going to take a brief break in the action to take inventory.

- Did Ray Floyd really spend the night at Golf Ball's house in Jackson, as Ball said?
- Did CBS really decide not to air that made-for-TV match when Mickey Wright and Barb Romack defeated Arnold Palmer and Dow Finsterwald, as Mickey said?
- Did Venturi really tell Palmer he was violating the rules when he played two balls that day on twelve at the '58 Masters, as Ken said?
- And who on earth filled out Fred's application for the 1979 U.S. Open?

The most thorough account of the incident on twelve that I have read is Herbert Warren Wind's *SI* game story in the issue dated April 21, 1958. But it has a significant omission: It never cites the actual rule that governed the action that Sunday. As I was trying to make sense of this cold case, it occurred to me that you had to have the exact language of the rule at your fingertips to really understand the dispute. I did not. I again turned to David Fay, the retired USGA executive director.

And David turned to the *Rules of Golf.* That is, the 1958 edition, unchanged since '56. He sent me a copy of the relevant page. The handwritten heading, the oval underneath it, the star in the margin, the wobbly underlining of the key passage, they're all his.

$R u l e \ 11-5$

RULE 11: *Disputes and Doubt as to Rights*
16   ~~RULE 12: The Honor~~

5. Stroke Play: Doubt as to Procedure

In stroke play only, when a competitor is doubtful of his rights or procedure, he may play out the hole with the ball in play and, at the same time, complete the play of the hole with a second ball. Before playing a stroke with either ball, the competitor must announce to his marker his intention to proceed under this Rule and must announce which ball he wants to score with if the Rules permit.

On completing the round the competitor must report the facts immediately to the Committee. If it be found that the Rules allow the procedure selected in advance by the competitor, the score with the ball so selected shall be his score for the hole. Should the competitor fail to announce in advance his procedure or selection, the score with the second ball shall be his score for the hole if played in accordance with the Rules.

Note 1: The sole purpose of this Rule is to enable a competitor to avoid disqualification when doubtful of his rights or procedure; a competitor is not permitted to play in two ways and then choose his score.

Note 2: *The privilege of playing a second ball does not exist in match play. A second ball played under Rule 11-5 is not a provisional ball under Rule 30.*

The complainant (Ken Venturi) maintained that Arnold failed to announce his intention to play two balls before he played his first. But the '56 rule book covers that situation: "Should the competitor fail to announce in advance his procedure or selection, the score with the second ball shall be his score for the hole if played in accordance with the Rules." On that basis, I could not see how Ken's complaint had any merit. It is true that later the language of this rule changed in a way that would have prevented Palmer from doing what he did. But can a player be required to abide by a rule that doesn't yet exist?

Regardless of all that, fairness is the fundamental principle of the rule book. Even Ken said that Palmer should have been given embedded ball relief. Had there been no special provision in the rule book, the Augusta rules committee—essentially, Bobby Jones—almost surely would have allowed the three Palmer made on the second ball to stand, because that would have been the fairest way to resolve a confusing situation. The starting point is that Arnold was entitled to embedded ball relief and didn't get it.

The rules can be complicated, but they usually have a sound logical basis. As a player and a broadcaster, Ken was not noted for being a rules expert, which makes him like most other players and broadcasters. This circumstance—playing a second ball in a disputed rules situation—seldom comes up and is something most pros know nothing about. I asked David Fay for his opinion: Did he think Ken actually told Arnold that he had proceeded incorrectly, right there on the spot, as Venturi maintained in his book and elsewhere? David's real-world experience took over: "There's no fucking chance."

Arnold got a bad ruling and dealt with it in a sensible way. I know that sounds like I am taking sides. What I am trying to do is sort through the known facts and reach a sensible conclusion. When I started to understand that, I started to realize that the incident wasn't about Arnold at all.

In Ken's telling, Palmer ignored both his caddie and Venturi, made that par on the second ball, followed up with an eagle on thirteen, then marched on to a one-shot win and an open lane to the good life. He then spent the next half century and counting being *Arnold Palmer* every single day, and he had a hell of a good time doing it. He stole the life that should have been Ken's. And Ken was not going to forgive him for that. Not ever.

15

I thought it was coming, and come it did: Mike said he was unsure about joining me when I went to see Curtis Strange. I wasn't getting much of an explanation, and I wasn't looking for one. Curtis and Mike were exact contemporaries, and the sense I got was that Mike felt it would be weird, sitting in Curtis's house asking him how he won this tournament and that one. I could see it. I wondered, though, if there was something else going on.

They were both born in 1955 and they had played in many of the same college and amateur tournaments. They had qualified for the senior tour at the same time. In between, they had played the regular tour together for years, although Mike will tell you his tour was different from the one Curtis played. Different hotels and restaurants, different equipment deals, different events (at times), different Thursday-Friday pairings, different results. Mike won once. Curtis won seventeen times, two of them Opens. Maybe Mike didn't need a reminder of those score-board tallies.

Not that Mike wasn't proud of his career. He was. Mike's first coach at Georgia Southern, who took away Mike's scholarship after one year for poor play, wrote a book about the psychology of golf. Many years later, he sent Mike a copy with this inscription: "To the man who went the distance." Mike had given it his best shot. What more can you do?

How it all plays out for any two people will never be the same, not in golf and not in anything else. At Memphis in 1987 Mike was standing behind the eighteenth green on Sunday, tied for the lead with four other guys and hoping for a playoff and his first tour victory. Curtis, in the last group, made a birdie on the final hole to win by a shot. Curtis was good at golf, better than Mike and most everybody else who ever played the game. Under pressure, he got even better.

The 1990 U.S. Open is best remembered for Hale Irwin's old-man win and Mike's gritty effort, but Curtis was exposed there, too. He had come to Medinah trying to win a third straight Open. When he didn't, a piece of him died. He never won again, on any tour. In Latrobe, Arnold had told Mike and me about what it means to *lose the edge*. Arnold had said that it had happened to him, to Big Jack, to every-one. In other words, Curtis and Mike and Mickey Wright and Randy Erskine and a thousand others. You have the edge, and then—poof—it's gone. Medinah, in a manner of speaking, was a cemetery for Curtis and Mike both. There's an unusual safe-travels exit sign at Medinah: ALLAH BE WITH YOU. Mike mentioned it to me once. Maybe it means more to him than he can know. After that sign, you're in suburban Chicago. And where do you go from there? What do you do when the edge is gone? How do you play out the rest of your life, as a competitor and as a man?

Mike and Curtis shared more than a birth year.

•   •   •

In the end, Mike decided to come. I didn't ask why. He flew from Fort Lauderdale to Atlanta, changed planes, and flew to New Bern, North Carolina, where he stayed overnight in the Courtyard Marriott. I drove from Philadelphia, picked up Mike in the old Subaru, and we headed to Curtis's home in Morehead City, in coastal North Carolina, about fifty minutes away.

Maybe Mike just wanted to see Curtis again. He had always liked him. He liked the way he played. He liked the no-nonsense way he carried himself (even if he did talk about himself in the third person now and again). To me, Curtis was a golfing god. When I was in high school, he was the dominant college golfer on the dominant college golf team. I don't know why, but those elite amateur and college golfers, whom I knew only from the occasional magazine article, seemed more unreal to me than Jack and Co. I would be going to college soon enough. But my college experience would never be anything like their college experience.

In the car, Mike was killing me with passive indifference.

"You want to get breakfast here?"

"I don't care."

No conversational question I posed did anything to engage him. The New Bern to Morehead City drive seemed longer than the drive from Mobile to Jackson. Something was wrong.

At Curtis's house, everything was fine. It's a rustic, nautical home by a creek that leads to Bogue Sound, which Curtis crosses regularly in his boat, *Lady Sarah*, on his way to the Atlantic Ocean, where he pursues large fish in deep seas with the zeal with which he once pursued golf. Curtis and the actual lady Sarah have two sons, both long out of the house, and three grandchildren.

I was struck by how quiet and still the house was, but maybe that was simply because Sarah was out, and the children and grandchildren, frequent visitors, were not there, either. When Sarah and Curtis got married, she was twenty and he was twenty-one. They had met as students at Wake Forest and had been through the wars of real life together: breast cancer (her), depression (him), the vagaries of a playing career that had many ups and some significant downs. Sarah was beloved on tour in the same way Barbara Nicklaus was. They were warm and caring. They softened their husbands' edges. Sarah and Barbara wouldn't tell you that, but their husbands would.

For a number of years, Curtis had been doing on-air work for ESPN. At one point, speaking of the seemingly unnatural swing Tiger Woods was then making, Curtis asked Mike, "When did the golf swing get so complicated?" He showed Mike swing-sequence photos from his days at Wake. "It was too loose, too erratic," Curtis said. Mike nodded knowingly. Too loose and too erratic, but still he beat everybody.

Working with Jimmy Ballard, Curtis narrowed his stance, changed the path of his downswing, and tightened his whole move. He was looking to hit fairways and greens. He made almost radical changes, and he did it in about a day. It took intelligence, maturity, and nerve to make such significant changes. That's what I felt. Curtis felt otherwise. "I'd have given that new swing about six weeks," he said. "If it hadn't worked, I'd have tried something else."

Curtis and Mike seemed happy to talk about old tournaments and old players. I stayed out of the way. Mike was waggling a beautiful persimmon-headed, steel-shafted fairway wood, and Curtis said, "Lemme see that thing." He likes to have things in his hands.

Curtis talked about how bored he gets, standing on the range hitting balls, and how frustrated he was by his poor play in senior events. He knew what a struggle it was for Mike just to get into those tournaments. When I thought about it later, I realized that the Champions tour, the professional circuit reserved for players fifty and over, can get right in a guy's head, even though it is barely a blip on the sporting landscape. That tour for old guys is right there, telling a veteran player about the state of his game, which he may or may not want to know at that point in his life. Nobody ever asked Dwight Gooden at fifty why he couldn't strike out twelve in eight innings anymore. But tour players are expected to pretty much maintain their peak level of play for the simple reason that a few of them are able to do so. It all makes you appreciate the wisdom of Ben Hogan when he said, "I am the sole judge of my own standards."

Curtis and Mike knew people who had won repeatedly and made fortunes on the senior tour. Some were Hall of Famers, like Hale Irwin and Bernhard Langer. Others were not, like Dan Forsman and Jay Haas, Curtis's Wake Forest teammate and Billy Harmon's close friend. The few golfers who are nearly as good at fifty as they were at forty are outliers.

At the time of our visit, Curtis had played in 115 Champions tour events over nine years and had just six top-ten finishes. You never would have predicted such modest results when he turned fifty. During those same years, Mike had played in only twenty-five events. On the regular tour, Mike played in thirty-eight events in 1988 *alone*. In the 1980s, nobody played more events on tour than Mike, and nobody won more money on tour than Curtis. Each, in his own way, was a big part of the show. What would possibly top *that*?

Mike told Curtis the story Ken Venturi had told us, how Curtis had challenged Ken over his critical commentary in the final round of the '85 Masters. That was when Curtis hit those shots into the water on thirteen and fifteen while contending in the final round. In Ken's telling, Curtis poked him during a heated discussion, and Ken said that if Curtis ever did that again he would slug him.

"That never happened," Curtis said.

Mike explained that he was just repeating the story Ken had told us.

"Did you believe him?" Curtis asked in his pointed way.

"No," Mike said, trying to be a good guest.

The truth is, at the time Ken told us the story, we had no reason not to believe it. It sounded plausible. Ken and Curtis were both hotheads. Over time, though, I was becoming less sure of Ken's stories, and I know Mike was, too.

Curtis said that he and Ken never had any sort of conversation about Ken's Sunday commentary in '85.

"Honest to God, on a stack of Bibles," Curtis said. "Nothing."

Curtis went to Wake Forest on an Arnold Palmer Scholarship. Sometimes Arnold would visit campus for a tournament or homecoming and play with the team, and Curtis and his teammate Jay Haas would try to get in a game with him. Curtis's father, Tom, played in six U.S. Opens and was a prominent club pro in Virginia and West Virginia. He knew and liked Palmer. Early on, Palmer was a Wilson guy, and so was Tom Strange. When Arnold started his own line of clubs, Tom signed on with him. Curtis remembered his father having dinner with Palmer at Venturi's U.S. Open. For some years, Tom Strange wore golf shirts with the Arnold Palmer umbrella logo sewn on them. Curtis grew up on Palmer. As a touring pro, he played Arnold's tournament at Bay Hill every year. Curtis would seek out Arnold at Augusta, hopeful that the four-time winner might unlock the secrets of the course for his fellow Demon Deacon. Curtis didn't get far. "Arnold didn't say a whole lot," Curtis said.

Curtis talked about Jack, too. Curtis got paired with Nicklaus at his first Masters, in 1975. Jack was at the height of his powers. Curtis was a college golfer on vacation. He was petrified. "I'm standing on that first tee Thursday with Jack Nicklaus and I'm over my ball and I'm saying to myself, 'Hold on, left hand, you're going for a ride.' "

In other words, he would grip the club hard with his left hand and barely at all with his right and thereby eliminate the chance of hitting an ugly snap hook. Curtis smoked his opening tee shot and then spent the next eighteen holes watching a Nicklaus exhibition in which the

Golden Bear nutted eighteen tee shots, pured eighteen second shots, and posted the easiest 68 Curtis had ever seen. Nicklaus hit every green and each of the par-fives in two and took thirty-six putts. No bunker shots. No chip shots.

Nicklaus went on to win by a shot over Tom Weiskopf and Johnny Miller in one of the greatest Masters ever. Curtis saw up close Nicklaus's classic forged MacGregor blade irons and MacGregor woods, packed in Nicklaus's shiny green-and-white MacGregor bag. In those days, MacGregor was in a class by itself.

Curtis played Wilson clubs in college and as a young pro but Mac-Gregor clubs in his professional prime. He won his two U.S. Opens carrying twelve MacGregor clubs. After his second Open win, Curtis signed a massive ten-year deal with MacGregor. But Curtis believes that Nicklaus, who owned a piece of the company, wanted him out. He never understood why. His new contract was not even two years old when a MacGregor executive started negotiations to buy Curtis out.

"It hurt," Curtis said, "because here's the greatest golfer of all time telling you, 'We don't want you.'"

Curtis said he got paid in full and retained the right to sign with another manufacturer, which he did. But it was a weird way to make a great big pile of money all at once, and it was not what he wanted. There are players who view their equipment contracts like Linus viewed his blanket. Sometimes the company-player relationship can make or break a player. Getting bought out by MacGregor certainly didn't help Curtis's confidence. For years, and with great success, Curtis had been a prominent son of clan MacGregor. And then he was not. I picked up the persimmon fairway wood that Mike and Curtis had been waggling and saw that it was a MacGregor 4-wood with Jack Nicklaus's perfect signature stamped on its soleplate. I showed it to Curtis. He smirked and said, "I know." Hurt has a long shelf life.

•   •   •

One of the press-tent jokes about Curtis was that if you wanted a quote from him, you went to Jay. Jay Haas and Curtis Strange had been friends forever, and I had always thought of them as being attached at the hip. You'd see them playing practice rounds together or talking on the driving range.

But when Curtis talked about their friendship with Mike and me it was clear that Curtis was far less social than Jay. They had a true friendship, but you could see there were limits. Curtis didn't really need a best friend on tour, just as Lee Trevino did not. (Trevino called Curtis "The Piranha.") Curtis told us that Jay often organized group dinners and always invited Curtis, and sometimes he came. But usually Curtis was content to order room service and eat by the light of the TV. That was all news to me, and I think to Mike.

I asked Curtis how he celebrated his first U.S. Open victory, won on a Monday in a playoff at the Country Club over Nick Faldo in '88. Mike had asked Arnold a similar question, about his first win at that '55 Canadian Open. Arnold's answer had stuck with me: "It was quiet."

I asked Curtis, "Who did you celebrate with?"

"It's got to be Allan, right?" Mike said.

Mike was referring to Allan Strange, Curtis's identical twin, who played the tour briefly and later became a stockbroker and financial adviser. Their father and golfing mentor had died when they were fourteen.

"Allan flew in that Monday morning," Curtis said, revisiting his playoff day. "I didn't even know he was coming."

That was telling. Allan figured Curtis had enough pressure on him. He wasn't going to bother him for a ticket.

"He got in coming right through the front gate, the security guys all thinking he was me. He was there hours before we started, walking around, drinking beer, and people are like 'What kind of shape is

Curtis gonna be in when he gets to the first tee?' I saw him. I knew he was there. But we didn't talk until much later that night.

"You don't really celebrate. I didn't. You do the trophy presentation and then you do a lot of press, then you go into the clubhouse and the members and the USGA give you a champagne toast, and after that you're on your own. Sarah and I looked at each other like 'What do we do now?' We went back to the hotel. It was quiet. When we got there it was past ten, ten-thirty. They served us dinner in the restaurant and we just sort of sat there and looked at each other and giggled. Like 'Can you believe where this game has taken us?' We were *driving* when we first came out, and here I was, the U.S. Open winner."

It was quiet. The exact phrase Arnold had used.

"At like two in the morning, I got Allan on the phone," Curtis said. "He had left right after I won. He told his buddies, 'If he had lost, I would have stayed, but he doesn't need me.' We talked about what I was thinking about on certain shots. Same as we did after a tournament for years and years. He was always the one person I could really trust to tell me the truth."

When Curtis won at the Country Club in 1988, he cradled the trophy as if it were a newborn baby. When he won in '89, at Oak Hill in Rochester, he cradled Sarah. The first signs of breast cancer had recently been diagnosed.

The sports psychologists will sometimes tell their golfer patients to imagine lifting the trophy on Sunday night before they play their first shot on Thursday morning. It sounds like a nice idea, but it was meaningless to Curtis and to Mike. Curtis was your classic one-shot-at-a-time player. Mike was not exactly the wish-it-true type, in anything.

On the Sunday night of the 1990 U.S. Open, Mike got a call from Lynn Roach, Fred's agent. "I'm going to fly in tomorrow morning," Roach told Mike, as Mike he remembers it.

"What for?" Mike said.

" 'Cause if you win this thing, you're going to need help."

"Lynn, if I win this thing tomorrow, I do a few interviews and I'm on my way." All the while he was thinking, *Lynn, if I win this thing tomorrow, all I'm gonna need is a limo and a driver and a map to Rush Street.*

Roach didn't come.

When he was through with his play on Sunday night, Mike went to his locker in the cavernous Medinah clubhouse. In it, he found a note from Curtis, wishing him good luck in the Monday playoff. Curtis wasn't rooting against Hale. He admired Hale. In fact, the best rookie advice he received was from Hale: "Keep your eyes open and your mouth shut." But Curtis understood the moment like everybody understood the moment. David would be playing Goliath for the U.S. Open, and Curtis was standing with David. He was rooting for the underdog. For the guy he played with in the '74 Western Amateur.

Writing that note and leaving it for Mike was some gesture, when you think about it. Given the depth of the disappointment Curtis had to be feeling then, at the end of his two-year run as the U.S. Open champion? The exhaustion he had to be feeling? He has spoken about that Sunday afternoon, how he felt something washing out of him when it was all over. Maybe that something was what Arnold would call *the edge*.

In any event, leaving that note for Mike was a generous, selfless thing for Curtis to do, and not the kind of thing he did on anything like a regular basis. Maybe it was the first act of the rest of his life.

We wrapped up with Curtis and got back into the Subaru, and Mike picked up where he had left off. It wasn't as bad as the silent treatment I got at Colonial in '86, but it felt about the same. The difference this time was that I didn't know what I had done wrong.

We stopped for sandwiches and talked about nothing. On the drive to the airport, I stopped making any effort and we drove on in silence.

Mike wasn't even telling me to slow down or warning me about on-
coming trucks. The silence was broken only when Mike wanted to
point out the next turn.

I was worried that any true rapport Mike and I had built over the
past twenty-five years and on our various stops with the legends had
somehow evaporated. I know it was bad, because later I told Christine
about it.

The state of Mike's golf game could not have been helping. That
day at the Cricket Club, Jaime had played better than Mike. For years,
Mike had played in nearly every qualifier he could for every senior
event, but he was no longer doing that. There was an underlying health
issue complicating matters. During a routine test, a cardiologist had
found an aortic aneurism and advised Mike to watch it closely. The un-
certainty distracted Mike, and his golf took a back seat. Eventually, he
received an aortic stent. Everything went well, but the whole process
didn't inspire Mike to go to the range and beat balls. All the while, he
was continuing to deal with the aftermath of a long relationship he'd
had with a lovely woman in Atlanta, a parting that came despite the
deep feelings each had for the other. Life and timing. For a bachelor
with no children, he had a lot going on.

Mike missed tournament golf. He missed the feeling of shooting
69 on a tough course with other tour players and the prospect of a good
payday. In 2012 he played in the U.S. Senior Open and got paired with
Damon Green, a tour caddie and a very good player. For some reason,
the guy bothered Mike, and not in a passing way.

"Enjoyed it," Mike said when their thirty-six holes together were
over.

"Well, I didn't," Green said, as Mike remembered the conversation.
Green was within spitting distance of the lead after rounds of 68 and 72.

This is Mike's version of the conversation, but Green told me it was
pretty much as he had remembered it, too.

"You didn't enjoy that?" Mike said.

"No," Green said. He was Zach Johnson's caddie and had won the 2007 Masters with him. "That's not my idea of fun." Green was wondering if he might have made more money caddying in a tour event.

"I missed the cut," Mike said. "And I can't think of anything more fun."

Green told me he was surprised to find himself on the receiving end of Mike's annoyance. He said he had always enjoyed playing with Mike and hearing his unvarnished views of golf and life. But on this day Green made a comment that crawled under Mike's skin and got lodged. Mike found Damon Green's response to his own good play in a major championship to be pretentious, and the game in Mike's day was anything but. Lee Trevino, Hubert Green, Lou Graham, these were not pretentious men. Damon Green had a big profile on tour and in Ryder Cups and on tournament telecasts. His best paydays as a caddie were likely better than Mike's best paydays as a player. When Mickey Wright wrote, "New game out there," she was talking (unintentionally) about Damon Green's game, the modern game: hard ball, long-shafted drivers with beastly heads, 9-irons that looked like 7-irons. Damon Green was playing smash-mouth golf, and he was good at it. Mike's game was the old game, the one he shared with Curtis, the one that rewarded power but demanded precision and finesse. Mike was Meyer Wolfsheim in *Gatsby*, remembering the old Metropole Hotel *filled with faces dead and gone*.

And in that scenario—in that mood—who was I? Just some guy going here and there, seeing the high priests, the Kings of Golf Road, asking a bunch of questions about a game that I would never really understand.

I dropped Mike off at the New Bern airport and pointed the Subaru to Philadelphia. A couple of hours in, I checked Mike's flights on an 800 number. There were delays in New Bern and in Atlanta. Exactly what I didn't want to hear. I drove straight through, stopping only for gas. I was eager to get home.

16

Remember Barb Romack? Rhonda Glenn's house-mate and friend who played with and against Mickey Wright as an amateur and as a pro? Eightysomething and *hot*? I am not saying she was a threat to my marriage, but we kind of hit it off. We talked. She knew Hogan, and Hogan liked her. She knew Arnold. She knew them all.

Fifty or more years after the fact, it was amazing how often Hogan and Palmer would come up in conversation, with Barb, with Billy Harmon, with Chuck Will and Mike and others. David Fay told me a story that Palmer had told him from a practice round at the '58 Masters. On that day, Arnold and Dow had played a money match against Hogan and Jackie Burke. Palmer and Finsterwald won. The four went into the clubhouse for lunch. Palmer and Finsterwald sat down. Hogan and Burke sat down at an adjoining table. Yes, a chilly move. Hogan said to Burke, referring to Palmer and loud enough for him to hear, "How'd that guy get invited to the Masters?" Arnold played smash-mouth golf, and Hogan could not relate.

I asked Barb about the match that Mickey Wright had told me about, the made-for-TV event in '61 at the Desert Inn in Las Vegas. That was where, as Mickey recalled it, Mickey and Barb had defeated Arnold and Dow on a course that comprised eighteen par-three holes. Mickey had said that CBS never aired it.

Barb remembered the day in vivid color. How the format was changed from stroke play to match play at the last minute. She remembered key shots. The extended break between the front nine and the back when Arnold went off for a long lunch while the gals sat around. The presence of Moe Dalitz, an old Jewish midwestern bootlegger and casino magnate who owned a piece of the Desert Inn. Mickey's extraordinary play.

"Mickey says CBS never even aired it," I said.

"No," Barb said. "They aired it."

"Are you sure?"

"Oh, they aired it. Definitely. We won, two up. That gave them a better show! It aired during our Open at Baltusrol."

I looked up that Open. It was played on the Lower Course at Baltusrol Golf Club in northern New Jersey, from June 29 through July 1, 1961. Mickey won by six and earned $1,800. Barb finished seventh and earned $350.

I contacted Robin Brendle, a longtime CBS PR person who has been helpful to me in good times (stories her bosses would like) and bad (stories they would not). In other words, a pro. She and her staff could not find any sign of the actual film in their archives. She did come up with a press release and sent it to me. On June 12, 1961, Robin's corporate ancestors mailed out this charming hand-typed release:

> Are women golfers ready to meet men club-swingers on equal terms?

With the ladies invading just about every field of endeavor these days, that question was bound to be asked sooner or later.

The answer will be revealed when a filmed record of the clash between two women golfers, hard-hitting Mickey Wright and precision-putting Barbara Romack, and two top men pros, Arnold Palmer and Dow Finsterwald, is presented in the "Golfing Battle of the Sexes" on "The Summer Sports Spectacular" series, Thursday, June 29, (7:30–8:30 PM, EDT) on the CBS Television Network.

The Wright-Romack vs. Palmer-Finsterwald match was played at the plush Desert Inn Country Club at Las Vegas, Nevada. A special eighteen-hole par-three course was constructed for the match with the women accepting no handicap.

Everything Barb said held right up.

It's not likely that Arnold found anything charming about losing to two female golfers. He has miles of televised exploits in his warehouse in Latrobe, in big round metal canisters often bought directly from the networks. But he has nothing from that day at the Desert Inn. As Barb tells it, Arnold in defeat said, "I'm not going to Colonial—they're gonna laugh at us!" That was the tour's next stop, in Fort Worth. But he went.

In subsequent years, when Barb and Arnold ran into each other, Barb would poke Arnold in the ribs and ask, "How's my pigeon?"

The show was years ahead of its time. Moe Dalitz was smitten by Barb and Mickey and their golf. He told Barb he wanted to bring an event for "the ladies" to another of his resorts, the Stardust. He wanted the event to be the biggest and the best. "What would you think about me putting up a purse of fifty grand?" Dalitz asked her.

"Oh, that's too high," Barb said.

But that conversation led to the women playing the 1962 LPGA

Championship at the Stardust for a fourteen-thousand-dollar purse, the biggest one they played for that year. The winner, Judy Kimball, earned $2,300. Moe and Barb became buddies. When she was in town, they'd have breakfast.

"I liked Vegas," Barb said. "I'd go for three or four days, just to get lost."

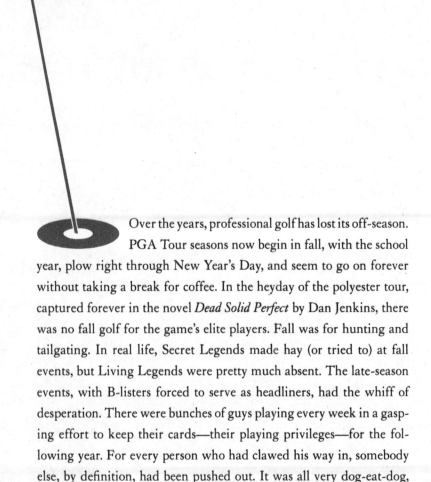

17

Over the years, professional golf has lost its off-season. PGA Tour seasons now begin in fall, with the school year, plow right through New Year's Day, and seem to go on forever without taking a break for coffee. In the heyday of the polyester tour, captured forever in the novel *Dead Solid Perfect* by Dan Jenkins, there was no fall golf for the game's elite players. Fall was for hunting and tailgating. In real life, Secret Legends made hay (or tried to) at fall events, but Living Legends were pretty much absent. The late-season events, with B-listers forced to serve as headliners, had the whiff of desperation. There were bunches of guys playing every week in a gasping effort to keep their cards—their playing privileges—for the following year. For every person who had clawed his way in, somebody else, by definition, had been pushed out. It was all very dog-eat-dog, except the antagonists wore Sansabelt slacks and played nice.

In 1988 Mike was playing his way off the tour. You needed to be ranked 125th or better on the year-end money list to be fully exempt for the next year—that is, to keep your card. After nine months in the eleven-month season, Mike was miles south of 125, the journeyman's magic number. With the season's curtain starting to drop he made an emergency late-September visit to see his teacher, Gardner Dickinson. Gardner was playing at a senior event in Roswell, Georgia, and Mike received permission to play nine holes with him during a practice round. Gardner saved Mike's career that day, or at least helped save it. That's Mike's view of it.

"When you come through the ball, I want you to feel like you're going to cut your left toe off with your hands," Gardner told Mike in Roswell. That's a pure Hogan move. Hogan's swing was so round. He didn't push the club down the target line. His swing was all turn, turn, turn.

Gardner worshipped Hogan. He wore the same style of cap Hogan wore, and he knew Hogan's swing backward and forward. Mike loved Gardner and learned a great deal about Hogan from him. Once, Mike and Gardner were able to get an audience with Hogan at Shady Oaks in Fort Worth. Mike remembers Gardner's nervousness on their way in. When we were in Latrobe, Mike had asked Arnold about Gardner. "Gardner was a Hogan guy, so we were never that close," Palmer said.

Mike started hitting beautiful, controlled draw shots with Gardner that day. Five days later he finished seventh at the Southern Open. He played eleven straight weeks to end the season, earning $118,509 in thirty-eight events for the year and finishing in ninety-sixth place on the '88 money list. His strong fall play made him exempt for '89, when he won his one tour event. The victory got him in the '90 Masters, where he shot his 64. Two months later, he carried his Augusta vibe to Medinah. Mike often speaks of "building a round." You grind, grind, grind. If there's a setback, and there will be, you dig even deeper. You fight with what you have, but not more. You're building a round. Do it often enough and well enough, and ten years in you've built a career. Invest wisely, and you've built enough of a nest egg that you never have to work again. As long as you don't have a wife and kids.

The 1990 U.S. Open is the highlight of Mike's golf career. Every career has one, and that is Mike's. We've had a hundred conversations about it over the years, how he needed to save one shot on Sunday to win in regulation, how he had Irwin on the ropes in the Monday play-off, how the whole U.S. Open experience was like a drug he found himself craving for the rest of his playing career. At Medinah, and maybe for a month or so after it, Mike felt like he had unlocked the secret to superior golf. It was not some new age power-of-positive-thinking mental trick. He was hitting the ball with more authority by virtue of a different and better swing. There was no "steer" in his shots. The faster he swung, the more control he had. Often golfers are afraid of clubhead speed. Mike couldn't get enough. His clubhead was coming from the inside on the downswing, striking the ball on a descending blow, and then returning to the inside. It was powerful. Not that he was hitting it so far. He wasn't. It was powerful because the shots were nipped. His ball was compressed against the clubface. The shots spun, held their line, stopped on command. It was nirvana. It was a fucking joy, is what it was. That's what Mike would tell you.

There was one instructor, Paul Marchand, Fred Couples's Houston teammate and longtime coach, who understood what Mike was doing. Paul helped Mike find his Medinah swing. But then, for whatever reason, that swing disappeared. It got papered over, or the head-to-body messages got confused—something happened. And when Mike tried to reclaim his old swing, one that was more reliant on good timing and more apt to produce hooks, he couldn't summon that move, either. Not that he really wanted to go back to that swing, because he didn't. He had seen what it was like to play golf at its highest level—at Curtis's level, at Watson's level, at Jack's level—and he'd discovered that there was nothing like it. Meanwhile, the missed cuts and high scores were adding up, and an odd sort of label was getting attached to him: *Mike Donald—poor bastard could have won an Open.*

And that was frustrating, because Mike would never think of himself as a poor bastard. Just the opposite. As Tiger Woods would say, what you overcome in life is more important than what you accomplish. Viewed that way, Mike's life was exemplary. His mother was a waitress and his father was a mechanic. For Christmas 1966, at age eleven, he received a starter set of junior Wilsons: two woods, four irons, and a putter. What luck.

What luck for Mike to take up golf in the middle of the Arnold Palmer golf boom, when courses were going up in South Florida as fast as drive-through banks. What luck that Mike had access to a par-three course, a nine-hole course, a city-owned course, a public course, sometimes even a private course.

What luck for Mike that he skipped school at fifteen to caddie in the 1970 Coral Springs Open and drew a lanky golfer from Texas named Bill Garrett, who won it. What luck for Mike that Garrett gave the kid on his bag a ridiculous sum, eight hundred dollars, which gave Mike enough money to play in any junior tournament that would have him for the next couple of years. What luck for Mike to come along when he did. We often think that, any of us, looking back in the right mood. But sometimes it's actually true.

Mike grew up with heroes you could touch if you figured out how to get close enough. Julius Boros lived in Fort Lauderdale, near Hollywood. One day he'd be on TV, the next in the grocery store. *Isn't that Julius Boros?* He had a face that belonged on Mount Rushmore. Mike knew people who knew him. He knew Julius's milkman. Mike was watching on the family TV when Boros won the '68 PGA Championship over Arnold Palmer by a shot.

Mike watched all the golf he could at a time when TV executives and advertisers were figuring out that televised golf was a way to deliver the good life to the masses. Golf programming was expanding every year, and there was Chirkinian and his sidekick Chuck Will pulling strings that Mike could not possibly see. The commercials would come on, and Mike would slip outside with a club in hand and wear a path through the coarse grass of his parents' narrow yard. One year he went to Doral, camera in hand, and got snaps of Arnold and Big Jack and the others. Mike is not one to save a lot of things, but those pictures are prized possessions. Yes, he almost got his name on a venerated trophy. But had he won, would his life have been richer? "It's just a sporting event," he once told me. Anyway, he got himself there. He started on a par-three course with seven clubs and got within a shot of winning a U.S. Open. So much of modern life is more, more, more. Mike is the opposite. He'll tell you that golf has given him everything he has, and he has a lot. Friends, family, financial security, good memories, few regrets. He has everything he needs and then some. He's grateful for what he has and for what golf has given him.

I have always enjoyed playing golf in the fall. The weak light and downed leaves make finding your ball a challenge, but courses in the fall are so *alive*, with tight fairways and fast greens and fewer people, owing to the call of football. Around Halloween each year, I host a little golf tournament called the Shivas Invitational, named for Shivas Irons, the celebrated Scottish golf professional. The event began in 1990, the year Christine and I were married.

I was covering the Oakland-Cincinnati World Series that October, knowing that if it went seven games without an earthquake delay it would conclude on October 24 in Oakland. We were getting married on October 28 on Shelter Island, a dot of land between the forks on the East End of Long Island. When the Reds swept in four I had a few extra days, so a group of friends and I had a small pre-wedding golfing get-together. We've been playing each fall ever since. My *SI* colleague Gary Van Sickle, an excellent golfer, won the stroke-play division of the tournament in nasty weather in a year when Bill Britton and Mike were also playing. Gary didn't milk it, at least not as much as he might have.

The Shivas medalist gets one-year custody of a framed picture of the Royal and Ancient clubhouse. But the prized annual award, presented at dinner, is the Shivas Trophy. The winner of this important piece of sporting hardware emerges in a handicap competition where the strokes are allocated in sealed conditions. In other words, you don't know your handicap, so the general advice is to play hard. Jaime Diaz won the trophy one year. In another year he spoke at dinner about golf's uncommon ability to promote empathy among its participants. He really captured something. Golf will let you share joy and also pain without anyone in your foursome ever having to ask, "So how did that make you feel?"

Michael Murphy, who knows Shivas Irons better than anybody, likes to say golf is yoga for Republicans. You could also say this: Golf is book group for men.

Eventually, I got an insight from Jaime about why Mike had me on verbal lockdown. That day when Mike, Jaime, Neil, and I played at the Cricket Club, more happened than I knew.

Jaime and Mike had been talking all through our first day and into the second. They both like to go deep or not bother. Walking down the fairway of the par-four eighth hole on the second day, Jaime said something to Mike about how relentless I find Mike because of his almost compulsive need to argue, debate, and examine. Jaime was accurate and of course meant no harm. Just the opposite. But he could tell Mike wasn't happy. If that was my shorthand take on Mike, he did not like it.

We got to the ninth, a long par-three, slightly downhill. From 210 yards I tried to hit a soft, fading 3-wood. But I hit it way too hard and pulled the shot, and the ball went left and over the green and into a bush. As we came off the tee, Mike asked what I had been trying to do with the shot. I started to say something about how that Cleveland 3-wood, with its stiff shaft, usually fades for me, but I quit my answer not even halfway through and said, "Yeah, you're right."

But Mike hadn't even said anything with which I could agree or disagree! And had he said something, it likely would have been correct, or at the least insightful, because Mike *knows* golf and the swing and the mistakes golfers make. You'd be a fool to dismiss what he says about any aspect of the game.

They were like a one-two punch, those brief exchanges on eight and nine.

Then, walking up the fairway on the par-four tenth hole, Jaime said something to Mike about my tendency to hit a lot of pulled shots. He wondered if I had an alignment problem or a stance problem, something like that. Jaime can talk about the technical aspects of the swing all day long. It's his hobby.

"Yeah, you know what?" Mike said to Jaime. "I'm done worrying about Michael's golf. I got my own problems to worry about."

Then came lunch and the final bit about the shoes he left behind at Rolling Green and his conflicted feelings about whether to see Curtis or not. By the time I picked Mike up at the New Bern Marriott he was barely talking to me at all.

I can offer you no dramatic story about how Mike and I worked things out. Once I understood this sequence of events, I called Mike and we reviewed what had happened on eight, nine, and ten. I apologized for being dismissive of Mike's efforts to help as we came off the ninth tee. As for what Jaime said to Mike on eight, something got lost in translation. A positive attribute got turned into a negative one. That quality, the desire to intensely examine any minute thing, is one I know well. It allows me to make a living. While reporting on a story, I once wrote to a German military affairs office, trying to find out what Bernhard Langer's father, a German soldier, did during World War II. My father helped with translation, and at one point said something like "You don't quit, do you?" Of *course* that quality can be annoying. A normal person wants to quit at some point. It's hard for me, and harder yet for Mike.

"Yeah, I just got fed up," Mike said. "Fed up and pissed off."

After that round in Philadelphia, Mike told me, he had made a vow: He would no longer offer unsolicited advice, insights, or observations, not to me, not to anybody else. His new program died on its second day.

We devoted about seven or eight minutes to this subject, cleared the air, and moved on. Maybe it seems like there should be more to it. There's not.

About seven months after Ken Venturi died, in the winter issue of his personal magazine, *Kingdom*, Arnold published a first-person tribute to Ken. It's beautifully written, and he surely got help with it. But its generous spirit is pure Arnold.

Ken became well known to casual golf fans when he joined the television booth in the late 1960s, but he was a force in the game as early as the late 1940s. A student of Byron Nelson and frequent playing partner of Ben Hogan, Ken was a formidable talent whose career was both sparked and unraveled by physical ailments. He first took up golf as a thirteen-year-old in response to his teacher's diagnosis of Ken as a "an incurable stammerer." He took up the loneliest sport he knew.

His ironman performance in winning the 1964 U.S. Open while battling severe dehydration remains the hallmark by which on-course toughness is measured. But ultimately it was another physical challenge, carpal tunnel syndrome, which forced his early retirement in the late 1960s and encouraged his transition to the broadcast booth.

Ken and I will likely forever be linked by a rules decision invoked while playing in the final round of the 1958 Masters. On the twelfth hole, I hit a 6-iron off the tee and my ball plugged into its own pitch mark on the back fringe of the green. The ground was wet and soft, and a local rule providing relief from an embedded ball was in effect all week. I was leading by a shot, and just to be safe I called over the rules official, the late Arthur Lacey. I proposed that I could lift, clean and drop my ball without penalty to a spot as close as possible to the original position and no nearer the hole (a stance with which Ken agreed), but Lacey disagreed, saying I had to play the embedded ball. I knew I was right, but I wasn't in much of a position to argue. Finally, I said, "I'm going to play two balls and appeal to the tournament committee." I knew I had that option under Rule 3-3a.

Lacey objected, saying, "No sir, you cannot do that either." I told him, "Well, that's exactly what I'm doing." I played the original ball as it lay for a five and then announced that I was about to play a second ball. I dropped to a clean lie and made par. Ken objected, saying that I was required to announce to him that I was going to play two balls before I played the original. The officials on site at the Masters reviewed the case, agreed with me, and I won my first Masters by a shot.

That incident affected our relationship. We both wrote about it in subsequent books, each of us insisting that we were right. I think the whole episode says more about the confusion built into the *Rules of Golf* than it does about me or Ken. I regret that the incident affected our relationship. Ken was a remarkable human being, and a warm and true friend to thousands of people in and out of the game.

How big-hearted. I know Ken would have disputed the part where Arnold says he announced his intention to play two balls before he played his first. Regardless, what Arnold did on that green in '58 was fine by the rules of the time. What Ken said and wrote about Arnold and what he did on that green was not. It was damning, misguided, mean-spirited. It was wrong in every way.

Ken confused Arnold. He thought they had been friends. *Why is he trying to discredit me like this?* But that was as far as he would go, from what I knew. Ken died, and nothing changed. Arnold had no interest in getting in last licks. He applied the rule book's spirit-of-the-game preamble, with its emphasis on courtesy, to life itself.

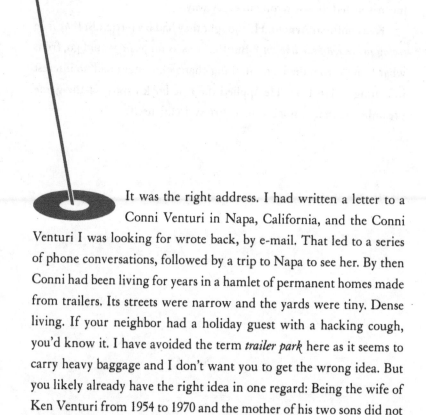

It was the right address. I had written a letter to a Conni Venturi in Napa, California, and the Conni Venturi I was looking for wrote back, by e-mail. That led to a series of phone conversations, followed by a trip to Napa to see her. By then Conni had been living for years in a hamlet of permanent homes made from trailers. Its streets were narrow and the yards were tiny. Dense living. If your neighbor had a holiday guest with a hacking cough, you'd know it. I have avoided the term *trailer park* here as it seems to carry heavy baggage and I don't want you to get the wrong idea. But you likely already have the right idea in one regard: Being the wife of Ken Venturi from 1954 to 1970 and the mother of his two sons did not provide Conni with anything like financial stability.

Conni told me about the fights she and Ken had as they were dividing their possessions. She said that Ken sold their two-seat Shelby Cobra for a song before the divorce was settled, and then bought it back as soon as the papers were signed. She said Ken's divorce lawyer collected a diamond pendant right off her neck, a piece of jewelry Ken had given her to mark his win in the '64 Open. Conni said Ken curried favor with the judge presiding over the case by giving him golf lessons. For years, Ken told people that he had been awarded full custody of their two sons, Matt and Tim. That was not true, Conni said. What was true, she said, was that the older son, Matt, chose to live with his father. The divorce tore the family apart. Conni spent her life trying to recover from it.

In our first conversation, I was struck by Conni's nasally, husky, distinctive voice, oddly similar to Carol Channing's. It so happens that in that first phone interview, I asked Conni about the night, shortly after Ken's U.S. Open win, when she and Ken went to see *Hello, Dolly!* on Broadway. In his telling, Carol Channing changed the famous lyric of its most famous number to "Hello, *Kenny*. Well hello, *Kenny*! It's so nice to have you back where you belong."

"Do you know how many times I heard him tell that story?" Conni said. "No, that never happened." There was no defiance in her voice. It was sad, if anything. "I remember it was sort of a scramble to get tickets, and we got them at the very last minute. I don't believe we were sitting anywhere near the stage, and I don't even know how Carol Channing could have known we were there. She never sang those words. But a lot of things Ken claimed never happened. He believed them, but they never happened."

Conni remembered the *SI* story I wrote about Ken in 1997. She especially remembered the scene in which Ken shows me the tape of his '64 U.S. Open win.

On the tape Venturi sinks his winning putt. With his hands and nose pointed up, he mouths the words "My God, I have won the Open." He turns the tape off hastily.

"Don't they show the trophy presentation?" a visitor asks.

"I think I had them edit that out," Venturi says. "I don't like

Beau to have to see Conni," he adds, referring to his wife, who's in another room, and his former wife, who lives in Northern California.

He continues to play the tape. There has been no editing. There is Conni Venturi—movie-star beautiful—embracing the winner.

"This is all show," Venturi says. "We're already headed for a divorce."

The phrase "who lives in Northern California" was added by an editor in fact-checking. I had nothing to do with it. I hadn't been able to locate Conni and filed the story not even knowing if she was alive.

Reading that story hurt Conni. The way I told it, it was all Ken. For that, I can only blame my inadequate reporting and myself. I should have found Conni and included her. I was writing about the dissolution of a marriage and had only one side.

Conni said, "I never understood why he said that," that they were heading for divorce. She said the marriage had issues, but there had been no discussion of divorce. Their focus was on making things better.

"We went to a Catholic church in Washington that week at Congressional. We actually knocked on the door of the parish house next door and asked them to open up the church, and they did. The parish priest prayed with us. That was the night before the first round of the Open."

Ken and Conni made a deal that night: If he won the U.S. Open, Conni would start taking Matt and Tim to church. That is, his church. Ken didn't want the boys going to the Presbyterian church with their mother anymore. He wanted all four of them in the same pew at his Sunday-morning Mass.

Conni showed no anger at being left out of the '97 SI story. I'm sure she was used to it. Ken's version of their marriage was the official one, the public one, because he was famous and she was not. I could see the sexism I had brought to my reporting and how I wrote in the thrall of Ken's celebrity and success. I made a vow not to make that mistake again.

Conni was eighty and open, intensely so. She had been enduring the cancer wars (colon). She was a devout Christian who often used the phrase *God bless you*. She was sometimes torn between protecting the public image of her only husband, chiefly for the benefit of her sons, and her desire to portray for once her version of her life.

In one conversation, she talked about what fun the player parties were in the fifties and sixties and how smashed some of the players and wives would get. She did not omit herself or Ken. She described a life that had a certain *Mad Men* sensibility. Not across the board, but in places. Intentions were pointed in her direction. They were not, she said, reciprocated. Not ever. This conflicted with something Ken had told others, that Conni had been (to use the word he used with me) "unfaithful." Conni said the opposite was true.

She said that in 1966 or '67, she had heard Ken was having an affair with a "barmaid at a key club." That is, a female bartender at a private club where members put their drinks on a running tab and proved their membership by showing a key. Conni went to the bar with three of her friends. She asked the barmaid in question for a martini, and the barmaid asked to see Conni's key.

"I don't have one, but my husband does," Conni said. "I'm Mrs. Ken Venturi."

The other woman's jaw practically hit the bar.

"I tipped her two quarters," Conni said. "My friends said I shouldn't have tipped her at all, but I thought that was more humiliating, giving her the two quarters.

"When Ken came home that night, I put out two fists. I opened one hand and said, 'Here's your friend at the bar.' I opened the other one and said, 'Here are the kids and me. You have to choose.' He said, 'I want you and the kids.' He was crying like a baby. But he never stopped seeing her."

Yet if Ken saw Conni having an intimate conversation with any famous man at a party—Arnold Palmer, James Garner, Chuck

Connors—he would erupt on the way home. Or even not so famous. In good times, and there were many, they would look at the modest and dutiful wife of this player or that one and joke about how much happier Ken would have been had he married "a little brown wren." Instead, he was stuck with a Sophia Loren look-alike.

When Conni suggested that Ken sign on with Mark McCormack, Arnold's agent and the founder of IMG, he became furious. He became furious when she made any sort of business suggestion. "I want you to be my wife, not my business manager!" he once yelled at her, as Conni recalled it.

She talked about Ken's collection of firearms, ten or twelve guns plus a gold-plated pistol given to him by Jerry Lewis after a night at the Lewis house when the comedian and the golfer practiced their Quick Draw McGraw routines. She said Ken would wave a gun around when he had been drinking, and that on one occasion he accidently fired a shot in their house. She said that one year at the Pine Inn, a popular hotel among the golfers playing in the Crosby, Ken locked her in a giant rectangular suitcase for several minutes, letting her out only because of her hysterical screaming. She said Ken was an alcoholic and that his drinking made his behavior erratic. She said Ken's biological father had been an alcoholic, too.

I had learned about Ken being adopted by Fred from a friend of Ken's. Conni was surprised that I knew about it. She said she had never talked about it with anybody. Over the years, she had heard many of the wise sayings Ken attributed to Fred Venturi. They puzzled her. "Ken's father was so quiet. He was simple. He said almost nothing. He was overwhelmed by his wife. Whenever I'd hear Ken quote his father, I'd think, *That doesn't sound like him to me.*"

Ken's own language, as Conni remembered it, could be rough. She said he used the most profane language when describing blacks, despite having good relationships with many of the African-American players on the circuit in the 1960s. In the 1970s, when Conni had a boyfriend who was an actor, she said Ken would sometimes ask her, "How's the little faggot?" Ken despised the acting profession. At the time of their engagement, Conni remembered Ken saying, "You have to choose: me or acting."

I'm sure her feelings for Ken are far more complex than I could ever know. She never considered remarrying and said that part of her wishes they had stayed married so they could have raised their sons together. But she also said, "I have not shed one tear since Ken died. Isn't that strange?"

We were sitting at a Starbucks near her house when she said that. Her eyes were clear. She was a striking woman, tall and slender, with long white hair, and she emitted an artistic vibe. Maybe it was her turtleneck-and-vest combo. She looked like somebody you might see at a community theater, either on stage or selling fund-raiser coffee at intermission. It was a warm, windy day in late December, and the shop was filled with the music and decorations of Christmas. Conni was wearing a sweet, heavy department-store perfume. In her candor, she reminded me of Golf Ball. It was like both of them wanted the truth out. So many of the older people we saw on our legends tour—Arnold, Sandy Tatum, Chuck Will, Ball—had a certain what-the-hell quality. They were far more open than most people my own age, and I sadly include myself in that assessment. Conni talked about smoking pot in the 1970s, her health challenges, her struggles with money, motherhood, love, God.

Like Arnold, she had a language that was from a certain place and time. In the early seventies, Conni had a bit role in a Clint Eastwood movie, *Magnum Force*.

"How's Ken?" Eastwood asked Conni. Eastwood was a golfer, active in the game.

Conni was surprised he hadn't heard. "Ken went south," she said. That is, he had split.

"Sorry," Eastwood said. He helped Conni as she tried to find her way in the movie business. He arranged for her to have a small role in his next Dirty Harry movie. But Conni was already in her early forties, and her efforts in Hollywood didn't go far. In time, she returned to Napa and worked as a nanny and answered phones and took other jobs to make ends meet. She was active in local theater. She worked on her relationships with her sons. She showed me pictures of her four grandchildren and one great-grandchild. She was close to them all.

Ken and Conni had met as students at San Jose State. Over sixty years later, Conni was saying that she wished she could have been the wife Ken needed and wanted. But she couldn't. She could not be that little brown wren.

She never understood Ken's dispute with Arnold over the 1958 ruling at the Masters. "Do you know that from that Masters until we divorced in 1970, I never heard him mention any sort of rules issue with Arnold? The first I heard about it was when that book came out.

"Arnold and Ken were good friends. They'd go out together. The four of us would go out together. We had dinner on the Saturday night of the '60 Masters! The Palmers had girls who were the same ages as our sons. Winnie and I went to supermarkets together. We went to Laundromats together. She was one of my very good friends on tour."

On tour, Conni called Arnold "Arnie." During summer, the kids would come out, Arnie and Winnie's daughters, Kenny and Conni's sons, lots of other children. Nobody on tour traveled with a nanny, but an enterprising mother could find a Saturday-night babysitter now and again.

"I remember one week, we were in—where were we? Maybe Ohio. Timmy was just a baby and Matt was maybe four, so probably summer of '60. Everybody was staying in the same motel. It was a Saturday morning. Arnold's door was open. He was sitting on his bed, no shirt, just in his shorts, eating cereal out of a bowl, watching cartoons.

Matt went down to his room, climbed up on that bed, and they watched cartoons together."

What a picture. That was Arnie, sitting on that bed.

Conni told me she had written a condolence note to Arnold after Winnie died and other notes on two or three other occasions. But she had never heard back, and wondered if the letters ever reached him. I said I could get her Arnold's office address in Bay Hill or Latrobe. No, she said. She wasn't going down that road again. I said I could hand-deliver a letter to Arnold, if that was something she wanted.

Months later, Conni mailed me a package. It contained a picture of Ken and Conni with Ed Sullivan, taken a day or two before they went to see *Hello, Dolly!* There was a review she had written of a local theater production of *Annie Get Your Gun.* There was an eight-by-ten head shot of her with salt-and-pepper hair, wearing a sweater with a shawl collar, all held up by her stage name in capital letters: CONSTANCE LORD. There was a poem she had written for Matt and Tim in 1979. There was a dazzling black-and-white AP photo of Ken and Conni from the night he won the U.S. Open. The caption reads: "DOUBLE REWARD—Ken Venturi, winner of the National Open, gets a big kiss from his wife, Conni, as he accepts the title-holder's silver cup after a searing final round on the Washington Congressional Country Club course yesterday."

This was 1964, when *man and wife* was still a boilerplate phrase of the American wedding vow. In that context, Ken was the king of golf-dom. It was all right there in the snap: the shiny silver cup, the glamorous wife, the dazzling his-and-her smiles. Once that AP photo hit the next day's papers, the whole world would see: Ken Venturi had it all.

There was one more thing in the mailer: a small pink envelope from Conni, bound for Arnold, his name written in black ink in her feathery eighty-year-old hand.

For years, deep within the culture of a tour life that is long gone and nearly dead, there were people who thought the real reason Ken could not let go of Arnold was because of an affair Arnold and Conni supposedly had. "That was never true," Conni said. "Never, never. Arnold wasn't even my type. If it were true, at this stage in my life, I'd admit it. I'd be proud to say that I had an affair with him. Why? Because he was such a gentleman. Not because he was Arnold Palmer. Because he was *Arnie*."

As the great thespian said: *Inside, we're all seventeen, with red lips.*

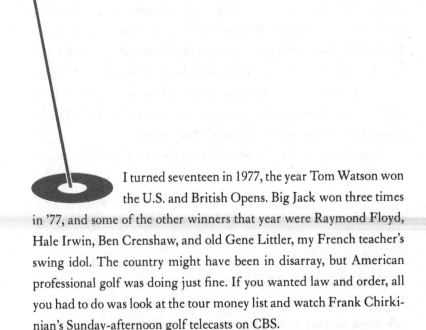

I turned seventeen in 1977, the year Tom Watson won the U.S. and British Opens. Big Jack won three times in '77, and some of the other winners that year were Raymond Floyd, Hale Irwin, Ben Crenshaw, and old Gene Littler, my French teacher's swing idol. The country might have been in disarray, but American professional golf was doing just fine. If you wanted law and order, all you had to do was look at the tour money list and watch Frank Chirkinian's Sunday-afternoon golf telecasts on CBS.

Crenshaw particularly resonated with me. His hair had something to do with it. The golf magazines would run pictures of him at impact, his blond hair would be flying everywhere. (My own was a helmet.) When Ben won or was trying to win, Frank Chirkinian would show us pictures of his young wife, the gorgeous Polly Crenshaw. Somehow it got lodged in my head that her family belonged to the Westchester

Country Club in New York, where they enjoyed the privileges of
wealth and status—poolside phones and that sort of thing. Somewhere
I had read that Ben met Polly while playing Westchester, likely at some
kind of dinner dance with champagne fountains and a sherbet course
after the entrée. I was seventeen, with an imagination that would fill
in the blanks.

Crenshaw never realized his collegiate promise. He was supposed
to be golf's next Nicklaus, but that never happened. He did, however,
win the Masters twice, the first time in 1984. The next year Herb Wind
wrote about him in the *New Yorker*. The glimpses we plebeians got
of our heroes' lives were different then, and I hung on every word.
I remember Wind including a bit about Crenshaw playing in his first
USGA event, the 1968 national junior championship at the Country
Club in Brookline, and Ben talking about how he would put on a
sweater in the New England morning cool. It was all so vivid. I could
almost feel the dew on the magazine's shiny pages.

Later that year, I was working on my first book in Patchogue, at
my parents' house. To pay for my typewriter ribbons and a new (to me)
cherrywood desk, among other necessities, I was selling *Encyclopae-
dia Britannica* and doing some freelance writing. One magazine piece
was about the National Golf Links in Southampton, a course I knew
and loved from a few go-rounds as a summer caddie and off-season
sneak-on. Nelson Doubleday, then the co-owner of the New York
Mets, was a member, and when I somehow got him on the phone to
talk about his club he was painfully terse: "It's a private club, and it's
none of your damned business." In reporting the story, I had also called
Crenshaw, already a noted architecture buff. One day after I returned
home from golf at Bellport, my mother said, "Ben Crenshaw called
for you." She had written down his 512 phone number. Austin, Texas.
Ben Crenshaw. I called back with tingling fingers. We still had rotary
phones.

In the ensuing years, I never spent any significant time with

Crenshaw, but whenever I was writing about a course or an architect I'd go to him, and he was always obliging. He was inexhaustible on these subjects.

I wrote the *SI* game story from the 1999 Ryder Cup at the Country Club, when Ben was the American captain and the U.S. staged an unlikely Sunday comeback. If you know about that event, you know about Crenshaw's I-got-a-feeling Saturday press conference and the way he kissed the green on Sunday at seventeen. That came when Justin Leonard made a putt from downtown Brookline and the team started celebrating as if they had already won. (They hadn't.) For an international goodwill team competition, it was way too much. All that was on the captain. He set the tone.

Still, Ben was Ben, and you couldn't stay mad at him for long. When I introduced him to Christine one year at Augusta he was the model of grace. A gentleman golfer of the old school.

I once took Tom Doak, a golf-course architect who does not lack for opinions, to the Philadelphia Cricket Club to play our A. W. Tillinghast course. We're all very proud of it, back at the club. Tillinghast was the genius who designed the courses at Winged Foot, Bethpage, and the San Francisco Golf Club. They're all enduring delights. On the par-four second hole, Doak pushed his shot wildly, and it landed on the roof of an old barn that is part of the clubhouse. In his *Confidential Guide to Golf Courses*, Doak later complained that the course was "cramped." I believe that statement to be demonstrably false, although now is likely a good time to trot out an old Herb Wind line: You may sooner insult a man's wife than his golf club. In any event, Doak wrote in his book, "I casually pushed my approach shot onto the roof of the men's locker room." I read his words with burning ears. In my mind, I worked up clever rejoinders. For example: *Your shot was lousy, sir, and it is that repurposed barn that gives the hole its old-time charm, as the Green Monster does at Fenway.* Something like that.

The next time I saw Ben Crenshaw, he said, "You still at the Cricket

Club? I love that course." This next part came without prompting: "I love that number two hole, the way that old barn comes into play."

It brought to mind a scene from *Annie Hall*. Alvy Singer, played by Woody Allen, is standing in a movie line with Annie, and some blowhard behind them is prattling on about the scholar and writer Marshall McLuhan. Alvy suddenly produces the real Professor McLuhan, who tells the man, "You know nothing of my work." Then Alvy looks at the camera and says, "Boy, if life were only like this."

Ben doesn't use e-mail, so to tell him about my legends list and his place on it, I wrote to him in care of his longtime manager, Scott Sayers. I should have just found Ben at a tournament, told him about what I was doing and Mike's role in it, and asked if we could arrange a visit. But I hadn't done that. I wrote to Scott, who wrote back telling me that Ben was going to pass. He was wrapping up one book and considering another. Plus, he had too many similar requests. My first rejection, unless you want to count Mickey Wright.

I was thinking of Conni Venturi when I decided to try to track down Ben's first wife. You may recall what Ball said when he learned that Polly Crenshaw, a native New Yorker, had moved back to Texas to sell real estate in Austin, where Ben lived with his second wife and daughters: "Well I'll be goddamned."

Polly suggested we meet at the Four Seasons hotel in downtown Austin. The hotel's front door was manned by a small army, the lobby smelled vaguely of burning mesquite, and the lighting was perfect for deal-making. The Texas State Capitol building was five blocks away.

I first met Polly as many of us did, in the mid-1970s over FCC-approved airwaves. She made a strong impression. Tom Watson had recently been in a British Open press tent recalling his win in the 1980 Open at Muirfield, and out of nowhere he mentioned Polly. He was describing how, while celebrating his victory that Sunday night, he and

Linda (Tom's first wife) and Ben and Polly (Ben's first wife) returned to the course, antique equipment and drinks in hand, with "Polly Crenshaw aerating the greens with her four-inch heels." Is that not the very picture of youthful glamour and half-drunk love?

And here was Polly, in all her late-fifties glory, walking into the hotel restaurant. Hair, jaw, teeth, carriage, looking for all the world like Christie Brinkley's kid sister, making long strides toward my table. You can be sure nothing like that ever happened to me in Patchogue. Or anywhere else.

Everything I thought I knew was wrong. Polly was not from a rich family, and no one in it had ever belonged to the Westchester Country Club. She met Ben in late August 1974 during the Tuesday practice round of the Westchester Classic. Polly was seventeen and about to start her senior year at Alexander Hamilton High in Elmsford, New York. Her father, Bob Speno, sold insurance. Polly had a twin brother and four other siblings. The three girls shared one bedroom. Everybody worked, Polly as a cashier at a supermarket. A checkout girl, as people said then.

Ben was twenty-two and in his first full year on tour. As a star player at the University of Texas, he was about as famous as a college golfer could be. Then he won his first tournament, the Texas Open, as a pro. He was dashing and talented and the world was at his feet.

"Dad said, 'Let's go to the golf tournament,' " Polly said. "He loved golf."

There was more going on than that. Bob Speno had good-looking kids, and he liked showing them off. He knew Polly would attract attention.

"I was wearing a shirt down to here," Polly said. She made a karate chop about three inches above her naval. "And *really* short shorts. Cutoffs."

The summer tan kind of announces itself in that description, doesn't it? You could tell Polly was very aware of herself physically. Then and now.

"We started following Ben, and my father said something to him about his golf and Ben said, 'Is that your daughter?' On Thursday, my father and Ben had lunch. On Saturday night, Ben and I had dinner in the clubhouse. He was very charming, very interested in me, a perfect gentleman."

She was going into a dream state as we sat there. Her crowded days didn't allow her to reflect often on her years with Ben. She seemed to live an in-the-moment life. There was something distinctly purposeful about her.

I asked, "Did it seem to you like you and Ben were in totally different places in life?"

In the summer of '74, Polly's next big thing was homecoming. (She was voted queen.) Ben's next thing was the Tournament Players Championship.

"No, it didn't," Polly said. "I never even thought of that."

Two weeks after they met, Polly stayed with Ben at the Southern Open in Columbus, Georgia. She remembers the words a player used to needle Crenshaw: *She's jailbait.* That was in September 1974. By January they were engaged.

The first half of the 1975 season was a long slog of mediocre play for Crenshaw. In May he took Polly to her senior prom. In June she graduated from Hamilton High, and Ben had his first good tournament of the year, finishing a shot out of the playoff at the 1975 U.S. Open at Medinah. The next week he and Polly were married.

By the time Crenshaw won the '84 Masters they were separated. Polly spent that week on a yacht in the Caribbean, doing shots of tequila and lines of coke and whatever else young beautiful people on a yacht in the Caribbean did in the eighties. Her second husband, the father of Polly's daughter, was on that boat. He later took his own life.

Ben won the '84 Masters by two over Tom Watson. The great Severiano Ballesteros, the defending champion, helped the new winner into his club coat in Butler Cabin.

Crenshaw had won the tournament he wanted most when his marriage was breaking up. He won his second Masters in 1995, days after burying his golf mentor, Harvey Penick. How unpredictable are these artist-golfers? I am thinking of Seve, Walter Hagen, Bobby Jones, Phil Mickelson, Payne Stewart. Crenshaw.

"Ben was always a such a nice guy," Polly said. "But there were three of us in that marriage. Ben, me, and Ben's golf. It was like his mistress."

Her life surely looked easy if you knew it only from TV. But real life, of course, is not an afternoon picture show on CBS. All the other tour wives were older. Polly had not earned the things she had except by way of her good looks. In the years when her high school classmates were going to college and easing into adult life—finding jobs in a tired economy, trying to keep four retreads on a used car, serial dating—she was married and living in the cloistered dream world of professional golf. At times she pinched herself. But often she was bored. She was closer in age and temperament to the caddies. She liked hanging with them, and the feeling was mutual.

Polly remembered Barbara Nicklaus as a warm and regal presence and Jack as a polite but standoffish one. She adored Arnold, "even if he might hug you a little too hard and a little too long." She described a mad, manic ride to an airport with Tom Weiskopf on a Friday afternoon when he had missed a cut. Tom was a drinker then, too. You could smell the booze in her stories.

Ben, Polly said, lost faith and interest in her during the last years of their marriage. He knew his wife had an alcohol and cocaine problem, and he made it clear he was not going to have children with her. She responded predictably. Sobriety came much later for her, long after their divorce was final, and after her second husband, Jack Price, committed suicide. When I saw Polly, she was working as a personal trainer, doing some acting and modeling, training for a triathlon, practicing yoga, and taking life one day at a time. She sold real estate in and around Austin under the name Polly Price, and sometimes under the name Polly Crenshaw Price. It was, she said, her legal name.

She has wondered what her father was thinking and doing on that Tuesday in August 1974 when he brought his daughter to the Westchester Classic in her cutoff shirt and shorter shorts. She was up for adventure that day, even if she could not possibly have imagined where it would lead. The way she described herself, she was not a young seventeen-year-old. Still, she was seventeen. Her father, worried about his daughter's future in an unpromising economy, was making a bet that she could secure it on her good looks. It's happened before.

Polly struck me as someone who had thought a lot about the vagaries of life and had come to terms with its setbacks and successes.

"Those years that I was out there with Ben, I think that was a different tour," Polly said. It was midafternoon, and the lunch crowd had thinned to nothing. Polly had that move where you shake your head just slightly and your hair does a dance all its own. "It wasn't corporate," she said. "It was about people. I think the commissioner—Deane Beman, right?—wanted a family atmosphere. We stayed at the same hotels. There were a lot of charter flights, all the players and their families together, going from one tournament to the next. There wasn't the really big money like there is today. It was *much* more like family. It really was. When I was out there, that tour was my family."

Get up everybody and sing.

The 1975 U.S. Open at Medinah, on the eve of Ben's marriage to Polly, turned out to be Crenshaw's best chance to win the national championship. His game, stylish but wild, didn't lend itself to the annual USGA grindfest. The reason the U.S. Open is both weirdly boring and great is because no tournament makes more demands on every aspect of a player's game, physical and mental, including the ability to plod along. If you win one Open, you've had a career. Winning two is freakish. Beyond that, you're on the mountain-top. Two men have won three Opens, and four giants have managed to win four.

The first person in the four-timers club was Willie Anderson, who died at thirty-one in Philadelphia and is buried a few miles from my house. The second was Bobby Jones, who is buried in Oakland Cemetery in Atlanta, a half-wedge from the Six Feet Under Pub and

Fish House, where there's a house drink called the Bobby Jones, which I have sampled in the name of research. The third was Ben Hogan. The fourth was Jack Nicklaus, who also had four second-place finishes. Tiger Woods won his third in a playoff with a double stress fracture in his left tibia, which lore and newspaper shorthand have turned into a broken leg. Hale Irwin won his third at forty-five, in his 1990 playoff with Mike. That sixsome is a list of golf's best thinkers. Just *playing* in a U.S. Open is exhausting, let alone winning. Curtis will tell you that. No tournament will do more to dull a player's edge. Arnold will tell you that.

Hogan kept the edge about as well as anybody. That is his mystique. He won his first U.S. Open in 1948. Eight months later, early one foggy February morning on a narrow bridge in West Texas, a Greyhound bus plowed into Hogan's Cadillac. The only thing that saved Hogan's life was that he threw himself on his wife, Valerie, to protect her. Had he not done that, the Caddy's steering column would have impaled him. The accident mangled his body and caused it to wither, and *still* he kept the edge. Likely, it got stronger. He won U.S. Opens in '50 and '51 and '53. The man was an original in every way.

In his ability to get his ball to follow directions, Hale Irwin is likely as close to Hogan as any golfer after Hogan and before Woods. (Feel free to make an argument for Nicklaus and Trevino and possibly Nick Faldo.) Irwin notched the first of his twenty tour wins in 1971. He won forty-five times on the senior tour. He was never an exciting or charismatic golfer. That was not his purpose. What he was, what he has been, is the ultimate golfing machine.

Irwin made a memorable first impression on me. I saw him in person for the first time at the 1985 Honda Classic. I was caddying for Brad Faxon, and Hale Irwin played through during a practice round as a singleton. Killer was caddying for Irwin, and Irwin was all business.

It was a perfect spring day in Florida and the man was grinding. Plodding. Brad was watching closely.

For some time, Mike and I had wondered whether we should see Hale together or if I should see him alone. Naturally, I was leaving it to Mike.

Over the years, oddly and inexplicably, Hale had been less than gracious when he spoke publicly about his win over Mike at Medinah. The final straw for Mike came in a 2010 interview Hale did with *Golf* magazine twenty years after the fact. When the interviewer asked Irwin what stood out for him about the playoff, he went straight to Mike.

IRWIN: His one big mistake. I'm down one. We get to the tee on eighteen. All day, Mike was using this metal-wood to hit fairway after fairway. He couldn't miss. I'm thinking, Mike, hit the driver! Hit the driver! And I'll be darned: On eighteen, he pulls driver and hooks it in the trees. I'm asked about the greatest shots I've ever seen. Well, Mike hitting driver was the antithesis of that. All he needs is to hit one more fairway and green to win. But he didn't. He made bogey. We tied. On the nineteenth hole, I hit a sand iron to ten feet. The rest is history.

INTERVIEWER: [Post-victory] you said, "God bless Mike Donald. I almost wish he had won." Why?

IRWIN: I felt for him. He had the U.S. Open won several times, but the moment escaped him. He didn't embrace it. Maybe he didn't see himself taking home that trophy. I wanted it. Deeply.

INTERVIEWER: What separates major winners from guys who don't close the deal?

IRWIN: Some of it is luck—a good or bad bounce from the golf gods. Also, Nicklaus, Watson, Trevino—they weren't locker room guys. They showed up, did their job, left. Mike was happy telling stories in the locker room at regular events. But regular events are very different than a Masters or U.S. Open.

Mike read the interview and was livid. In the next issue, this letter ran, above Mike's name and below the headline HALE NO!

I read with interest the interview with Hale Irwin in the June issue, particularly the parts about his win in the 1990 U.S. Open at Medinah in a nineteen-hole two-man playoff. I'm the guy he beat. In the interview, talking about the eighteenth hole of the playoff, Irwin says, "I'm asked about the greatest shots I've ever seen. Well, Mike hitting driver was the antithesis of that." He describes himself rooting for me to pull driver on that eighteenth tee and not the metal wood he says I had been hitting well all day. I can't even imagine thinking like that, hoping for a guy to make a mental blunder. But the most ridiculous part is that Hale has it wrong. I didn't hit my MacGregor Eye-O-Matic driver there. I hit my metal wood, a TaylorMade twelve-degree Original One. You can see it plain as day on the tape. Hale's standing right there. I pull-hooked it, it finished in the left rough and I made bogey. It was a bad swing. But it wasn't, as Irwin describes it, bad judgment.

Anyway, when I think about the greatest shots I've ever seen, I think of the drawing 2-iron with a cross wind that Hale hit to ten feet on sixteen in our playoff. That shot was pure class.

Mike wasn't done. There was a senior event in Birmingham, Alabama, right at the time the interview was published. After playing in the tournament qualifier, Mike left a letter for Irwin in his locker, taping it from a top shelf so it would be at eye level when Irwin opened the door. Mike concluded with this: "In the future, when you're talking about me, get your facts straight and your arrogance in check."

Mike was in his car, in the parking lot of the Holiday Inn Express on the east side of Birmingham, when Irwin called him.

"I'm shocked," Hale said. "Shocked by the venom."

They spoke for maybe twenty minutes. Hale suggested that they have dinner. Mike wasn't interested, and the conversation ended.

After he hung up, Mike realized he hadn't really said what he wanted to say. He called Irwin back, and they arranged to have an early breakfast at the tournament clubhouse the next morning. This time Mike did most of the talking, and the essence of his message was this: *Hale, you've got the crown and all the jewels. It's twenty years later, and I don't get what you're doing. Medinah was one of the great weeks of my life, and every time you go negative on me, it's like you're stealing from me. And I don't like it.*

When Mike revisited that breakfast conversation for me, I asked how Hale had responded to it all.

"He was sorry about being wrong about the driver. He said, 'I always thought you hit driver there. I wish I had known.' He didn't have much to say about the other stuff. But he had already talked. This was my turn. He did say one thing. He said, 'You know, Mike, the way I see it? A champion is a champion. You either win or you don't.' "

I saw Hale at a senior event in Boca Raton, held on a newish development course called the Old Course at Broken Sound. I introduced myself, told Hale about my project, and presented him with the exciting news that he was on my legends list. Hale said he could see me the following week, across the state in Naples, at a tournament being played there. He was matter-of-fact but polite. He's given a thousand interviews. It would be no big deal to give one more.

At Broken Sound, Wayne Levi was working on his putting, with his wife standing behind him. The same Wayne Levi who was at the back of the van at the Kemper Open in 1979. Now, thirty-five years later, his wife was giving him advice on his stroke and Wayne said, loudly enough to be heard easily by others, "I can make 'em here, I can't make 'em out *there*." In 1990 he won four times, but sooner or later, everybody loses the edge. Even Hogan. If there was ever an exception to that, it was Irwin.

Mike played in the Tuesday qualifier for the Naples event, the week after the tournament at Broken Sound.

"How'd it go?" I asked him. I try not to do that. Usually I am able to look up the scores before we talk, but this time I had not.

"Eighty-five," Mike said. "Played with Gary Hallberg. He shot eighty. We finish and he says, 'Are we gonna turn these in?' I'm like, 'I've got no problem turning it in.' It's an embarrassing score. But it's what I shot."

Mike had a sore right hand, and I asked if that had contributed to his poor play.

"That had nothing to do with it," Mike said. "I hit it so bad it was a joke. I got no speed, no idea where it's going. I had to hit five provisionals." That is, emergency shots in case you are unable to find your original ball. "I found four of 'em. Otherwise, I would have shot ninety."

I told Mike I was seeing Hale in Naples. He said, "You should probably just go see him yourself."

With almost every other legend on my list, I had various paths to the person. We knew the same people, or I had intersected with said legend at an event or on a story. That was not the case with Hale Irwin. I had never even talked to him. I met him in the locker room at the TwinEagles Golf Club in Naples and followed him to a quiet spot in a massive, cold ballroom where breakfast was being served for the players and the pro-am participants. I told him that Mike was also one of my legends. I felt he should know.

I asked Hale how he started in the game. Successful golfers are asked that question to the point of boredom, but Hale took right to it. He told me about putting on sand greens as a kid, getting $2.75 to caddie and paying $2.25 golf fees. He described a solitary childhood. The Irwins had no TV, and the family moved from Missouri to Kansas to Colorado. I didn't ask him the Proust Questionnaire classic—"When and where were you happiest?"—but I'm sure he was answering it. Hale had played football and baseball in the fifties and sixties and liked it. But teaching himself golf—no instructor, no teammates, no gambling games—brought him the most pleasure. That was happiness for him, to be alone on a golf course, figuring it out all by himself. Fay Vincent, the former baseball commissioner, once asked Warren Spahn how he learned to pitch. The great lefty said, "Hitters taught me how to pitch." Hale's instruction was equally direct: The flight of his ball taught him how to play. "I loved hitting it where you were supposed to hit it," he told me.

When he first got on tour in 1968, Hale was still learning how to play. "What I realized was that body type dictated swing. I saw Jack Nicklaus, with those tree-trunk thighs, and I realized he hits the ball with his lower body. I remember the first time I saw Arnold Palmer coming out of the shower, seeing how big he was through the chest, how muscular. I realized that that's how he hits the ball, with his chest. I figured out for myself that there was no one swing. There was a swing for your body."

That was a telling phrase: *I figured out for myself.* When I asked Hale who his closest friend on tour was, he said, "Dale Douglass was very nice to me." The subtext was clear: *I didn't need friends.* Not on tour, anyway. Hale's friends were at home. On tour, his most meaningful relationship was with the golf ball at his feet.

Hale said, "I didn't get on the tour thinking, *I hope I can make it.* I am a compulsively driven person."

Another interesting phrase. I would say Tiger Woods is a

compulsively driven person, and that Hogan was. Palmer, Watson, and Mickey Wright were, too. Big Jack? Hard to say. Probably not.

Hale spoke with genuine affection about his first driver—cut down to size by his father, who put a tape grip on it—a club on display in his locker at the World Golf Hall of Fame. He talked about going to his first golf tournament, the 1960 U.S. Open at Cherry Hills, where he saw Ben Hogan practicing with brand-new balls. He'd never seen anybody do that. Hale had just turned fifteen. Somebody gave him a sleeve of brand-new balls that week. U.S. True Blues. He never used them.

Long before that morning in Naples, I knew about Hale's extreme competence at golf. Everybody in golf respected his game and was impressed by how he had maintained it, like a vintage race car that always turned right over. But until that day, in that cold ballroom, I never had any sense of how lodged the game was deep within him. It made him more likable for me. The odd things he had said over the years about Mike seem incongruous. In his own way, he was a soul golfer.

We talked about the 1983 British Open, about what Hale did on the fourteenth hole of the third round, when he "whiffed" a tiny putt, maybe six inches long. Whenever it is written about or discussed, *whiff* is the word people use, but it's not really correct. Irwin attempted to backhand that putt in, as many players do. His downswing actually stopped when he stubbed the putter head into the turf short of the ball. He counted that stroke without any hesitation or discussion. Irwin could have claimed it was an aborted swing and that he did not intend to hit the ball. That claim likely would have saved him a shot. "It would never even have occurred to me to do that," Irwin said. "I was trying to hit it." He finished second, a stroke behind the winner, Tom Watson.

We went through his three U.S. Open wins. When he talked about the '74 U.S. Open at Winged Foot, Tom Watson's name came up. (They were in the final group on the final day. Irwin shot 73 and

Watson shot 79.) When he talked about the '79 Open at Inverness, Sandy Tatum's name came up. When he talked about the '90 Open, Mike's name came up.

For some reason, and despite a vague plan I had going in, I suddenly didn't feel like reviewing the history of Hale's relationship with Mike, or revisiting Hale's commentary. Mike had already figured out what Hale had just told me, that he was compulsively driven. That quality will cloud a man. What was there to add?

I did ask Hale about his enduring quote, on national TV, right after the playoff: "God bless Mike Donald. I almost wish he had won." I always thought that was a genuine and gracious comment. Mike was always dismissive of it. I asked Hale why he said it.

Hale considered my question in an instant, smiled thinly, and said, "*Almost.*"

It was, you could tell, something he had said before. He paused briefly and then summarized the whole thing in one familiar sentence: "The cold, harsh reality is that I won and Mike didn't."

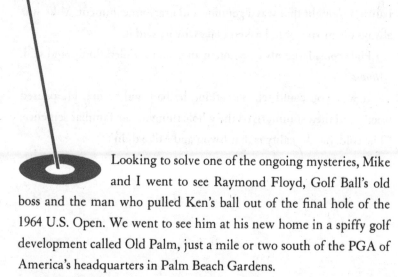

Looking to solve one of the ongoing mysteries, Mike and I went to see Raymond Floyd, Golf Ball's old boss and the man who pulled Ken's ball out of the final hole of the 1964 U.S. Open. We went to see him at his new home in a spiffy golf development called Old Palm, just a mile or two south of the PGA of America's headquarters in Palm Beach Gardens.

Raymond looked like a movie star. He was seventy-one, trim and tan, with smooth skin and no gray hair. I had never seen him look better. He told us he gets a daily home massage.

He showed us his book collection, an inviting group of titles separated into three categories: art, golf, and baseball. One of the baseball books was *The Boys of Summer*, the Roger Kahn classic in which the author catches up with some of the 1950s Brooklyn Dodgers long after they made their final outs. I started to mention something about the book to Raymond but quickly changed gears. Raymond loves baseball and the Chicago Cubs in particular, but Kahn's book—that is, its actual contents—did not appear to interest him.

He was leading an expensive life. The house in Old Palm was spacious and beautiful and seemed to enjoy the services of a daily housekeeper, who tiptoed through the house with plastic bags around her running shoes. Raymond also had a summer home in Southampton and a farm in Vermont. He had memberships at Seminole and Shinnecock Hills, among other places. How he got so rich, I could not tell you. I mean, how many people have *two* vacation homes? I never would have guessed that Raymond Floyd, with his Palm Beach tan and manicured nails, would be someone to own a gentleman's farm, but people will surprise you. If Raymond was making cheddar cheese up there in the Green Mountain State, good for him.

He remembered pulling Ken's ball out of the final hole at the '64 U.S. Open. "He was a zombie," Raymond said. "He was shaking it in the hole there at the end. I had tears in my eyes when it was over."

I asked, "Could you hear him say, 'My God, I've won the Open'?"

"No," Raymond said. "I didn't hear him say that."

We talked about Ken and Arnold and Ken's obsession with the '58 rules dispute at Augusta.

"He blamed Arnold forever," Mike said.

"That's because he's Italian," Raymond said. "It's part of his culture. It's a way of life, really."

Raymond called Arnold "my mentor." He told us a story about how he wore madras plaid pants one day at the Masters, and Arnold told him madras plaid was not appropriate for Augusta National. Raymond banished *all* madras plaid from his wardrobe from that point on.

He had such a long career. He was on the scene when Arnold was at the height of his powers and he was there when Greg Norman was at the height of his. The names coming out of his mouth were the ones who lured me into the game: Jack Nicklaus, Tom Watson, Johnny Miller, Curtis Strange, Tom Weiskopf, Gary Player, Lee Trevino, various others. He wasn't name-dropping. He was remembering his life and high times.

We turned to Dolphus Hull. Raymond talked about Golf Ball's ability to read greens and players. He said that Golf Ball could get him straight for a round by making a single suggestion or comment. "He was loose, like his body," Raymond said. "He kept me loose. Those old black caddies like Golf Ball were very observant. If I was off, Golf Ball would say, 'Man, what you done with your swing today?' If the ball was starting left, he'd say, 'Man, put that ball back in your stance.' "

I asked Raymond the question I needed to ask: Had he ever seen Golf Ball's house in Jackson?

"I picked him up once there."

"At his house?"

"No. I've only been to Jackson one time. Didn't get past the airport. I flew in private, met Golf Ball at the airport, brought him to a senior event, I think in Birmingham. That must have been in the mid-nineties. He couldn't work anymore, but it was a chance for him to say hi to the guys."

"So you were never at his house?"

"No."

Ball had said another thing altogether. He had Raymond staying overnight in his house. He had him playing little gambling games with the other guests at his welcome-home party. He was specific. The two stories were in obvious conflict.

Maybe Golf Ball had a fantasy. Regardless, I don't doubt for a minute Ball's recollection of how he joined the circus in 1963. Eight caddies, two cars, his mother's words rattling in his head: *Don't forget to send me back some of that money.*

Raymond wasn't always a private-plane guy. He drove the tour all through his early years, sharing a highway with Ball and a gang of others, the whole bunch of them running toward their dreams.

"We were Gypsies," he said.

• • •

Mike played his final tour event in 2006, at the Honda Classic. His place in the field was a parting gift from Cliff Danley, the tournament director, who was making his own farewell that year. Cliff had started working for the tournament as a volunteer in the early seventies, when he was in his mid-twenties. In those days, the event was named not for a Japanese car manufacturer but for an American entertainer, Jackie Gleason. *The Jackie Gleason Inverrary Classic*. Inverrary was (and is) a period-piece 1970s Fort Lauderdale country club that Jerry Ford played often, hatless in the Florida sun, his collars flapping as he rode shotgun in a Rolls-Royce golf cart owned and operated by Gleason, who was the king there.

Sometime after 2006, with the tournament being run by Jack Nicklaus's people, the Honda Classic turned into a high-profile event. Some of Jack's extended neighbors, including Rory McIlroy and some-times Tiger Woods, started playing in it. It was given a new lineup spot, batting first in the Florida Swing. It had found a long-term home on a better course. The marketing budget exploded. Jack brought star power, spruced it up, made Honda an international event.

But before all that, Honda was the kind of local event—like the much older stops in Hartford and Fort Worth and Honolulu—on which the tour was built. It was a perfect tournament for Mike, and he played in it every year between 1981 and 2001. In the years when he wasn't exempt, Cliff got him in. Yes, he was playing favorites. Cliff once told me that of the hundreds of players he had met over the years, none made a bigger impact on him than Mike.

One warm winter night, Mike, Cliff, and I met for dinner at Il Bella-gio, a popular restaurant at an outdoor mall in the heart of West Palm Beach. The restaurant is not as fancy as it sounds, and over the years Mike and I have had many leisurely meals there, always on the outdoor patio, overlooking a series of hyperactive fountains and various chain stores devoted to the good life, American-style. These dinners were an opportunity for us to marvel at the health of the American economy, or at least a segment of it, and to settle the issues of the day.

But on this night, with Cliff as our third, the focus was the tour. That is, the tour that Cliff came up on. Cliff was a tournament administrator with no use for the word *metrics*. He didn't do focus groups. His stock-in-trade was relationships, and his most significant gift was the ability to read another person's motives and needs. Cliff, who was in his mid-sixties, was only twenty-four when Jackie Gleason gave him a delicate assignment: chaperoning the Great One's lady friend at his tournament. He did it well. He kept the cart out of lagoons only he could see. Cliff had a set of skills that are not taught at the Harvard Business School.

Some time after our outdoor dinner on that warm winter night, I called Cliff and asked what I could not in front of Mike: How did he get Mike into the 2006 Honda, when Mike was fifty and not even a regular presence on the senior tour? How—and why?

"It was an emotional, acrimonious time," Cliff said. The lid was coming off quickly. "I knew it would be my last year running the tournament. The tour was making changes. A new board was coming in, and I was going to be out of a job. I was going to be fine, but I was worried about my staff. Would they be able to land on their feet?"

It's always like that, isn't it? The manager gets fired, and the pitching coach takes his kids out of parochial school. He knows he could be next.

"We had six exemptions," Cliff said, spots in the field for friends of the tournament. "I didn't care about five of them. I knew I wanted one of them to go to Mike. People used to call Mike a journeyman, but I prefer *consummate professional*. That's really what he was. And he was before that 1990 U.S. Open, during that Open, and after it."

What an insight. Medinah in '90 might have changed the way Mike thought of himself as a golfer. But the experience didn't change him, not at his core.

The Honda tournament gives the players brand-new Hondas to drive around for the week. Courtesy cars. Cliff can tell you, chapter and verse, where these courtesy cars have been left and in what condition. He has known players who asked for courtesy cars for their wives, nannies, girlfriends. He knows the players who used the backseat as a recycling bin for Anheuser-Busch products. Mike had no interest in driving a Honda courtesy car. For one thing, Honda was a home game for him, and he was perfectly content driving his own car. More to the point, he figured the tournament was already giving him enough. Throughout his career, Mike was critical of tour greed, especially in his four years on the Tour Policy Board. It's in his nature not to grab free stuff. But he also understood that a measure of modesty would serve the tour well in leaner times.

"There are people who will tell you that Mike is blunt," Cliff said. That put it mildly. "But to me, he was just telling it like it is. You ask him a question, he answers it. We'd have lunch, and I'd tell him what I knew and he'd tell me what he knew. And he knew a *lot*."

That all sounded familiar.

"People have no idea how generous he is. How many caddies he helped, how many people he loaned money to or just gave money to. How he talks to people and tries to help them. You'll never meet anybody with a bigger heart.

"You have to get approval from the tournament board for these sponsor exemptions. I told the board I just needed one, for Mike. I told them: 'This is personal to me,' " Cliff said, his voice catching.

He was a large, decidedly earthbound man, hardened by a long series of corporate wars. For years his life had revolved around that golf tournament. As we spoke, his entire history with it, and with Mike, had to be racing through his head. The tournament had brought him a livelihood, standing, friendship. It was to him what Raymond was to Ball.

"Normally, you have to tell your board all these reasons for your candidate, make a case, do all these things. I didn't do any of that.

I went in there without my usual line of shit. This was going to be my last tournament, and I knew it was probably going to be Mike's final tour event. They were fine with it. I'm sure the vote was unanimous. They knew what it meant."

I met Mike at the '85 Honda and I had been to many Hondas, including the one in '06. Mike's appearance wasn't exactly Arnold playing his final Masters (which I witnessed twice). I don't think Mike felt any heightened emotion about it. He wished he had played better. He was grateful for the opportunity Cliff had given him. It was the 550th and last tour event of his career. He had made 296 cuts and earned $1.97 million.

Mike did not come close to making the cut at the '06 Honda. But he came back on Sunday, when Luke Donald won. No relation, and the surname coincidence barely registered with Mike. He came back on Sunday because he wanted to be there when Cliff turned off the lights for the final time.

You have to be brave to answer the Proust Questionnaire honestly. Chuck Will, in his late eighties, and Sandy Tatum, in his early nineties, could do it. Billy Harmon and Mike could, too. *When and where were you happiest?* What a question. It's one thing to answer in the privacy of your own mind, and another thing to answer for others to see. Could I do it? No, but I am closer now than when I started this whole thing. Like they say in the self-help section, it's a journey.

I can do what we all do: close my eyes and drift. I am now remembering a wet and windy day from the summer of 2010. Mike and I were both in Scotland. He was there to try to qualify for the British Senior Open. I was there to cover the regular British Open, which was in St. Andrews, with its stout cathedral and buckling gray walls. The weather was south of appalling. Second-round play was suspended twice because the wind was so strong that balls would not stay put on the exposed greens. It was like being in Maine: A squall would come through, and with it a drenching rain followed by cat-and-mouse sunshine. The Scottish golf fans were unperturbed. With everyday nonchalance, they put on their foul-weather gear in the distant carparks, hiked to the ancient playfields in their rubber boots, and watched "the golf."

Late on that Friday afternoon, Mike and I became transfixed by an odd sight: Tiger Woods and Tom Watson simply standing in close proximity to each other. Watson was in the group behind Woods, but play had ground to a halt and the two groups had nowhere to go as they waited on the second tee.

Eight months earlier, Woods had run over a fire hydrant in the middle of a November night. In a short burst, everything went wrong for him. People were screaming for his head. Everybody he had ever met seemed to have a lawyer and a publicist. Woods went deep into a cave, far from the cameras that could not get enough of his various casual girlfriends, looking for their fifteen minutes or a payday or something. The manhunt for Woods was frenzied and finally ended with the publication of a hideously invasive photo of Woods at a rehab center. I don't think any of this is what the Framers had in mind when they defined free speech, and I felt for Woods, no matter what he did to bring it all on himself.

About the only people showing any decorum or sense right about then were the old boxer Larry Holmes and Big Jack. In their primes, Holmes and Tiger had used the same Las Vegas trainer. When the story was breaking, I tracked down the Easton Assassin for his take on the whole thing. He said, "You're Tiger Woods—you're some famous athlete or show biz celebrity, whatever. The girl's got you in the corner. She's in your face. You're like, 'No, no, no, I can't do this. I got the wife at home.' But she's pushing and pushing, and finally you give in. It don't mean nothing. It's just thirty seconds. But it feels so good you want it again and again and again. They're a toy to play with. And that's all you are to them. You give them some money and they go away." He was encouraging people to take a deep breath. Nicklaus was, too. He said, "It's none of my business."

Elsewhere the message seemed to be that Woods had somehow *let us down*. The fog of sanctimoniousness would have halted play. Tom Watson was especially critical, telling the world (via CNN) that Woods needed "to clean up his act." He complained about Woods's on-course comportment and how it didn't measure up to the standards of their golfing forebears.

And there at the Old Course, where golf has been played for six hundred years, Woods and Watson stood near each other, saying nothing, making no eye contact, each staying in his corner, slightly bent in the heavy sea air. Finally, after a wait that seemed to last for an hour but was actually not even ten minutes, the coast was clear and Woods played off number two.

"Man," Mike said, "was that weird."

The weather conditions were not improving, but Mike and I, following the code of lunatic golfers everywhere, decided to go play. We left the Old Course around six P.M. and made the back-road drive across Fife to a golf course in the tiny seaside village of Elie. It's an unusual and windswept layout, with sixteen par-fours and two par-threes on a pale-green peninsula of linksland. It's one of my favorite courses anywhere.

Mike and I, as a twosome, had balls in the air a little before seven. Summer golf in Scotland. Like most private courses there, Elie is happy to have paying visitors, especially for evening play, but there was nobody around to collect our green fees. Okay: We sneaked on. The opening hole goes uphill and downhill, and there's a giant periscope on the first tee for the purpose of making sure the coast is clear. We didn't need the periscope. The place was deserted.

On a short into-the-gale par-four, Mike smashed a driver and then a 4-wood and was still maybe eighty yards short of the hole. Score was meaningless in those conditions. There were only upwind shots and downwind shots and tending to our running noses between shots. It was nearly ten P.M. when we got to the eighteenth tee.

Across tiny Links Road from Elie's last tee is a cozy spot called Golf Tavern, with good drink and food from a kitchen that I knew from past experience closed at ten. We abandoned the last hole, parked our clubs outside the tavern's front door, and fell into the moist warmth of a dozen or two Friday-night merrymakers. Mike checked in with his lady friend, and I did the same with mine. Then we focused on the matters at hand: the peculiar joys of Elie, Watson and Woods and St. Andrews, the number of spots available in Mike's upcoming Senior Open qualifier. A good time.

More than that. Our golf that night, on a spit of land between a town and its beach, was pure joy. That round on the Elie links was years in the making. Did we drive there from St. Andrews, as I remember it—or did the wind somehow deposit us on the course, like Dorothy and Toto being airlifted to Oz in that trippy twister? I cannot say. I can say that golf is a windblown game, and it produces energy like nothing I know. I've never been happier than I was that night. Not playing golf, anyway.

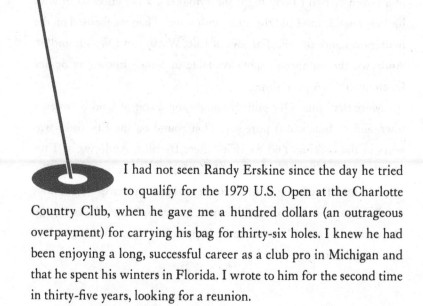

22

I had not seen Randy Erskine since the day he tried to qualify for the 1979 U.S. Open at the Charlotte Country Club, when he gave me a hundred dollars (an outrageous overpayment) for carrying his bag for thirty-six holes. I knew he had been enjoying a long, successful career as a club pro in Michigan and that he spent his winters in Florida. I wrote to him for the second time in thirty-five years, looking for a reunion.

When I first tracked him down by phone I realized immediately that his distinctive voice, so midwestern and accommodating, had been filed in my head, unused, since the day I last saw him. I suggested breakfast at Testa's, a reliable family-owned spot in Palm Beach that was a short drive from an apartment where Randy went in winter. He knew it and liked it, and we were on.

In the eighties and nineties, when I was covering more baseball and there was a lot of Grapefruit League play on the east coast of Florida,

I ate breakfast at Testa's often, always after getting the morning papers a few doors down at Main Street News, where they pipe in the smells of newsprint and tobacco. One morning during spring training in 1994, I picked up the papers and over breakfast with Christine read two or three stories about a final bash at the Kennedy estate in Palm Beach before it was being sold off. JFK had used it as his winter White House. The *Miami Herald* piece mentioned that Sargent Shriver was at the farewell party, along with his son Tony and Tony's wife, Alina. I asked Christine, who was pregnant, what she thought of that uncommon name. "It's a beautiful name," Christine said. As I sat down for breakfast with Randy, I thought of our daughter, who was away at college and closing in on twenty. It goes fast, doesn't it? A sportswriter is gone a lot, but (in my case) home a lot, too. I was able to watch Alina grow up and become a beautiful young lady.

In May 1979 I was nineteen, and Randy was thirty and had been married to his University of Michigan girlfriend, Judy Monahan, for eight years. At the time of the 1979 Kemper Open, they had three young children, a girl followed by two boys, the second of whom had been born four weeks earlier. By the morning of our Testa's visit, Randy was sixty-five, he and Judy had been married for forty-three years, and their three children had brought ten more young people to this earth of ours. Talk about your march of time. It brings to mind something the Stage Manager says in Thornton Wilder's *Our Town*: "You know how it is: you're twenty-one or twenty-two and you make some decisions; then whisssh! you're seventy: you've been a lawyer for fifty years, and that white-haired lady at your side has eaten over fifty thousand meals with you."

It was thoroughly enjoyable, being with Randy. The game had been good to both of us, and I think we were celebrating that, too. Randy was wearing shorts and running shoes. When I met him in '79, he was trim, blond, sun-bleached, and he was wearing Sansabelt slacks. (They all were back then.) Now his hair was white but he was still fit and active and he still played golf at a high level. He had snorkeled and scuba-dived all over Florida and once in Australia. He was in excellent shape all the way around.

As a tour player, Randy spent more than he made. After his tour days were over, he had developed three or four regular sources of income. He was a club pro in Michigan. He was the paid commissioner of a series of golfing junkets for amateurs and their professional friends. And he owned nine rental apartments in a retirement community in West Palm Beach. He also made some nice vacation money playing tournament golf. He had won the Michigan Open five times, the '79 title among them.

As a real estate man Randy did nearly all the work himself. He could paint, wire, and plumb. Randy speculated that he had inherited his entrepreneurial spirit and restlessness from his father's father, Albert Russel Erskine, who was the president of Studebaker, the car manufacturer, from 1915 through his death in 1933. Randy's namesake grandfather was an active golfer.

Randy played with Arnold Palmer in a tour event—one of his career highlights—and he readily recalled seeing the King when we were together at the U.S. Open qualifier in Charlotte in '79. "I remember watching the people watching Arnold," he said. His stated goal that morning was to qualify for his first U.S. Open. He finally played in one in 1985, when the Open was at Oakland Hills, outside Detroit. Randy's path to that Open was a high-speed straight shot on I-275. Bob Tway had pulled out early on opening day, and Randy got a call from P. J. Boatwright of the USGA at 6:38 that morning, inviting him to take Tway's spot and fill out the threesome going off at 7:36. Randy was in his bed in Ypsilanti, fifty miles from the course. He drove like a wild man, changed shoes at a red light, and made it to the first tee with nine minutes to spare. Yes, it was insane. Dangerous, really. But it was the U.S. Open. Randy shot 76-73 and missed the cut.

Randy graduated from Michigan in 1970. Though he was aware of the teach-ins and the antiwar protests, they made little impact on him. In his graduation picture, he looks like he could pass as the kid brother of Steve Bolander, the class-president schoolboy played by Ron Howard in *American Graffiti*. Randy was an all-American golfer who graduated in four years and managed not to get drafted. With his framed diploma on the wall, his plan was to make a living selling insurance and to live the American Dream, Wolverine-style. Marriage, kids, Sunday golf, maybe save up for a cabin in the woods. It was all going fine, except golf kept nipping at him and in 1973 he turned pro.

In his short career, Randy played in 144 tour events and made sixty-five cuts. You could make a living playing like that in the Tiger Era, but you couldn't in the seventies. You'd go broke.

"What was the difference?" I asked. "What was the difference between you and the guys who made it?"

Randy thought for a moment and said, "I think they were more sure of themselves. Over every shot, they were more sure that they could do what they wanted with that shot. And it's funny, because I didn't see many players who could play shots that I couldn't play. But over the ball I had more doubt."

This whole area is a recurring subject for Mike and me. The sports psychologists want to preach the importance of confidence and faith and trust, and Mike, as you would expect, is comically dismissive. "Here's the truth," he once told me. "Some guys just have more talent. You know where trust comes from? Results. To get the results, you have to have talent." But I think Randy was saying something else. I think he was saying he had enough talent on Tuesdays, but on Fridays (cut day) and Sundays (payday) something was preventing him from *proving* his talent. He was talking about confidence and talent as two different things.

Mike's point is irrefutable. On the PGA Tour, your scores *are* your talent. I once heard a player say, "It's a results-oriented business." Exactly. But only Randy could know what golf was like for him in Michigan, playing against the best players in the state, and what it was like on tour, playing against the best players in the country. I think there is a mental makeup by which some people can get out of their own way and others cannot.

Randy talked about playing well at the 1973 Tour Qualifying School and how Crenshaw, who won, finished *twenty-two* shots ahead of him over the eight rounds. Crenshaw ended up twelve shots ahead of the guy who took second. Randy finished in a tie for sixth. He told me how nervous he was. His PGA Tour card was on the line, and he often felt like vomiting. His caddie, he said, kept him in the game.

"Who was that?" I asked.

"Dolphus Hull," Randy said.

"Golf Ball?"

Golf Ball.

When Mike and I were with Ball in Jackson, he had brought up Crenshaw's performance at that '73 Q School. In fact, Ball had said in passing that he'd been working for somebody named Randy Watkins. But it wasn't Randy Watkins. It was Randy Erskine!

I told Randy that I had recently seen Golf Ball and that I had his phone number. I don't think either of us could believe how the global village was shrinking right there in front of our morning eggs. Randy called Ball from our breakfast table. I could hear Ball.

"Golf Ball? This is Randy Erskine."

"Randy Erskine!"

"You used to caddie for me."

"I know!"

"I haven't spoken to you in over thirty years. How you doing, buddy?"

"Hey, man—how you doin'?"

"Good, good. I'm a club pro in Michigan. I'm going to retire this year."

They talked. Randy asked Ball if he still played. He remembered him as a good player.

"No, man," Ball said. "Can't use my legs."

Randy could not have known.

"You still hanging around with that Barney Thompson?" Ball asked. Barney Thompson played the tour in the seventies and eighties.

"I spoke to Barney just the other day," Randy said. He was amazed how quickly Ball had remembered his friendship with Barney. "I'm gonna see him in a little bit here."

"Man, he played golf with a *pea* for a brain," Ball said.

Randy laughed. Barney was not noted for his course management. "Barney got himself on the senior tour, but just for one year," Randy said. "How old are you now?"

"Seventy-one," Ball said.

"Seventy-one? You're all grown up!" Randy said. "I remember back in the day you were put away wet many, many a night."

You could hear Ball giggle all the way from Jackson.

Randy and I sat at Testa's for hours, comparing notes. Lunch was well under way by the time we were done with breakfast. Randy insisted on paying. I told him how grateful I was for the chance he had given me thirty-five years earlier in Charlotte, when we were both far from home. He seemed to remember our week together with fondness.

"I've always been amazed by one thing," I said. I couldn't even use first person for this next part. "You've got this college kid caddying for you. You don't know him at all. He doesn't know what he's doing. And you give him the spare bed in your hotel room. What were you thinking?" Had the tables been switched (to use an Arnold phrase), I could not imagine myself doing the same. I wish I could say otherwise.

Randy answered instantly. "You were part of the team!" he said. "Gotta keep the team happy and strong."

I wish I could express how good that made me feel, to know that for a week in late spring 1979, at the age of nineteen, I was a valued member of Randy Erskine's team.

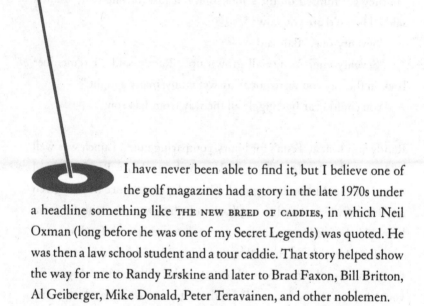

23

I have never been able to find it, but I believe one of the golf magazines had a story in the late 1970s under a headline something like THE NEW BREED OF CADDIES, in which Neil Oxman (long before he was one of my Secret Legends) was quoted. He was then a law school student and a tour caddie. That story helped show the way for me to Randy Erskine and later to Brad Faxon, Bill Britton, Al Geiberger, Mike Donald, Peter Teravainen, and other noblemen.

Peter is one of a kind. In retirement, he will sometimes hit balls in the lanes created by well-ordered rows of blueberry bushes. Likewise, there will never be another Neil Oxman. Neil, in his life as a political consultant, knows a lot of reporters, and we met sometime after I arrived at the *Inquirer* in 1986. He was dismissive of me at first. He had logged years as a real tour caddie. He paid his way through Villanova (undergraduate) and law school (Duquesne) with money he earned on tour. In law school, he had an almost perfect absentee record, owing to the call of the tour. Since 1972, there has never been a year when he didn't caddie in at least one tour event, and over forty-plus years he has worked about five hundred tournaments, senior and junior events combined.

It embarrasses me when Neil tries to talk to me as a fellow caddie. He knows that I know I was out there on a tourist visa. Neil has a long list of preferred pejoratives, and one of them is *fucking dilettante*. I typed my way out of Neil's basement and am relieved to say that I am now (I think) what Neil calls a *real person*. Classic Neil sentences are often variations on this theme: "Michael, these people in Philadelphia's Sixty-sixth Ward in the Great Northeast aren't fucking dilettantes like your rich friends on the Main Line in their Gucci loafers. These are real people."

Neil has a range of moods, and I'm sure he brings a boxer's energy and disdain for an opponent to his work at his company, the Campaign Group. On tour, he's a different person. He loves the players, the caddies, the stories, and the action. Polly Crenshaw and Neil came of age at the same time and in the same place, in the all-together-now tour of the seventies. It stamped Neil for life.

It is sometimes said, among the people who discuss such things, that Neil "introduced" Bruce Edwards to Tom Watson, which would make Neil the best matchmaker in the history of caddie/player marriages. Neil should get the credit, but this is how it actually went: In the summer of '73, Neil and Bruce were young caddies traveling the circuit. They were in the parking lot of the Norwood Hills Country Club in St. Louis a few days before the start of the St. Louis Children's Hospital Golf Classic. Neil had work, and Bruce was looking. Watson was walking across the parking lot, bag on his shoulder. Upon seeing Watson, Neil yanked Bruce up from the ground and said, "That's Tom Watson. Why don't you ask him?" Bruce did, and with a few absences

Watson and Bruce were together for most of the next thirty years. When Bruce got sick in 2003, Neil stepped in. Bruce died the next year.

Neil and I stayed in the same hotel during the week of the 2009 British Open at Turnberry. On the Saturday night before the Sunday finale—when Tom Watson, at age fifty-nine, had a one-shot third-round lead—we sat in the hotel dining room talking for hours, not a minute of it devoted to what might happen. I knew not to talk about Sunday. I didn't want to add to Neil's anxiety. He had spent years schlepping around courses with some of the most unheralded players in golf history. Now he was in a position to see golf history being made from the best seat in the house. When Julius Boros won the '68 PGA Championship at age forty-eight, he became the oldest player to win a major championship. Watson was six weeks short of *sixty*. He was thirty years past his prime and ahead of everybody. The prospect for something amazing to happen was *right there*. But Neil and I talked about the Phillies, movies, politics, newspapers, mutual friends. Watson's name did not come up. Neither did that of Harry Vardon (the only golfer with more Open wins than Watson). We did not speak of the final round.

Late on Sunday, Watson came to the par-four eighteenth hole needing a four to win. He drove it down the middle and was left with 170 yards to the front edge of the green, with the pin back another twenty yards. He did what he wanted to do. He hit a full, flush 8-iron and it pitched on the front of the green. But the ball hit a hard spot, bounded crazily, and settled just over the green. Links golf, like life itself, is unpredictable.

Watson, siding with caution, used a putter from a slightly fluffy lie. He was left with an eight-footer to win, but his putt, half yippy, never had a chance. He tapped in and dragged his way through the four-hole playoff like a man out of gas.

Anyone who thinks that Neil could have or should have talked

Watson into hitting a 9-iron knows nothing about Watson or links golf. In links golf, especially, it's not the club you pull, it's how you decide to hit it. As for a 9-iron, it could have left him way short of the green. There's no way to say. Anyway, Watson makes his own decisions. If his caddie, Alfie Fyles, talked Watson into hitting that fatal 2-iron at the Old Course on the Road Hole on Sunday in 1984, the first time he was trying to win his sixth Open, Watson has never admitted it. Maybe he did, and maybe that was a turning point in his career, I don't know. Watson contended in a dozen or more major championships after the '84 Open but never won. Turnberry was likely the last of his chances (though you never know). It was a beautiful loss, Watson's to Stewart Cink in 2009, as all I-gave-it-my-best losses are.

Arnold Palmer knew why Watson lost. It wasn't because he was fifty-nine and playing on an artificial hip. It wasn't because he had an unlucky bounce on that approach shot to eighteen. No. He didn't win because he had lost the edge.

As best I can tell, this is *the edge*: There's a line deep in your head with *go* on one side of it and *stop* on the other, except you can't see the line, let alone those words. You don't decide on which side of the line you fall. In fact, you don't even know the line is there at all. That's what I had gleaned from Arnold. I can't vouch for this definition. It's like golf on the moon. How many people are qualified to describe that?

With his loss Watson had the opportunity to give to the game what it had already given him. He took full advantage. He gave to Stewart Cink the same present Nicklaus had bestowed upon him thirty-two years earlier, in the same place and circumstance. I am speaking of the warmth with which Watson congratulated Cink, the candor with which Watson talked to reporters, the cooperative way he posed for pictures at the Turnberry hotel that night. It was Watson at his best, and it was more significant than what he did during the U.S. Open at Pebble in '82, when he pitched in from the hay on seventeen on Sunday and beat Jack again, as great as that was. Bruce was right there for that one, just as Neil was at Turnberry twenty-seven years later. For a few real-time hours, Neil was at the center of the sporting universe. In terms of memory, he'll be there forever.

I wrote my original legends list at the Ryder Cup in Medinah in 2012, with Watson on the Living Legends side and Neil batting in the Secret Legends lineup. Two years later, Watson was the U.S. Ryder Cup captain and Neil the unofficial captain of the caddies. The gig did not go well for Watson.

After another American defeat, reports emerged of dissension between some of the American players and Watson. The carping, anonymous and otherwise, was unnecessary and unattractive. The real reason the Americans lost was because the European team had better players who played better golf and better team golf. Same as forever. But the lack of connection between Watson and some of his players surely did not help. I could imagine the disconnect. I have seen Watson be cold and aloof with me and with others. A terrible know-it-all. But there's more to him than that. I am thinking now of the obvious admiration he showed that day at Whitemarsh for his friend Sandy Tatum as Sandy talked about golf and life and his memories of the '36 Olympics in Berlin.

Ted Bishop was the PGA of America official who had recruited Watson for the job. After he returned home from the Ryder Cup—*his* Ryder Cup—he told me how disappointed and upset he was with how it all unfolded. He said he had been commiserating with Watson about it. "And Watson said, 'You gotta talk to Ox.' And I did. Neil was really the one guy who had perspective on the whole thing."

Neil understood the Ryder Cup as the players saw it, as the NBC executives saw it, as the reporters saw it, as the PGA of America saw it. He has a profound understanding of conflict, which makes him a natural as an amateur movie critic. It also makes him successful at his day job, where he helps politicians get elected or learn something from defeat for the next time out. Understanding conflict made Neil valuable in the inner-circle cauldron of another acrimonious Ryder Cup. Bishop said Neil cited a list of reasons why that Ryder Cup was over before it began. But to me, Neil's journey to the team room at Gleneagles was the most amazing thing. It started in that parking lot in St. Louis.

The Ryder Cup at Gleneagles was not the way Watson wanted to close out his competitive career, but ends are never pretty, are they? At best they're wistful.

When Watson won the Senior British Open at Turnberry in 2003 Bruce Edwards was in serious decline. Neil caddied for Tom that week in Bruce's name. Bruce's death, from the same disease that killed Lou Gehrig, came on the first day of the 2004 Masters. Later that day, Watson, with Neil carrying his bag, left an egg salad sandwich for Bruce on the bench by the thirteenth tee, in the most remote part of Amen Corner. That was Bruce's sandwich, and that was his spot to eat it. Bruce inherited a rooting interest for all Philadelphia teams— *EaglesFlyersSixersPhils*—from his father, and that rooting interest was one of Bruce's bonds with Neil. That and coming of age on tour in the doubleknit 1970s.

A few weeks after that Ryder Cup in Scotland, Neil was a host of an event on a rainy, gloomy October night in Philadelphia. His friend John Lahr had written a biography of Tennessee Williams, and Neil had helped arrange for Lahr to speak at Philadelphia's grand central library. There was a reception for Lahr. Our former mayor Ed Rendell was at the library that night, among other people afraid to say no to Neil. Neil's devotion to the library is inspiring.

In his introduction, Neil recalled a piece Lahr had written for the *New Yorker* about Cole Porter. Neil then took a quick detour and talked about working at the Sammy Davis Jr. Greater Hartford Open one year in the 1970s. His man had missed the cut, and on the weekend

Chuck Will hired Neil to be a CBS spotter, helping to relay on-course information to Ken Venturi in the broadcast tower over the eighteenth green. Late one day Neil found himself alone with Sammy in the open-air broadcast booth. He asked a question that Sammy could not have been expecting in that setting: "Did you ever meet Cole Porter?"

It is unlikely that anybody else in the library that night could have combined golf in the seventies, Ken Venturi, Cole Porter, John Lahr, and Sammy Davis Jr. into a single two-minute story. John Lahr—son of Bert Lahr, who played the Cowardly Lion—came up to the podium, and Neil exited stage left to warm applause. What an image: Sammy Davis and Neil talking about Cole Porter, surrounded by all that golf. This Neil Oxman (to use one of Mike's constructions) has been on one long, strange trip. It's hard to imagine him ever getting off the tour bus. Why would he?

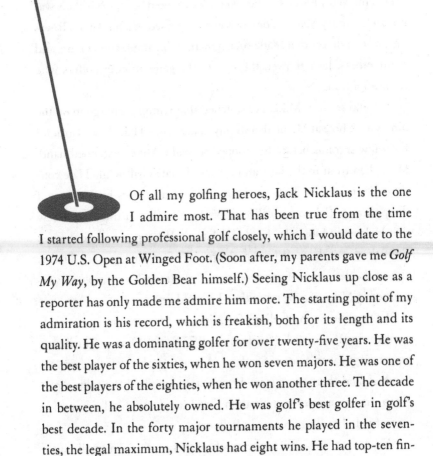

Of all my golfing heroes, Jack Nicklaus is the one I admire most. That has been true from the time I started following professional golf closely, which I would date to the 1974 U.S. Open at Winged Foot. (Soon after, my parents gave me *Golf My Way*, by the Golden Bear himself.) Seeing Nicklaus up close as a reporter has only made me admire him more. The starting point of my admiration is his record, which is freakish, both for its length and its quality. He was a dominating golfer for over twenty-five years. He was the best player of the sixties, when he won seven majors. He was one of the best players of the eighties, when he won another three. The decade in between, he absolutely owned. He was golf's best golfer in golf's best decade. In the forty major tournaments he played in the seventies, the legal maximum, Nicklaus had eight wins. He had top-ten finishes in all but four of those forty events. He was the runner-up seven times. Think of what that takes, to bring it again and again and again. (Woods in his heyday had that same quality.) As a golfer, Nicklaus was relentlessly consistent. As a person, the same. I've never known him to be anything other than decent.

Some of those second-place finishes left a permanent mark on me. For a Mets fan in my era, the underlying message was that losing was noble. Even when the Mets did win pennants—most notably in 1969 and in '73, when Yogi Berra managed a club that was three games over .500 to the World Series—they weren't supposed to. But Nicklaus was not an honorary Met. No one was ever surprised when he won. It was his grace in defeat that made such a memorable impression on me and many others. Jack showed the way to the generation of golfers who came after him.

I could see it in Mike. He watched that winning putt go in on the ninety-first hole at Medinah and stayed put while Hale danced around for a few seconds before he stopped to shake Mike's extended hand. Mike then went to the hole and retrieved Hale's ball while Hale continued to celebrate. Those winning balls from majors have a way of disappearing. (I know a collector of them.) Mike instinctively knew that Hale would someday be glad to have it. What presence he showed right then and there. What an awareness of another person. That is almost the definition of courteousness. I'm sure Jack's example was ingrained in Mike, maybe more than he could know.

I can winnow my feelings for Nicklaus down to one moment. It came during the Saturday finale of the 1977 British Open at Turnberry, on the craggy west coast of Scotland. A heat wave had left the fairways parched, and there were large brown stretches amid the rolling pale green carpets, a color combination that brought to mind my modest home field, the village course in Bellport.

Every iron shot off Turnberry's firm turf produced a small mushroom cloud of exploding dirt. Over the first three days, Tom Watson, who in April had won the Masters, shot rounds of 68, 70, and 65. Meanwhile, Nicklaus, who had finished second in that Masters, *shot the exact same scores*. The photo in the Saturday sports section in the *New York Times* showed Watson and Nicklaus sitting on massive rocks on the beach while a passing storm suspended play. They are in short sleeves and wearing golf shoes with kilties, the little fringed flap that once covered the laces on all your better golf shoes. No minions were hovering. I read the paper in our kitchen in Patchogue and watched the final round on our living-room RCA. We didn't watch much TV in our house, and never in the holiness of Saturday morning. But there I was.

It seems odd now, but the last round of the British Open was played on Saturdays then, a nod to the Old Course, which is closed on Sundays. ("If you gentlemen dinna need a rest on the Sawbath, the links does," the Custodian of the Links, Old Tom Morris himself, once bellowed out his window, which looked over his course.) On that second Saturday in July 1977, Nicklaus came to the tee of Turnberry's par-four eighteenth hole trailing Watson by a shot. Watson striped his drive, and Nicklaus pushed his into the right rough. As he came off the tee, Nicklaus slammed his driver head against the firm turf. Golf cannot be played at any level without emotion.

Watson was away and, with those drumstick arms, hit an 8-iron to thirty inches. *Thirty inches!* The quality of the golf they were both playing was astounding. Nicklaus then smashed an 8-iron out of the heavy rough and onto the green.

The Golden Bear, with his distinctive white-haired Greek-American caddie, Angelo Argea, tending the pin, holed his last-gasp putt for three—from thirty-five feet. Watson, wearing green plaid pants with western pockets held up by a thick white belt, did not fuss. He stepped right in and quickly made his. They both had closed with birdies. Nicklaus had shot 66 and Watson 65.

They walked off the home green bathed in sunshine and applause.

Nicklaus, nearly ten years older than Watson, draped his arm around the winner, and Watson did the same to the man he had just defeated, fair and square. That was it for me. That moment.

Is what Nicklaus and Watson did that week at Turnberry— playing four rounds of golf on a sparkling seaside Scottish course in 266 and 265 shots—some kind of artwork? Something you can discuss alongside twentieth-century masterworks like Marc Chagall's tapestries at Lincoln Center and Dr. Seuss's *Oh, the Places You'll Go!* and Mike Nichols's *The Graduate?*

In a quiet voice: *yes.*

I was almost giddy when Mike and I met in the parking lot of Golden Bear Plaza, on Highway 1 in North Palm Beach, on the still weekday morning in spring when we were on the docket to see Big Jack. Our tour through yesteryear had reached its terminus.

I make no claims that our Mike-and-Mike show had been any sort of epic road trip, like the Dead's summer tour in '67. We had made several long hauls, but we did a lot of day-tripping, too. In '81, when Mike played thirty-five tour events by car, that was a road trip. In '91, when Christine and I traveled in Europe for seven months as newly-weds, that was a road trip. Mike and I hadn't been from Tucson to Tucumcari. My wife said it well: "Your thing with Mike was more of a mental road trip."

If golf is not a form of hunting, it is at least a goose chase. Reporting is, too. I remember calling Mike once as I was driving south on U.S. 17 in South Carolina, on a particularly beautiful and marshy stretch. I was chasing whatever I was chasing, in the name of the magazine, and I felt happy. I don't say that daily. I gave Mike a status report, and he responded by telling me about being on a practice range at the B. C. Open one year with Bill Britton, who was back out after a prolonged absence. They were hitting balls side by side when Bill said,

"I feel *alive* again." All our legends had one thing in common: Golf coursed through their veins.

We saw Jack in his office, overlooking the Intracoastal Waterway and the Lost Tree Club, where Nicklaus and his family have lived for decades. Jack sat in his special chair to preserve his ever-recovering back.

Jack was never a tall man, and age and his back issues have rendered him shorter, but we were all at the same height when we sat. Anyway, Jack's eyes have always been his main asset. He focuses on you. Whatever the opposite of ADD is, he has it. He knew Mike, he knew me, and even though I was excited, I was also oddly comfortable. I think Mike felt about the same. Mike had once told me about an exchange he had with Nicklaus on the practice range at Augusta National, late on Thursday afternoon of the 1990 Masters, after Mike had shot 64. Nicklaus walked fifty yards out of his way to Mike's workstation and said, "That was a wonderful round of golf, Mike."

Jack had recently seen Arnold at Augusta, where it was obvious to Jack that Arnold's walking was more labored than ever because of his back issues. Jack sounded like an osteopath, talking about Arnold's medical condition. Jack is ten years younger than Arnold but sounded like the older, prudent brother in the relationship.

Jack at one point said, "Arnold is as close a friend as I've got." I think because that sentence is true, and because Arnold knows it is true, Jack was comfortable talking about Arnold in an honest way. Jack made a reference to how good Arnold is in a crowd and at golf-course openings. Both Arnold and Jack had been prominent for decades in golf-course design.

"I don't want to cut the ribbon or do the cocktail party," Jack said. "Arnold wants to cut the ribbon. He wants to do the cocktail party. We were always different that way. I'd invite Arnold to dinner, but Arnold would rather go to a party with forty people he didn't know than go to dinner with one friend. That's the difference between the two of us. I'm not criticizing Arnold. We're just different."

I asked Jack about Winnie. Jack knew her well, and Winnie Palmer and Barbara Nicklaus had logged many hundreds of hours in each other's company, walking courses, eating dinners, attending PGA and USGA and PGA Tour receptions together, to say nothing of various events hosted by Mark McCormack and IMG.

"Winnie understood who Arnold was and what Arnold was and she understood how to handle him, and she handled Arnold beautifully," Jack said. "And that's probably why Barbara handles me the way she does. I think that Arnold had his freedom to do pretty much what he wanted to do except when Winnie said, 'Arnold, we're not doing that.' She let Arnold be Arnold, and then all of a sudden she'd say, 'We're not doing that.' And he responded very well to her. Barbara pretty much lets me be me until she sees me a little offline or out of kilter."

I asked Jack when he first met Arnold.

"I first *saw* Arnold in '54, at the Sylvania Country Club in Toledo, at the Ohio Amateur," Jack said, ever precise. "I was playing a practice round. It was pouring down rain, and I was the only person on the golf course. When I came in, there was only one guy on the practice range, hitting knee-high nine-irons. It looked like Popeye out there.

"So I sat back and sort of watched from the back of the range for about ten minutes or so, and then I went into the clubhouse.

"I said, 'I know I'm crazy for being out there in this silly rain, but who is *that* idiot?'

" 'That's our defending champion, Arnold Palmer.'

" 'Oh, *that's* Arnold Palmer.' I was fourteen and he was twenty-four."

Arnold won that '54 Ohio Amateur in Toledo. Then he won the U.S. Amateur in Detroit. After that he went to Fred Waring's Shawnee

Inn, on the Delaware in eastern Pennsylvania, where he won the Waite Memorial, met Winnie, and asked her to marry him.

Jack talked about playing in the 1962 Phoenix Open with Arnold during Jack's rookie year. Arnold was running away with the tournament, and they were paired together in the last round.

"He put his arm around my shoulder and we walked to the eighteenth tee," Jack said. "And Arnold said, 'Come on, you can finish second here. You can birdie this hole. Just relax.' It was a pretty nice thing to do. I birdied the hole and I finished second. Arnold won by twelve. He just nipped me, 269 to 281."

Arnold made $5,300. Jack made $2,300.

"Arnold was very good to me when I first started," Jack said. "He used to come over and pick me up in Ohio in his plane, and we'd go globe-trot the United States and play exhibitions. In those days, the tour allowed you three weeks a year to play exhibitions, and we'd take eight days and go play eight exhibitions three times a year. That's the only place you'd make any money. You didn't make any money playing golf, but you could make a couple grand or three grand playing an exhibition. You'd play eight of them and put twenty grand in your pocket for the week. That was pretty good."

"How was Arnold as a pilot?" I asked.

"Well, I guess I trusted him."

"Was there a copilot?"

"No, just Arnold. He'd pick me up, and we'd go fly around and play exhibitions."

I loved that picture, two guys in one little plane, golf bags in the back, a map on the pilot's lap as he pointed the nose of his plane to some new place. Ball, speaking loosely here, was beneath them in his yellow Grand Prix, doing about the same thing.

"Arnold made an interesting comment when we were at lunch with him," Mike said. "He said that if he hadn't won the U.S. Open in 1960, he would have won three or four other ones. He said he won there in Cherry Hills and then he lost the edge."

"Interesting comment," Jack said. "I make a similar comment every time I sit down in front of an audience and talk about that 1960 Open. I say the best thing that ever happened to me was *not* winning the U.S. Open in 1960. Because if I had won that Open, I would have been too smug or too self-confident and felt like however I had prepared my game was ready. But I was growing into the game then. Arnold had already won two Masters. He was at the top of the game. He *had* the edge."

Arnold had the edge and then he lost it. Yes, he won at Augusta twice after that '60 Open, he won two British Opens, he won scores of other events. He needed all those wins to become the public icon known as *Arnold Palmer*. But that day in Latrobe Arnold was not talking about the public person we all know, whose signature was on the front door of a thousand Dunkin' Donuts, in the name of some new tea-and-lemonade combo. That day in Latrobe our host was talking about *Arnie*, as Arnold's father called him, as my father-in-law called him, as Conni Venturi called him. He was talking about himself as the son of a greenkeeper who had U.S. Open dreams for his big-boned boy. Arnold was telling us that something had changed after he won the national open in 1960 at Cherry Hills. After that, whenever he was contending in his national championship, the one that he wanted most, he could not find fourth gear. That's a far from perfect image, because the real issues had to be much more mental than that. But the point is that Arnold had lost the ability to will it in when he needed it most.

Maybe this has all become less meaningful, this discussion of the U.S. Open and edge, even for American players. The game has become much more international, and the prestige of the Masters, with its United Nations of a field, has increased immeasurably. In Jack's day and Arnold's day, the Masters was a nice invitational tournament, but it wasn't a *championship*. Golf's championships were the PGA, the British Open, and the U.S. Open. Jack told us the Masters was a reward for playing well in other events, but he valued his national open far more. "As an American, the U.S. Open to me was the number-one tournament in the world," he said. Its status was assigned to him on January 21, 1940, in Upper Arlington, Ohio, on the occasion of his birth.

Jack was a plodding player, often annoyingly so. But he was also careful, and he was never involved in any sort of rules dispute. He called penalties on himself in the rare instance when something went wrong, but there was never a time when anybody accused him of being anything less than completely faithful to the rule book. Hundreds of thousands of shots, and never an issue.

"When you start playing as a kid, your dad teaches you good sportsmanship and to live by the rules," Jack told us. "That's what my dad taught me, and I'm sure that's what Arnold's dad taught him. The rules are the rules. That's golf. I remember when I was eleven years old, I was playing a qualifier for a district junior tournament. We were playing at the Army Depot Golf Course, and I missed one like this." Jack took his two small, tanned hands and held them about ten inches apart. His thumbs have always had a pronounced curve. "I got mad and I whacked the ball down the fairway. Everybody just stood there."

It was stroke play. There were, of course, no given putts. Every hole had to finish with the ball at the bottom of a cup. But in his anger, little Jack lost track of that basic fact.

"So then I went down the fairway and played it back up to the green. I ended up shooting eighty-one that day instead of shooting seventy-eight. I was playing with Larry Snyder. S-N-Y-D-E-R, if you use it. We played some junior golf together."

"Is your memory that good for everything?" I asked.

"I remember things that were impactful," Jack said.

He continued on the subject of the rules. "This was at Royal Lytham, at the Open in 1979. Fifteenth hole. Final round. There was a bunker about sixty, seventy yards short of the green. I put it in that bunker, right up against the face of it. When I swung, I took the face out and dirt went flying."

All manner of debris came at Nicklaus. The ball stayed in the bunker. Joe Dey, by then the retired first commissioner of the PGA Tour, was working that Open as a rules official. He had been walking with Nicklaus, with whom he was close.

"I felt something come down and hit me," Jack said.

It could have been a stone or a clump of dirt or his own ball. In those days, if you were struck by your own ball, it was a two-shot penalty.

"So I turned to Joe and said, 'Joe, I got hit by something.'

"Joe was right there. He said, 'The ball didn't hit you.' "

Nicklaus asked Dey again before he signed his card whether the ball might have hit him, and Dey again said that it had not. So Nicklaus signed. He finished in a tie for second with Ben Crenshaw in the 1979 British Open at Lytham, three shots behind Seve Ballesteros, who won with 283. Jack has never felt sure about the 286 next to his name for that week. He has never felt sure about the scorecard he signed on that fourth round when he failed to get out of the bunker on fifteen on his first attempt.

"It still bothers me," Jack said. "Because I think that ball might have hit me."

Near the end of our visit, I attempted to express to Jack what he meant to me, as a golfer, as a model of grace, as a role model. I'm sure he's heard the same from many others. Still, he seemed to appreciate it. This was a serious piece of business for me. Jack gave my life a direction it would not have had otherwise. He helped a gangly kid, not particularly good at anything, find a path to adulthood. I was lucky to have the chance to say it in person to Jack. I could tell he understood what I was trying to say.

"If you go back to Turnberry, to when Tom and I embraced each other, that to me really is what it's all about," Jack said. "When two people get done, they shake hands and say, 'Well done.' You say, 'You beat my rear end. I'll get you next week.' I love that about golf. When I congratulated Tom on his win, I could do it with meaning because I'm the guy he beat. And when I beat Arnold, he'd shake my hand and say, 'Congratulations, well done.' And I knew he meant it."

Mike and I had come far. We were now sitting with the greatest golfer ever, and he was discussing his wins and losses and opponents and friends with casual, genuine intimacy.

"Your character comes through in golf," Jack said. "If you're pissed at the world the whole time, you really can't enjoy your wins, and in many ways you can't really—what's the right word?—you can't really understand the meaning of your defeats. To get beat is very healthy. Particularly when you've really given it your best effort. If you win every time, you don't learn anything. You don't learn anything about yourself. You don't learn anything about the other person. You don't learn anything about the game. You don't learn anything about *life*."

25

When we were done, Mike and I walked slowly across the parking lot of Golden Bear Plaza. I was half in a daze. Who today is talking about the lessons learned from losing? Jack Nicklaus has to be as thoughtful, in his plain and practical way, as any world-class athlete has ever been.

Jack had told us about a note he had sent Bubba Watson after Bubba won his second Masters: *You play a game with which I am not familiar.* Bobby Jones once said that of Nicklaus. Nicklaus's father, Charlie, offered Jones to his only son as a role model. Joe Dey, from the PGA Tour and the USGA before that, passed along much of what he knew about Jones to Charlie and Jack, and he knew a lot: When Jones completed the Grand Slam in 1930 at Merion, Dey was there as a cub reporter, covering it for Philadelphia's proper afternoon paper, the *Evening Bulletin.* Four years later, Jones started a tournament at Augusta in his own image. Eighty years later, Rhonda Glenn was in Augusta during Masters week to accept an award at a banquet dinner from the Golf Writers Association of America for outstanding contributions to the game. For that dinner, Rhonda kindly invited me to join her and her people. I sat at a round table up front in a banquet room at the Augusta Country Club with Barb Romack, '56 Curtis Cup cover girl for *SI*. Two months after that Masters, I saw Barb and Rhonda again when the two U.S. Opens, the men's Open followed by the women's Open, were played at Pinehurst. One night at the Carolina Hotel, Jaime Diaz told Rhonda, Barb, and me about a lesson Barb had given him *forty-five* years earlier. The ladies laughed. Eight months later, Rhonda died. Pancreatic cancer. That lifetime GWAA award went to the right person.

As I shut things down here, and finally clean out the back of the car, I realize I have not nailed down every last thing. Fred, for instance. I knew from experience that getting Fred Couples to sit down for any sort of interview is about as easy as getting a rhino into a dental chair. I sent Fred an e-mail through his agent, told him about the legends list and his place on it, and Mike's place, too. Fred got back to me by text, his preferred form of communication. I got back to him, and after that the line went dead. If someday I find out the answer to Mike's question—*Fred, who filled out your application for that '79 U.S. Open?*— I will figure out a way to disseminate the answer. If you hear first, please let me know. It's not easy being a detective in the Golf Division. You need all the help you can get (and I got a lot), and still your work is never done.

After Nicklaus won the Masters at age forty-six in 1986, he took off a week and then played the following week in Houston. Gordon S. White, Jr., covered that Houston tournament for the *New York Times*. He wrote about a tour caddie following Nicklaus as he played and used a phrase that was new to me: *busman's holiday*. In the ensuing years,

I have come to realize that the busman's holiday is an elemental part of my life. Actually, I don't know where my work life stops and my recreational life begins. Mike is the same way. Visiting these various legends, secret and otherwise, felt like one long busman's holiday.

For all his verbal intensity, I find being with Mike relaxing. For one thing, he's an excellent storyteller. Somewhere in our travels he told me about going to Portugal to play in the European Senior Tour qualifying tournament. Upon arrival, he hired an English caddie who, he soon discovered, reeked of body odor. Mike suspected his caddie was sleeping outside. After a morning practice round, Mike brought his man to a supermarket and bought him soap, a toothbrush and toothpaste, deodorant. Mike gave him a pep-talk on personal hygiene. That afternoon, when Mike was on the range hitting balls, the caddie returned smelling like a rose. But the next morning the smell was rancid again. Reluctantly, Mike fired the man several holes into the round. Naturally, Mike paid him in full. Mike's philosophy is pay in full and part as friends. I've learned a lot from him.

I find that I don't have to put up any fronts with Mike. What an energy saver. It's helpful that he knows a lot about my everyday life. Nothing has to be perfect in my accounts. I can tell Mike things I can't tell others, in part because he lives a thousand miles away, but also because I know he will understand what I am saying and what I am trying to say. I feel no compulsion to be successful around Mike. What a relief.

Our night on the Elie links in 2010 was a prime example of a busman's holiday, and so was a trip we made out to Long Island to watch the Walker Cup three years later. The Walker Cup is a competition in which a team of the best American amateurs plays a team of the best amateurs from Great Britain and Ireland. The first Walker Cup was held in 1922 at the National Golf Links of America on the East End of Long Island. In 2013 the Walker Cup returned to the National

Golf Links for the second time. There was no paid parking, no security check, no security check, no gallery ropes. You could just wander the property and enjoy the golf, the course, and the people on it. Or not. Leaving the course after the Saturday round, Mike and I played Twenty Questions. To start the game, Mike offered this hint: "On the course today, I saw the biggest douchebag in all of golf." I know it's been a while since you've heard Mike in full. I didn't want him to fade out quietly here.

The National was designed by Charles Blair Macdonald with a major assist from a Long Island engineer named Seth Raynor, who designed the course I grew up playing in Bellport. NGL and Bellport are about thirty miles apart. They are both old-timey links built on brackish bays, and they both offer more than a nod to the motherland. As a young golfer I took many of my cues from Scotland, from Bellport, and, in a less direct way, from the National. Not the National as it actually was, because I surely didn't know it. But the National as I imagined it, circa 1979, as a course populated (sparsely) by well-mannered gents who accepted life's bounces, good and bad. I extrapolated wildly from there. I was a dreaming teenager.

On the Sunday morning of the Walker Cup, Mike and I played Bellport. When I go to Bellport, it all comes flooding back: putting for quarters with Stuart Feldman; caddying for my high school principal and holding his pipe between shots; playing through dark on summer nights with Larry Lodi. If I were asked which course I would play if I were down to my last game, there would be no debate. To join Bellport as a kid, all I had to do was fill out a piece of paper and hand the clerk in the village hall fifty dollars. I still have my junior-member Class E tag on my current bag, now woefully expired (good through June 1, 1980). But in my mind my membership has not lapsed and never will. Where would golf be without public courses? Where would I be?

On the Monday after the Walker Cup, I paid a visit to somebody I had not seen in close to forty years, Don Greenlee, my gym teacher in eighth grade. Mr. Greenlee was a good golfer, and it occurred to him that his favorite sport should be offered at South Ocean Avenue Middle School, "even though Patchogue was not an affluent community," he said. "So I filled out a requisitions form and ordered a bunch of five-irons, and I think the class you took, Mike, was the first one I ever taught." I was Mike again.

The whole class, held in winter, was conducted inside on the basketball court. We hit plastic balls off plastic mats, aiming for the backboards. It was enough to get me hooked. Mr. Greenlee taught me how to hold a club. Years later, Ken Venturi complimented my grip.

Mr. Greenlee talked about trying to qualify for a few USGA events and winning a club championship at Spring Lake, a public course where our high school team practiced and played. Mike came with me, taking it all in. Mr. Greenlee was retired, and he and his wife divided their time between central Florida and Suffolk County. Mike was impressed by Mr. Greenlee's prudence, the care with which he had managed his life. Mr. Greenlee asked about my mother, who taught English at South Ocean Avenue for a number of years, and he remembered the day when Fred Couples came to Bellport for an exhibition, though he didn't go. "I wish I would have availed myself of that opportunity," he said. He talked about the pleasure golf continued to give him. He looked remarkably unchanged, though I noted that he no longer had a mustache. Turns out he had shaved it off thirty years earlier.

Near the end of our visit, Mike said to Mr. Greenlee, "You taught Mike well." What a nice thing for Mike to say, both for my benefit and for the man who changed my life. *Better living through golf.* I know the concept. Mr. Greenlee does, too. As does Mike Donald, Golf Ball, Arnold Palmer, Chuck Will, Fred Couples, Jaime Diaz, Billy Harmon, Randy Erskine—you know the list. Maybe you're on it.

As we got up to leave Mr. Greenlee in his tidy home, it occurred to me that I had arrived empty-handed. At the British Open a couple of months earlier, during registration in the press tent, each reporter was given a tiny metal pin, a replica of the Claret Jug that the Open winner receives. I immediately took mine out of its tiny square plastic bag and attached it to the collar of the white golf shirt I had on that day. I never wear such things, but that's what I did. The pin stayed put through many subsequent washings, and I was wearing that white shirt with the pin that day at Mr. Greenlee's house. In the three years I had played varsity golf at Patchogue-Medford High School, we were given something similar, along with our varsity letters: a little gold-colored pin in the shape of a golf bag. Christine has one of them on a coat.

"I wish I had something better to give you," I said to Mr. Greenlee as I handed him the pin. "Thank you for all that you did for me."

His eyes welled.

I had seen Arnold a half-dozen times since the first stop on our tour, when Mike and I saw him in Latrobe. Once, sitting with Arnold in his heavy leather-and-wood Bay Hill office, I asked him if he was one to dream.

"Oh, I dream all the time," Arnold said.

"Really," I said.

"Oh, yes."

He then told me about a recent dream he'd had in which he could not get a business matter to work out no matter what he tried.

I asked if golf appeared in his dreams.

"All the time," Arnold said. "I had one last night where I made a twenty-footer to take the lead, but I didn't get to the back nine. I'd like to know how that one ends. I never get to the eighteenth in any of my golf dreams. It's never a specific tournament or course. I never recognize the other players."

He seemed disappointed by that last revelation, as if he'd like another shot at the old gang.

I asked Arnold how often he dreamed of golf. "About a quarter of the time," he said.

Arnold is a numbers-oriented man, and he then did a little round-number accounting. Golf accounted for a quarter of his dreams. Business issues, he said, occupied another quarter, and flying a third quarter. I asked about the remaining quarter.

"Other," Arnold said.

Arnold was leaving a whole category for himself. Who could blame him? *The secret dreams of Arnold Palmer.* I'm going to take a wild guess that Arnold wanted what Ken wanted, what Mike wanted, what I wanted, what millions of men the world over want: to get the trophy and the girl. Is that asking too much? Arnold did it. He got both and never gloated about it. The opposite. He let us in.

One day at Bay Hill when Mike and I were visiting, Arnold introduced Mike to his daughter Amy and said, "Mike and I played the tour together." Arnold has an astounding capacity to make people feel good. On that same day, Arnold called his wife and asked if she wanted to join him at lunch. Kit said, "Can I have fifteen minutes?" Arnold said, "Take as much time as you need." Talk about your models of manly grace.

After lunch on a different day, I absentmindedly had my right forearm in the window of Arnold's SUV as he sat in the driver's seat with the window down. By way of good-bye, he placed his right hand in the middle of my forearm. I don't know how any one person could exude more warmth. It must be in his DNA.

In the end, after Jack, there was one more *final* final stop on *Farewell to Persimmon Tour '79*: Arnold in Latrobe. (You got to stop somewhere, right?) I drove from Philadelphia to Latrobe to see him. I made the drive wearing sandals, and when I arrived in Latrobe I was chagrined to discover that amid all my paraphernalia in the trunk of the Subaru I did not have a pair of real shoes. The only shoes back there were running shoes and a pair of white wing-tip golf shoes still wearing the dirt of their last game. I went to the men's room in the lobby of the SpringHill Suites, at 115 Arnold Palmer Drive, to clean them up.

A short while later, I was sitting with Arnold in his office. I was right beside him at his desk, and I noticed that he was looking in the general direction of my ankles.

"Arnold, are you looking at my shoes?"

"No," Arnold said, "I'm looking at your socks!"

They had horizontal stripes and were semi-ridiculous. I took that opportunity to apologize for wearing golf shoes (with little rubber nubs on the soles) to his office.

"That's not a problem," Arnold said. He picked up his right foot and pointed the bottom of his black leather shoe in my direction. He was wearing golf shoes himself, along with a schoolboy smile. It was like he was getting away with a spitball. *Golf shoes in the office!*

I filled Arnold in on the legends Mike and I had seen: Sandy Tatum, Ken Venturi, Golf Ball, Chuck Will, Jack Nicklaus at the end. I told him about David Fay sending me the relevant page from the 1958 edition of the *Rules of Golf* and how it was clear that Arnold had proceeded within the rules on the twelfth green at Augusta on the Sunday of the '58 Masters. Arnold put his thumb in the air. I doubt I was telling him anything new.

In the rounds Mike and I had made, nobody made a stronger impression on me than Golf Ball, in his bed at the nursing home in Jackson. I was awed by his acceptance of his station in life and moved by the obvious pleasure he took in the memory of his tour years, when he was at-large. I asked Arnold if he was satisfied with his life. Arnold did not pause.

"*Noooooooo!*"

For one thing, he wasn't piloting his own airplane anymore. For another, he was playing tournament golf only in his dreams, and in those tournaments he never made it to the seventy-second hole. Age had crept into his body and robbed him of his best moves. He didn't like it.

In the big picture, yes, he had led a rich life. He continued to lead a rich life. He had accomplished so much, in golf and in business. He had married twice and both times well. He had loving relationships with his two daughters. He had true friends and great wealth that did not trap him. He had a good appetite. His older grandson was trying to play his way to the tour and getting closer. But *satisfied* with his life, as a day-to-day proposition? The truthful answer was no.

I told Arnold about seeing Conni Venturi, about her health issues and how she lived by herself in a trailer park in Napa. Arnold shook his head with a certain sorrow. "Wasn't Ken paying her?" Arnold asked.

I said that they had been through the alimony wars, but those payments had ended a long time ago.

"How did she support herself?" Arnold asked.

I told him about her various jobs, her movie-star dreams as a girl, and her devotion to local theater as an older woman.

Arnold asked if Conni had ever remarried and seemed surprised to learn that she had not. He remembered her two sons.

"I always thought she was great," Arnold said. "Just . . . *great*."

Arnold was eighty-four, with health challenges of his own. It had been sixty years since he had won his U.S. Amateur on a week off from selling paint. Mike and I were lucky we saw Arnold the day we did, when he relived for us, chapter and verse, those fast weeks when he went from amateur to professional, and from bachelor to married man.

I gave Arnold the pink envelope from Conni, with her handwriting in black ink on its face. It had been burning a hole on my desk at home.

Arnold held the envelope up to eye level, looked at it, gave it a little shake, slid open the top drawer of his desk, and dropped it in.